THE NEGRO'S GOD

THE NEGRO'S GOD

as Reflected in His Literature

BENJAMIN E. MAYS

NEW YORK / RUSSELL & RUSSELL

FIRST PUBLISHED IN 1938
REISSUED, 1968, BY RUSSELL & RUSSELL
A DIVISION OF ATHENEUM PUBLISHERS, INC.
BY ARRANGEMENT WITH BENJAMIN E. MAYS
L. C. CATALOG CARD NO: 68-26870
PRINTED IN THE UNITED STATES OF AMERICA

IN MEMORY
OF
MY PARENTS

PREFACE

A few years ago, Robert Russa Moton wrote a book entitled *What the Negro Thinks*. It was a revelation. He presented to the American mind a written document containing the Negro's most advanced thoughts on social, economic, and political questions. Here, the aim of the author is to tell America what the Negro thinks of God. The purpose is to trace historically the development of the idea of God in Negro literature, "mass" and "classical," from 1760 to 1937.

As strange as it may seem, this book represents the first attempt to study the development of the idea of God in Negro Literature. It has been taken for granted that the Negro is over-emotional and super-religious. It has been assumed by many people that the ideas of God expressed in Green Pastures are wholly representative of what the Negro thinks of God. Although the author did not set out in this study to disprove anything presented in Green Pastures, the data themselves show that the Negro's idea of God is *not* now and has never been what Green Pastures may lead some people to believe.

The Negro's ideas of God grow out of the social situation in which he finds himself. This is true in all three areas in which the ideas of God are developed. Whether they are developed along compensatory lines, are used to effect social change, or whether they show a growing tendency toward communism, they develop at the point of social crisis. This being the case, the study presents a challenge to America, since stifling social conditions may produce varying types running the gamut from the Communist who seeks a way out through atheism and revolution, to the religionist who seeks refuge in the other world.

The author does not intend to appraise any idea of God recorded here as valueless or detrimental to the best interest of the Negro. For example, compensatory ideas of God or ideas that portray atheism or agnosticism are not condemned and judged as harmful simply because they are compensatory or atheistic. On the other hand, views of God developed along the

Preface

lines of social rehabilitation are not adjudged as being superior to the other ideas. The object of the writer is to achieve a high degree of objectivity in the presentation and analysis of data.

The author does not claim to have utilized every idea of God expressed by Negro writers in their literature. He does claim, however, that the examples given are highly representative of what the American Negro thinks of God.

The author is greatly indebted to the publishers and individuals who gave him permission to quote from their works; to individuals whose counsel was frequently sought and given during the five years this volume was in process of preparation; to Edwin E. Aubrey from whom the author received much help throughout the first two years of the study; to Samuel C. Kincheloe, Donald W. Riddle, Howard Thurman, William Y. Bell, Charles H. Wesley, Benjamin G. Brawley, Jason C. Grant, Jr., and William E. Carrington who read the manuscript and criticized it helpfully; to Dorothy Porter who placed at the author's disposal necessary data; to Mabel Madden who read the galleys and checked the accuracy of quotations used; to Howard H. Long, Chief Examiner in the Public Schools of the District of Columbia, who gave a critical appraisal of the manuscript, and to his wife, Sadie G. Mays, who was helpful in discussions and who encouraged the author to publish this volume.

BENJAMIN E. MAYS.

School of Religion
Howard University
April 22, 1938

TABLE OF CONTENTS

I.	Introduction	1
II.	Ideas of God in the Literature of the Negro Masses	19
III.	Ideas of God in "Classical" Literature 1760–1865	97
IV.	Ideas of God in "Classical" Literature 1865–1914	128
V.	Other-Worldly "Classical" Literature (after 1914)	156
VI.	The Impartiality of God and the Unity of Mankind	162
VII.	Miscellaneous Ideas of God in "Classical" Negro Literature (1914–1937)	189
VIII.	Ideas of God Involving Frustration, Doubt, God's Impotence, and His Non-Existence	218
IX.	Summation	245
	Bibliography	257
	Index	265

THE NEGRO'S GOD

CHAPTER I

Introduction

In this chapter terms are defined, the dominant trends in Negro life that developed during the period of the study are indicated, the main arguments are briefly outlined, the reason for specializing in the Negro group is given, and the method of approach is set forth.

Negro literature includes the chief productions of Negroes from 1760 up to the present time—slave narratives, biography, autobiography, addresses, novels, poetry, and the writings of social scientists. These are labeled "classical" Negro literature. Negro literature also includes modern Sunday School productions, prayers, sermons, and Negro Spirituals. These are called "mass" Negro literature. They contain the ideas of God that reach the masses primarily through the church and through the minister in public utterances. The time-span of the investigation, from 1760 to the present, is divided into three epochs. The first epoch embraces the period from 1760 through the Civil War. The second epoch runs from the Civil War to 1914. The third period covers the time from the beginning of the World War to the present.

It is logical to begin with 1760 because in that year appeared the single poem of Jupiter Hammon who, as far as we know, was the first Negro poet to develop on American soil. It is logical to close the first epoch with the Civil War because a new day dawned for the Negro with emancipation. At the beginning of the first era, certainly before the close of the eighteenth century, sentiment in some quarters was growing in favor of the emancipation of the Negro; while, at the same time, the number of slaves was greatly increasing, particularly in the South. The war with England, resulting in the independence of America, with her declaration that "all men are created free and equal," and the basic teachings of Christianity, aroused a few clergymen and political leaders to cry out against the institution of slavery before the close of the eighteenth century. These preachments were not very effective, as evidenced by the fact that in 1770 there were approximately 700,000 slaves in the thirteen colonies as against 4,000,000 at the time of emancipation—this increase being due to importation, smuggling, and natural increases. As slave labor proved to be more and more profitable, it became intensively more difficult to arouse sentiment against it. However, between 1830 and 1840 there had developed not only an anti-slavery movement but a movement to abolish slavery on the ground that it was a moral evil and contrary to the law of God. It should prove a revelation to observe how the Negro thought of God in the period from 1760 to 1865. During the latter part of this era the pro-slavery and anti-slavery forces were engaged in bitter controversy. In this era slavery reached its peak and culminated in a great Civil War. The result was the emancipation of the slave.

The second era, from the Civil War to 1914, is also significant for the study of the development of the idea of God in Negro literature. The first part of this epoch includes the period of Reconstruction. Perhaps no phase of American history has caused more bitter controversy than the Reconstruction Era, and possibly no section of American history has been treated with so much passion and bias. Be that as it may, during this period, from 1865 to 1880, Negroes played a great part in the affairs of government. The Southern Negro in the Reconstruction Era helped to shape the affairs of state in a way not since realized by him. The period was followed by the disfranchisement of the Negro, his domination by white workers, and the development of deep-seated race prejudice. What did this era contribute to the Negro's idea of God? This second period is significant again because it includes the years in which two distinguished Negroes were rising to fame: Paul Laurence Dunbar and Booker T. Washington. Race consciousness began to dawn quite strikingly with Dunbar and he became the first great interpreter of Negro life. In this period Booker Washington did his most effective work. Without doubt he was one of the most distinguished Americans of his day.

The third era begins with 1914 and merits a more detailed analysis than the other two periods, not only because of the great social and economic upheavals resulting from the World War, but also because there developed in this period an awakened race consciousness and increased educational advantages for the Negro, as shown by the numerous literary productions of the period.

The greatest social, economic, and religious upheaval of the Negro since emancipation occurred during the migratory period (1914–1925) when Negroes moved from South to North and from rural to urban areas. Although Negroes have migrated from the South to the North since 1815, and since the exodus to the West (1879) there has been a steady migration of Negroes from the South to points in the North, the most colossal and significant movement began around 1914. The reasons for this are not difficult to state. As foreigners residing in America returned to Europe to participate in the World War and as the War put a stop to the great influx of Europeans to America, the Negro was sought to work in the industries of the North. It is conservatively estimated that from 1914 to 1915, owing to the World War, the number of foreign immigrants to the United States decreased from 1,218,480 to 326,700. Almost simultaneously with the World War was the devastation of the one crop system of the South by the boll-weevils and the occurrence of unusual floods in the main cotton states during 1915. These calamities further encouraged the migration of the Negro.

When the War began, the Negro served actively abroad as a participant in the struggle to make the world safe for democracy. As a result of this experience the Negro gained a new appreciation of his importance in the world. Almost over night, Negroes from the most backward and restricted areas of American life were transplanted to Europe to fight alongside white Americans,

Frenchmen, Englishmen, and Italians in a common cause. Also his experience of freedom from discrimination in France was something new to him. His experiences in Europe gave him a new conception of his status as a person, a conception which flowered forth in much of the post-War literature. This new estimate of himself could not have been achieved apart from this larger experience. A more detailed analysis of the period should further justify the dating of the third period from 1914.

The boll-weevils and the flood made life on the farm very unstable and precarious for the Negro. The traditional custom of mortgaging the crop before it was produced suddenly broke down. The landlords dismissed Negro tenants by the hundreds and thousands and commissaries by which thousands of Negroes lived were forced to close. Banks and merchants ceased to extend credit, since cotton could no longer be relied upon for security. In this situation Northern industries, since the number of foreign immigrants had greatly decreased owing to the War, seized the opportunity to bid for Negro labor, offering attractive wages.[1] Many Negroes looked upon these circumstances as blessings in disguise and considered 1914 the dawn of a new economic era for the race.

The movement of Negroes to urban centers, though largely economic in character, was accelerated by the deficiency of the rural school system in the South; the denial of the ballot to Negroes in virtually the whole of the South; the brutal and inhuman treatment of Negroes in the courts; the inferior accommodation on railroads and busses; lynching; and the fear of the mob.[2] That Negroes considered this crisis an opportunity to escape from the crippling restrictions of the South is affirmed by *The Crisis* magazine.

"It is lynching, forced labor, and discrimination that is sending the Negro North. When he comes North he may

---

[1] Scott, Emmett J., Negro Migration During World War (New York: Oxford University Press), p. 14 ff.
[2] The Chicago Commission on Race Relations, The Negro in Chicago (University of Chicago Press, 1922), Chapter III.

find mobs and hostile labor unions, but he will also find the law and the law will be enforced."[3]

That the period from 1914 to the present is a significant one for our study is shown by the actual number of Negroes who migrated. It seems clear that the city-ward movement of Negroes took place slowly between 1900 and 1910; but rapidly from 1910 to 1920 and between 1920 and 1930. T. J. Woofter, Jr., writes:

> "The Movement from 1900 to 1910 merely drained off some of the natural increase of the Southern rural districts, leaving a slight decrease in Negro rural population. But from 1910 to 1920 and 1920 to 1930 the Movement was so rapid that the cities not only absorbed all the natural increase of the country districts, but actually depleted the rural population by about one-half million in twenty years."[4]

In other words, Woofter says that from 1910 to 1920, the Negro city population increased sharply and from 1920 to 1930, more than a million Negroes migrated from the Southern rural district—650,000 to Southern cities and 450,000 to Northern cities.[5]

The third period is significant religiously too, both as to the increase in the number of urban churches and the moral status of the migrant. The following quotation is pertinent:

> "This shift of the Negro population had led to a rapid increase in the number of urban churches and an increase in membership, especially in Northern centers. According to the Federal census of Religious Bodies, there were in 1916 a total of 127 Negro Baptist churches in Chicago, Detroit, Cincinnati, Philadelphia and Baltimore. In 1926, the Federal census of Religious Bodies reported 319 Negro Baptist churches in these five cities, an increase of 151 per cent. The reported membership of the 127 churches in 1916 was 59,863; the membership of the 319 in 1926 was

---

[3] The Crisis, "Editorial Section" July, 1917, p. 114.
[4] Woofter, T. J., Jr., The Economic Status of the Negro (Mimeographed: June, 1930), p. 25.
[5] Ibid, pp. 24, 25.

reported to be 178,637, an approximate increase of 200 per cent." [6]

It is a sociological principle that an individual becomes a person in group relationships and that it is essential to morality and integrity of character that the individual have an important role to play in his group. That is the reason why it is often dangerous to dissociate a person from a group in which he is known and has status, and transfer him to a larger environment where he plays no important role in group activity. It is one of the main arguments in the study *The Negro Family in Chicago* that many Negroes suffered morally and religiously when they were suddenly ushered into an urban environment from the rural and small towns of the South.[7] This fact is further illustrated by this testimony:

> "He (a Detroit pastor) expressed the conviction that many Negroes in Detroit, formerly faithful church people in the South, had suffered moral and religious shipwreck because they could not make the necessary adjustment and the resident Christians did not always have the requisite sympathy, imagination, and resourcefulness to make them feel at home and to introduce them gradually to new ways of life and thought." [8]

This period has religious significance in a larger sense than that of race. The War brought disillusionment which has shaken our way of thinking about God. The period which led up to the War and the period of the War itself was permeated with social optimism. A wave of progressivism swept through both the Republican and Democratic parties under the leadership of Roosevelt and Wilson. The social gospel was the most popular message of the period. The World War was not out of harmony with the social idealism of the time because we were fighting to

---

[6] Mays & Nicholson, The Negro's Church (New York: Institute of Social and Religious Research, 1933), p. 96.
[7] Frazier, E. Franklin, The Negro Family in Chicago (Chicago: The University of Chicago Press, 1932).
[8] Mays & Nicholson, The Negro's Church (New York: Institute of Social and Religious Research, 1933), p. 98.

INTRODUCTION 7

make the world safe for democracy. It was a "war to end wars." It was preached from the pulpit, public platform, and the press that after the War "human institutions were to be reconstructed on the basis of ideal justice." To exonerate God from the crimes committed, some made Him finite.[9]

Spiritual depression and skepticism followed the War. Institutions were not reconstructed and a new earth did not appear. Humanism spread while men like Joseph Wood Krutch asserted the illusoriness of human values and the futility of human existence.[10]

The period from 1914 up to the present time constitutes the most outstanding period for the Negro educationally since his arrival in America in 1619.

In 1928, Monroe Work published *A Bibliography of the Negro in Africa and America*. The volume is "a select reference bibliography on the Negro with more than 17,000 entries covering the most worthwhile publications in different languages issued before 1928." Those produced by Negroes are starred. As one examines the productions by years, it is revealing to note that the stars become more numerous as we enter the second decade of the twentieth century, which includes the beginning of the third period of our study.[11] Had Negroes produced no more literature from 1914 to 1935 than they did from 1760 to 1914 this study would have been considerably less fruitful.

Beginning with 1909, the facts on this point are even more astonishing.

"It is estimated that from 1820 to 1909 inclusive, a period of eighty-nine years, 3,856 Negroes were graduated from American colleges with A. B. degrees, and that the total at the end of 1925 was 10,000. According to the education numbers of the *Crisis*, between 1926 and 1931 inclusive, a period of six years, 9,257 Negro men and women received college degrees from American institutions. In

---
[9] Horton, W. M., Theism and the Modern Mood (New York: Harper and Brothers), Chapter I.
[10] Ibid, Chapter 1.
[11] Work, Monroe N., Bibliography of the Negro (New York: H. W. Wilson Company, 1928.)

other words, approximately four times as many Negroes were graduated from college between 1909 and 1931, a period of twenty-two years, as in the eighty-nine years previous to 1909. In 1930 and 1931, 4,051 Negro students were graduated from college, which is more than the number graduated in the eighty-nine years between 1820 and 1909." [12]

The educational numbers of the *Crisis* (August numbers), 1932 to 1937 inclusive, show that approximately 12,500 Negroes graduated from college during these six years.[13]

It is interesting to observe that the vast majority of Negroes who have won Phi Beta Kappa honors earned them in the period from 1914 to 1936. From 1874 to 1936 inclusive, 155 Negroes were awarded membership in the Phi Beta Kappa Society. Of that number 121, or 78 per cent, received their Phi Beta Kappa Keys since 1914.[14] Of course, this is to be expected in the light of the fact that the number of college students increased enormously during the same period.

Similarly, most of the Negroes who have earned Ph.D. degrees, received them since 1914. From 1876 to 1936 inclusive, 132 Negroes had earned the Doctor of Philosophy degree. Of that number 117, or 88.6 per cent, received the degree since 1914.[15]

The Negro's perspective was enlarged during this period. His race had fought in every war in which America had been engaged. But never before had a war been the occasion of creating within the Negro a view of world significance and a new sense of his importance, as was the case in the World War. It helped to arouse in him a sense of worth that will never be eradicated. Brawley points out that the Negro placed a fighting

---

[12] Mays & Nicholson, The Negro's Church (New York: Institute of Social and Religious Research, 1933), p. 49 ff.
[13] The Crisis, 69 Fifth Avenue, New York.
[14] Work, Monroe, N., The Negro Year Book (Tuskegee Institute, Alabama, Negro Year Book Publishing Company, 1937–1938, p. 2.
[15] Ibid, p. 2.

force of 400,000 men at the disposal of his country and that more than 200,000 of them saw active service in Europe. A total of 1,200 received commissions as officers. "Sixty Negro men served as chaplains; 350 as Y.M.C.A. secretaries; and others in special capacities." The Negro invested millions of dollars in Liberty Bonds and War Savings Stamps. He also contributed generously to relief agencies such as the Red Cross and Y.M.C.A.[16]

Brawley says further that:

"The remarkable record made by the Negro in the previous wars of the country was fully equaled by that in the Great War. Negro soldiers fought with special distinction in the Argonne Forest, at Chateau-Thierry, in Belleau Wood, in the St. Mihiel District, in the Champagne Sector, at Vosges and Metz, winning often very high praise from their commanders. Entire regiments of Negro troops were cited for exceptional valor and decorated with the Croix de Guerre—the 369th, the 371st, and the 372nd; while groups of officers and men of the 356th, the 366th, the 368th, the 370th, and the first battalion of the 367th were also decorated..... The 370th was the first American regiment stationed in the St. Mihiel Sector, it was one of the three that occupied a sector at Verdun when a penetration there would have been disastrous to the allied cause; and it went direct from the training camp to the firing line.

"Noteworthy also was the record of the 369th infantry, formerly the Fifteenth Regiment, New York National Guard. This organization was under fire for 191 days, and it held one trench for 91 days without relief. It was the first unit of allied fighters to reach the Rhine, going down as an advance guard of the French army of occupation." [17]

Participation in the world-wide struggle, the experiencing of a temporary war-time democracy, and the receiving of actually less social proscriptions in Europe, particularly in France, than he was accustomed to experience in America, naturally kindled in the Negro a firmer belief and confidence in his real worth in

---
[16] Brawley, Benjamin G., Social History of the American Negro (New York: The Macmillan Company, 1921), p. 351.
[17] Ibid., p. 351 ff.

the world. These are the chief reasons why we say the third period of the study is to include the time from 1914 to 1937.

In another sense, it is justifiable to use the time span from 1865 to 1937 as the second and third eras of the study because during this time definite social and economic trends in Negro life developed. These trends furnish an excellent background against which the ideas of God are traced and developed.

1. During the latter part of the second period Booker T. Washington and his philosophy dominated almost the whole of Negro life and influenced greatly the thinking of white America with respect to the Negro. He emphasized industrial education for the masses of Negroes and believed that it was folly for the Negro to try to force the dominant group to accept him socially and politically. He believed that as the Negro made himself proficient and indispensable in the industrial and mechanical phases of life, he would eventually win his way in the other areas of life. Rights and privileges, he believed, were to be achieved. The Negro was advised to let down his bucket where he was and prove to white America that he was an asset and not a liability. The desire for economic security was uppermost in Washington's mind. Though a few leaders like DuBois and Monroe Trotter opposed Washington in his program, their voices were feeble in comparison with that of Washington who made a strong impression on American life. His ideas are perpetuated in Tuskegee Institute.

2. Opposition to Washington's ideas became organized in 1909, the year the National Association for the Advancement of Colored People came into existence. In 1910 the *Crisis* was born, the official organ of the N.A.A.C.P. Though organized in the second period of the study, the greatest work of the Association and the *Crisis* was done during the War and in the post-War era. The N.A.A.C.P. was and is primarily civic and political in character. It would be safe to say that the N.A.A.C.P. came into existence for the express purpose of making actual those rights and privileges theoretically guaranteed to the Negro in the 13th, 14th, and 15th amendments

to the Constitution of the United States. The following quotation proves the assertion and shows that the social trend of the N.A.A.C.P. differs widely from that of Booker Washington and his followers:

"Common justice and equality of opportunity for the Negro are as essential for white America as for black America. The N.A.A.C.P. exists to defend the full civil, legal and political rights of fourteen million colored Americans and to obtain for them full equality of opportunity with all other citizens. To make fourteen million Americans physically free from lynching, mob violence and peonage; mentally free from enforced ignorance; politically free from being held voteless; and socially free from insult." [18]

The N.A.A.C.P. wants not only economic security but civic, political, and social security. It demands recognition, social response, and the opportunity for new experiences in areas closed to the Negro.

3. The third social and economic trend of our period is represented in the National Urban League which was organized in 1910. It was incorporated as the National League on Urban Conditions among Negroes in 1913, one year before the beginning of the third epoch of our investigation. The Urban League is chiefly concerned with the Negro's advancement in industry—his opportunity to get work on the basis of efficiency and as far as possible without discrimination; his opportunity to improve and to be promoted on the job; and to promote the idea of equal pay for the same calibre of work done. The League is also concerned with the making of scientific investigations to set forth the facts pertaining to the Negro as a worker and to stipulate his industrial and economic needs. It seeks to improve urban conditions among Negroes in matters of health, recreation, delinquency, and crime. It endeavors to get the doors of organized labor opened to the Negro. Like Booker Washington, the National Urban League expresses the Negro's desire to be

---

[18] The N.A.A.C.P., Its History, Achievement, purposes (New York: The National Association for the Advancement of Colored People, 1933).

economically secure. The next trend also reveals the desire to be economically protected.

4. There is emerging now a new emphasis with respect to the economic status of the Negro—an emphasis that differs widely from that of the National Urban League, but is related to it in its economic substance. It might be stated as the emphasis of the Negro Business League and other leaders who reflect the view of the Negro Business League. Instead of seeking to become integrated with American business generally, this group argues that from necessity the Negro must build up a separate and distinct group economy of his own or he will be completely crushed or forever exploited. W. C. Matney says:

"It is the opinion of the writer that the Negro is faced with two alternatives: continued exploitation in the present economic order; or economic and industrial opportunity through an ever widening co-operative society of the Negroes' own making." [19]

Dubois writes:

"A new organized group action along economic lines, guided by intelligence and with the express object of making it possible for Negroes to earn a better living and, therefore, more effectively to support agencies for social uplift, is without the slightest doubt the next step. It will involve no opposition from white America because they do not believe we can accomplish it. They expect always to be able to crush, insult, ignore and exploit 12,000,000 individual Negroes without intelligent organized opposition. This organization is going to involve deliberate propaganda for race pride. That is, it is going to start out by convincing American Negroes that there is no reason for their being ashamed of themselves; that their record is one which should make them proud; that their history in Africa and the world is a history of effort, success and trial, comparable with that of any other people." [20]

---

[19] Matney, W. C., Exploitation or Cooperation (Crisis: Vol. 37) January, 1930.

[20] DuBois, W. E. B., Article: "On Being Ashamed of Oneself" (September Crisis, 1933) p. 200.

5. The fifth trend is set forth by the Association for the Study of Negro Life and History. This Association was organized in Chicago by Carter G. Woodson, September 9, 1915, one year after the beginning of the third epoch of the study. In brief, the Association aims to create in the Negro group esteem and group self-respect. It seeks to do this primarily by unearthing the history and past accomplishments of Negroes and publishing these in books, articles, and in the Journal of Negro History, the official organ of the Association. It seeks further to develop group esteem and group and individual self-respect by urging Negroes to study their history and by urging the teaching of Negro history in Negro schools. It is the belief of the Association that the Negroes will never be an upstanding, respectable people as long as they despise their history and look upon themselves with eyes of inferiority. This desire for status is to be achieved primarily by getting the Negro to accept and appreciate himself.

6. The last trend of the period is embodied in the ideas of Communism. This is wholly a post-War trend and is built upon the belief that the hope of the Negro lies in the Communist Party where the barriers of race are almost completely abolished —a philosophy built upon the conviction that the present economic order must be completely uprooted and the Communism of Russia instituted in its stead. The uncompromising stand which the International Labor Defense has taken in its efforts to save the lives of the Scottsboro boys, its heroic work in the case of Angelo Herndon, and the nomination of a Negro for the office of vice-president by the Communist party in 1932 and again in 1936—all are potent factors intended to convince the Negro that his opportunity for social justice lies in Communism.

It should be noted here that these trends do not appear in chronological sequence and they do not appear in isolation. There is overlapping, and often more than one appear in the writings of the same period or man.

It is against the social, economic, and educational background portrayed in the preceding pages that an effort is made to prove the fact that the idea of God in contemporary Negro literature is developed along compensatory, social, and atheistic lines.

The Main Contentions

The main emphases of the study are placed upon the development of the idea of God in its relation to certain trends revealed in contemporary Negro literature.

1. In much of the "mass" literature and in an appreciable amount of the "classical" Negro literature, ideas of God adhere strictly to traditional, compensatory patterns. They are traditional in the sense that they are mainly those of orthodox Christianity as set forth in the Bible, with primary emphasis upon the magical, spectacular, partial, revengeful, and anthropomorphic nature of God as revealed in the Old Testament; the New Testament ideas of a just, impartial God; and those ideas of God that are being rapidly discarded in an age of science. The ideas are compensatory when used or developed to support a shallow pragmatism. That is, a belief or idea may be accredited as true if it satisfies our desire, "if it uplifts and consoles;" or if it makes us "happier to believe it" even though the belief or idea does not fit observed facts. A dependent mother who believes in a God who answers prayers and who prays to him twice daily asking him to bless her sons, preserve their lives, and cause them to prosper (thinking her task is done when she does this) is typical of an idea of God that supports such pragmatism. The idea influences her behavior—it leads her to pray; it helps her to feel better; it saves her from much worry; it enables her to sleep at night. This person's behavior is different from that of a person who does not believe in this sort of praying. It has value for the mother but it is an idea of God used to perpetuate compensatory thinking. Furthermore, ideas of God that are used to support an other-worldly view are ideas that adhere to traditional, compensatory patterns, those ideas that encourage one to believe that God is in his

heaven and all is right with the world, and finally, those that tend to produce negative goodness in the individual based on a fear of the wrath of God here or in the next world.

2 There is a constructive development of the idea of God to support a growing consciousness of needed social adjustment. This necessary social adjustment may be differentiated as follows:

> a. Social adjustment that is universal in scope but inclusive of the needs of the Negro.
> b. Social adjustment that is confined primarily to the social and economic needs of the Negro.
> c. A psychological adjustment in which the idea of God is interpreted to support the growing conviction that the Negro is not an inferior people and for that reason is entitled to the social, economic, and political privileges exercised by other groups.

3. There is a growing tendency or threat on the part of the younger post-War writers to abandon the conception of God "as a useful instrument" in social rehabilitation as evidenced by the following facts:

> a. There is a tendency to doubt God in respect to His being of value to the Negro in his effort to rise.
> b. There is a denial of the existence of God.
> c. God is described as having outlived his usefulness.

The development of the idea of God in relation to these trends constitutes the heart of this study. The main purpose is to discover the authors' ideas of God and see how the ideas have developed in the period covered. Though discovering these three major developments of the idea of God in Negro literature, the writer is well aware that it is not always possible to draw a sharp line of demarcation, for example, between a compensatory idea and one that is socially derived.

The literature of the Negro group is used because the author is interested in the Negro race and because the Negro represents one of the minority, underprivileged groups in American society. Since the behavior of the suppressed groups tends to differ from the behavior of dominant groups, the needs of the suppressed may be different. It is certainly true that the opportunity for achieving economic, social, and political needs is less available to the Negro than is usually true of American people at large.

Then, too, in social and psychological areas the reactions of suppressed groups are more than likely to be different from those of the dominant groups. This leads to the assertion that the social and psychological needs of the Negro group are likely to be different from those of the dominant, ruling majority. This idea is implied by Herbert Miller when he speaks of the oppression psychosis of oppressed groups—meaning by oppression "the domination of one group by another, politically, economically, or culturally—singly or in combination." He means by psychosis "those persistent and exaggerated mental states which are characteristically produced under conditions where one group dominates another." Miller points out that an oppressed group is abnormally subjective. There is likely to be an incapacity to view its own problems objectively. The group is hyperaesthetic to itself and its members are likely to go around with chips on their shoulders. Supersensitiveness to insult is highly characteristic of oppressed groups.

In addition to being highly subjective, the suppressed group is usually suspicious—constantly on guard. It is also characteristic of oppressed groups to develop what psychology calls the "inferiority complex." Often they are unnecessarily aggressive in their effort to make up for "their inferiority." Likewise the oppression psychosis tends to create a group solidarity which could not otherwise be created.[21] It goes without saying that the characteristics just described are applicable to the Negro.

These are some of the chief reasons why it is felt that the needs of the Negro group are sufficiently distinct to warrant the attempt to see how the idea of God has developed in Negro literature.

---

[21] Miller, H. A., *Reaces, Nations and Classes* (Philadelphia: J. P. Lippincott Company, 1924), p. 32.

The Method of Approach

"Classical" Negro literature and "mass" Negro literature are examined and analyzed. The various ideas of God are pointed out. Special attention is paid to the desires, needs, and fundamental wishes expressed in the references containing the ideas of God. Following the analysis the ideas of God are appraised in the light of the trends already outlined.

The ideas of God in the "mass" literature (Sunday School literature from three major Negro denominations, prayers, sermons, and the Negro Spirituals) are used for the purpose of furnishing a basis of comparison between the ideas of God in that literature and those in the "classical" Negro literature. It is important to know to what extent the ideas of God in church services and the church literature are reflected in "classical" Negro literature, and to what extent that literature is in harmony with or is a protest against the ideas of God as found among the masses.

The ideas of God expressed by a writer at different periods in his writings are compared and analyzed. For example, it is highly conceivable that one's idea of God prior to 1914 may be quite different from his idea of God since 1914. The concepts of God expressed by authors prior to 1914 are compared with the concepts expressed by authors since 1914. It is shown here that the World War and its aftermath, the larger outlook that the Negro developed during the War, and the disillusionment that followed, wrought changes in the Negro's conception of God.

Finally, the ideas of God, previously indicated in the main emphases, are studied against the Negro's social and economic background—to see to what extent his ideas of God are developed out of his social and economic environment, and the psychological needs born of that environment. This is a vital point because there are various approaches to a conception of God, and to see which approach the Negro has made is revealing in the light of the social situation in which he lives and of his minority status in American life. Further exposition clarifies the point.

There are people who arrive at the fact of God and the nature of God through the experience of nature. Those who argue for God on the basis of cosmology and teleology are illustrative of this type. It is of interest to note the reflection or non-reflection of the cosmological and teleological ideas of God in Negro literature. There are others who reach their conception of God by observing progress in nature. Shailer Mathews argues that the emergence of personality shows progress in nature and he defines God as the personality producing activity. Other nature approaches to God are seen in Bergson's *Elan Vital* where God is identified with some kind of evolutionary process; the Holistic Principle of Smuts (though it is not called God by Smuts); the idea that God is the struggle toward the next higher level as represented by Alexander; the view of H. N. Wieman, (similar to Smuts') that God is progressive integration; and the mystical approach whereby one experiences a feeling of mystery in the presence of nature.

There is a mystical approach to God in which one experiences a sense of wholeness—a feeling that one is a part of the whole. This may lead to a type of uno-mysticism, complete absorption in the Deity.

Some people approach God through the sense of moral struggle against sin and evil in which case God reveals himself in the struggle with man. Some approach God through the intellect as did Hegel; in which case God becomes absolute truth. "God is that which makes logically possible the unity of our experiences." There is still another approach which is akin to the ethical approach. It may be expressed as follows: one may approach God by accepting the traditional views of God, taking God for granted as Jesus and the prophets did, but in an effort to achieve fulness of life, emphasizing those ideas of God that support one's desires and struggles to achieve the needs for existence. It is highly possible that the man who is suppressed and feels the injustices of society, would emphasize the justice of God. Whatever approach or approaches to God the Negro takes in his literature, it will be of value and will shed light on the Negro's religion and theology.

CHAPTER II

Ideas of God in the Literature of the Negro Masses

A. The Spirituals.

The "mass" literature includes the Spirituals, sermons, prayers, and Sunday School literature. It is the literature which contains the ideas of God that are taught to church goers through the channels named; ideas that reach the people in sermons and through the minister in public utterances. These ideas are distinguishable from those that are more likely to be concealed from the masses in literary productions other than sermons. The ideas of God as found here and their relation to the main emphases in Chapter I are compared with those found in "classical" Negro literature. Since the Spirituals grew out of slave experiences and subsequent conditions similar to slavery, they are representative of ideas of God held by the masses in the whole period of study.

In treating the ideas of God in the Negro Spirituals, although they follow the traditional, compensatory pattern, it should be stated here that the Spirituals represent one of the greatest contributions to American culture. The creation of the Spirituals was hardly an accident in Negro life. It was a creation born of necessity in order that the slave might more adequately adjust himself to the new conditions in the new world.

Speaking of the Spirituals in another connection, the writer says:

> "These songs are the expressions of the restrictions and dominations which their creators experienced in the world about them. They represent the soul-life of the people. They embody the joy and sorrow, the hope and despair, the pathos and aspiration of the newly transplanted people;

and through them the race was able to endure suffering and survive. Clearly, the Negro Spirituals are not songs of hate; they are not songs of revenge. They are songs neither of war nor of conquest. They are songs of the soil and of the soul." [1]

It is this "soul" quality of the Spirituals that makes their contribution to American life and culture a unique one. James Weldon Johnson senses the quality and value of the Spirituals in the last two stanzas of "O Black and Unknown Bards":

"There is a wide, wide wonder in it all,
That from degraded rest and servile toil
The fiery spirit of the seer should call
These simple children of the sun and soil.
O black slave singers, gone, forgot, unfamed,
You—you alone, of all the long, long line
Of those who've sung untaught, unknown, unnamed,
Have stretched out upward, seeking the divine.

"You sang not deeds of heroes or of kings;
No chant of bloody war, no exulting paean
Of arms-won triumphs; but your humble strings
You touched in chord with music empyrean.
You sang far better than you knew; the songs
That for your listeners' hungry hearts sufficed
Still live,—but more than this to you belongs:
You sang a race from wood and stone to Christ." [2]

The Spirituals, having their origin in slavery, or under conditions comparable to slavery, are characteristic of ideas of God held by many Negroes throughout the entire period, from 1760 to now. The ideas of God in the early sermons and those in very recent sermons are very similar to the ideas set forth in the Spirituals. Thus, it is in order to begin the survey of "mass" literature with the Spirituals.

It is legitimate to use the God-ideas of the Spirituals and *God's Trombones* because, as will be seen subsequently, the

---
[1] Mays & Nicholson, The Negro's Church (New York: Institute of Social and Religious Research, 1933), p. 2.
[2] Johnson, James Weldon, The Book of American Negro Spirituals (Binghamton, New York: The Vail-Ballon Press, 1925), p. 12.

God-ideas of one hundred sermons published in 1933 reflect to an amazing degree, those found in the Spirituals and *God's Trombones*.

The ideas reflected in the Spirituals may be briefly summarized: God is omnipotent, omnipresent, and omniscient. In both Heaven and earth God is sovereign. He is a just God—just to the point of cruelty. In the very nature of things sinners will be punished by God. He will see to it that the wicked are destroyed. God is revengeful. He hardened the heart of Pharaoh for the express purpose of trapping him and his host in the Red Sea. This indicates that God is a warrior and He fights the battles of His chosen people. "Go Down Moses" and "Joshua Fit de Battle ob Jerico" are filled with the confidence that God takes care of His own.

He will also see to it that the righteous are vindicated and that the heavily laden are given rest from the troubles of the world. The Spirituals, "Mos' Done Toilin' Here" and "Members, Don't Git Weary," are illustrative of the assurance that God will give rest to those who toil here below.

This rest comes after death. God saves for Heaven those who hold out to the end. He provides golden crowns, slippers, robes, and eternal life for the righteous. The principal reward comes in the other world.

God is near and there is a feeling of dependence upon Him. In times of distress, He is ever present. The idea that God comforts and consoles in hours of trial is brought out in the Spirituals, "Keep Me From Sinking Down" and "Give Me Jesus When I Come to Die." There is no doubt that God is ever present.

He answers prayers. It makes no difference what one does or what the situation is, "A little talk wid Jesus makes it right." Complete reliance on God is clearly seen in the belief that God answers prayers and rewards those who pray. God is observant. He sees all you do and He hears all you say. It is implied that one is judged by God for all deeds whether in words, thoughts, or actions. All the desires and wishes of mankind are to be fulfilled through the handiwork of God.

The desire for response, though overlapping with other desires, particularly the craving for recognition, is pregnant throughout the Spirituals. The lonesome, troubled, weary soul, failing to get proper attention and sympathetic understanding from man, seeks warmth, satisfaction, and recognition from Jesus and God. "Nobody Knows de Trouble I See, Nobody Knows but Jesus"; "Sometimes I Feel Like a Motherless Child"; "Every Time I Feel the Spirit"; "Oh, When I Come to Die, Give Me Jesus"; and "Steal Away to Jesus" are fair examples of the yearning on the part of the Negro to get the emotional satisfaction that comes to one who feels that his environment is friendly and that his friends can and do enter into sympathetic appreciation of the difficulties that beset him. There is, however, a strain of pessimism so far as this world is concerned. The response is expected to come not from man and not from the earth but from God and Heaven.

The Negro not only seeks response in the Spirituals but he seeks physical and emotional security. This is especially true during turbulent times. "Sometimes de forked light-nin' an' muttering thunder too, of trials an' tem'-tation make it hard for me an' you, but Jesus is our friend, He'll keep us to de en'." Though mingled with response, the following shows a yearning for security: "Now Lord, I give myself to Thee, 'Tis all dat I can do. If Thou should draw Thyself from me,—oh, whither shall I flee?.....Lord, if I go, tell me what to say, Dey won't believe in me." Economic security is not sought here. It is protection from danger and the desire to feel safe and secure in a world that is none too friendly. Emotional security and the desire for response are revealed in the Spiritual, "I'm troubled in mind. If Jesus don't help me I sho'ly will die—Jesus my Saviour, on Thee I'll depen' when troubles am—near me, you'll be my true friend." In chaotic and distressing times, one can feel safe and be sure of protection because Jesus is near. The Spirituals, "I got a home in a dat rock.....poor man Laz-rus, poor as I, when he died he foun' a home on high. He had a home in dat rock," "My Soul's been Anchored in de Lord" and the

Spiritual, "Save me, Lord, save me. I, me, yes, I want God's heab'n to be mine," are fair samples of the desire for security to be experienced outside the process of history.

The desire for new experiences expresses itself too, though at times, it is difficult to distinguish new experiences from the desire for security. The following quotation expresses both desires: "In dat great gittin' up mornin' I'm—a goin' to tell you 'bout de comin' of the Saviour, fare you well, fare you well.....Dere's a better day a-com-in', fare you well, fare you well.....In dat great gittin up morn-in', fare you well, fare you well. Dere dey live wid God for-ever." Other expressions of the desire for new experiences are: "Walk in Jerusalem jus' like John"; "Oh, yes! oh, yes! Wait 'til I git on my robe"; "Death come to my house he didn't stay long; hallelu-u-u—O, my Lord, I'm gwine-ter see my mother again"; "Gwinter ride up in de chariot soon-a in de mornin'—gwine-ter meet my brother dere, yes, soon-a in de morn-in', "; "'Zekiel saw de wheel"; "My ship is on de Ocean—I'm go-in' away to see de good ol' Daniel, I'm go-in a-way to see my Lord"; "Walk to-gether children, don't get weary—There's a great camp meeting in the Promise Land"; and, "Some o' dese morn-in's bright an' fair, death's gwine-ter lay his cold i-cy hands on me, I'll take-a my wings an' cleave de air." In the light of the foregoing analysis, it is now necessary to consider the relation these ideas of God bear to the main emphases or trends stipulated in the introductory chapter.

Clearly the ideas of God in the Spirituals adhere to the traditional, compensatory pattern. For the most part the authors of the Spirituals appropriated the ideas of God found in the Bible, particularly the magical, spectacular, and miraculous ideas of the Old Testament; either that or the ideas of God in the Spirituals were stimulated by those contained in the Bible. They adhere to the compensatory pattern because they are ideas that enable Negroes to endure hardship, suffer pain, and withstand maladjustment, but they do not necessarily motivate them to strive to eliminate the source of the ills they suffer. This holds true for the ideas found in the one hundred twenty-two Spirituals examined in this connection. Most of them are other-worldly—that is, they lead one to repudiate this world, consider it a temporary abode, and look to Heaven for a complete realization of the needs and desires that are denied expression here. It is strongly implied in the following quotation that God will supply the needs of His "chillun" not in this world but in the world to come. It is implied that patience and suffering endured here will be trebly rewarded in Glory. The Spiritual, "I got a robe, you got a robe, all o' God's chillun got a robe. When I get to heab'n I'm goin' to put on my robe, I'm goin' to shout all ovah God's heab'n," illustrates the point. This idea of God helped Negroes to endure their troubles and sing to their oppressors: "Ev'rybody talk-in' 'bout heab'n ain't goin' dere; heab'n, heab'n, heab'n, I'm goin' to fly all ovah God's heab'n." "Deep river, my home is over Jordan" is a denial of this world and implies that God provides rest and security in heaven. "O, by an' by, by an' by—I'm gwinter lay down my heavy load" shows that the Negro is tired and that he is looking forward to the time when troubles will be over. The idea is that God is preparing a place for him in Heaven where the heavy loads borne here will no longer need to be carried. The same idea is inferred in the Spiritual, "I know de udder worl' is not like dis." No idea of God is so dominant in the Spirituals as the belief that God will make things right in Heaven.

Those ideas of God which support the traditional view that even though things are not right here, and will probably not be made right in this world, they will be made right in Heaven, are ideas which adhere to traditional, compensatory patterns. Since this world is considered a place of temporary abode, many of the Negro masses have been inclined to do little or nothing to improve their status here; they have been encouraged to rely on a *just* God to make amends in Heaven for all the wrongs that they have suffered on the earth. In reality, the idea has persisted in some areas that hard times are indicative of the fact that the Negro is God's chosen vessel and that God is disciplining him for the express purpose of bringing him out victoriously and triumphantly in the end. The idea has also persisted that "harder the Cross, brighter the crown." Believing this about God, the Negro, in many instances, has stood and suffered much without bitterness, without striking back, and without trying aggressively to realize to the full his needs in this world.

The idea that God will punish sinners and those who torment His chosen people is also prevalent in the Spirituals. Pharaoh and his host were drowned because they interfered with God's plan for the chosen Israelites. As God protected the Jews from Pharaoh, the Negro masses have believed that God in His good time and in His own way would protect and deliver them. Until recently, they have never doubted that as God delivered Daniel, He would also deliver them in some magical, mysterious way, and in His own opportune time. This compensatory idea, that God will bring His own out victoriously in the end, has had a profound influence upon Negro life. In the midst of the most stifling circumstances, this belief in God has given the Negro masses emotional poise and balance; it has enabled them to cling on to life though poor, miserable, and dying, looking to God and expecting Him, through miraculous and spectacular means, to deliver them from their plight. The idea has made Negroes feel good; it has made life endurable for them; and it has caused them to go to church on Sunday and shout and sing and pray. It has sent them back to their unbearable situations on Monday strengthened to carry on another week, consoled by the fact that "troubles don't last always." Equally consoling has been the idea that God is near, He understands. I can tell my troubles to Him when no human being can understand or sympathize. "When my father and mother forsake me, then the Lord will take me up." This belief, too, has made the burden easier to bear.

The fact that these ideas of God, as portrayed in the Spirituals, have had profound compensatory influence upon the Negro can be authenticated not only through logical processes, and by an analysis of the data themselves, but it can be validated in Negro life. Thousands of people, particularly Negroes, have seen the compensatory result of these ideas in their own communities. Long before I knew what it was all about, and since I learned to know, I heard the Pastor of the church of my youth plead with the members of his congregation not to try to avenge the wrongs they suffered, but to take their burdens to the Lord in prayer. Especially did he do this when the racial situation was tense or when Negroes went to him for advice concerning some wrong inflicted upon them by their oppressors. During these troublesome days, the drowning of Pharaoh and his host in the Red Sea, the deliverance of Daniel from the Lion's Den, and the protection given the Hebrew children in the Fiery Furnace were all pictured in dramatic fashion to show that God in due time would take things in hand. Almost invariably after assuring them that God would fix things up, he ended his sermon by assuring them further that God would reward them in Heaven for their patience and long-suffering on the earth. Members of the congregation screamed, shouted, and thanked God. The pent up emotions denied normal expression in every day life found an outlet. They felt relieved and uplifted. They had been baptized with the "Holy Ghost." They had their faith in God renewed and they could stand it until the second Sunday in the next month when the experience of the previous second Sunday was duplicated. Being socially proscribed, economically impotent, and politically browbeaten, they sang, prayed, and shouted their troubles away. This idea of God had telling effects upon the Negroes in my home community. It kept them submissive, humble, and obedient. It enabled them to keep on keeping on. And it is still effective in 1937.

It is not surprising that the ideas of God in the Spirituals adhere to compensatory patterns. Speaking of the situation that gave rise to Negro Spirituals, and one might add the situation still exists in all too many places, James Weldon Johnson says:

"At the psychic moment there was at hand the precise religion for the condition in which he found himself thrust. Far from his native land and customs, despised by those among whom he lived, experiencing the pang of the separation of loved ones on the auction block, knowing the hard taskmaster, feeling the lash, the Negro seized Christianity, the religion of compensations in the life to come for the ills suffered in the present existence, the religion which implied the hope that in the next world there would be a reversal of conditions, of rich man and poor man, of proud and meek, of master and slave. The result was a body of songs voicing all the cardinal virtues of Christianity, patience—forbearance-love-faith-and hope..... It is not possible to estimate the sustaining influence that the story of the trials and tribulations of the Jews as related in the Old Testament exerted upon the Negro. This story at once caught and fired the imaginations of Negro bards, and they sang, sang their hungry listeners into a firm faith that as God saved Daniel in the Lion's Den, so would He save them; as God preserved the Hebrew children in the Fiery Furnace, so would He preseve them; as God delivered Israel out of bondage in Egypt, so would He deliver them. How much this firm faith had to do with the Negro's physical and Spiritual survival of two and a half centuries of slavery cannot be known." [3]

Not only have the ideas in the Spirituals developed along traditional, compensatory lines, but they have developed out of the social situation in which Negroes found themselves, at the point of social crisis. It has already been indicated, and it is common knowledge, that the Spirituals developed out of slavery or conditions equivalent to slavery. Seeing no opportunity for rest in this world the Negro looked to Heaven for rest. Accepting the fact that trouble in this world was inevitable, the Negro sang "I'm So Glad Trouble Don't Last Always"; "I Know De Udder Worl' Is Not Like Dis." Despairing of conditions here the Negro has looked to God and Heaven for deliverance.

History bears testimony to the fact that compensatory,

---

[3] Johnson, James Weldon, The Book of American Negro Spirituals (New York: The Viking Press, 1925), pp. 20, 21.

other-worldly ideas of God are usually developed at the point of social crisis—at the point where justice is denied, hopes are thwarted, and plans shattered. The compensatory, other-worldly ideas of God arose in Jewish history at a time when Israel had been subjected for generations to domination by one or another of the imperial powers. When the Jewish people, after prolonged suffering and persecution, accepted the idea that they could never hope to gain lasting political supremacy in this world, the belief in an age to come in which justice would hold complete sway came more conspicuously to the front.

The other-worldly idea of God, therefore, finds fertile soil among the people who fare worst in this world; and it grows dimmer and dimmer as the social and economic conditions improve. It is pointed out in *Middletown* that "it is in matters of belief that the churches apparently retain their most complete dominance over the lives of their members in certain groups of the working class, who on the one hand, have less opportunity for other approaches to problems than the business class, and, on the other, have fewer enjoyments in this life and more urgent needs," that "it will be made up to us in heaven."[4] It is not surprising, therefore, that the compensatory idea of God in Negro life has developed out of similar situations.

Although the majority of the Spirituals are compensatory and other-worldly, it would be far from the truth to say that all of them are of that character. Even in the Spirituals the Negroes did not accept without protest the social ills which they suffered. "Go Down, Moses," "Oh, Freedom," and "No More, No More, No More Auction Block For Me" are illustrative of the Spirituals that revolt against earthly conditions without seeking relief in Heaven. It seems that the Negro was accustomed to interpret Negro slavery in terms of Egyptian bondage. Throughout such interpretations, he implied that as freedom came to the Hebrews it would come to the Negro. The approach is subtle. "When Israel was in Egypt's land, Let my people go;

---

[4] Lynd, Robert S., and Helen Morrell, Middletown (New York: Harcourt, Brace and Company, 1929), p. 405.

Oppressed so hard they could not stand, Let my people go; Go down, Moses, 'way down in Egypt's land; Tell ole pharaoh—Let my people go." "Oh, Freedom!" is more militant. It shows that the Negro was determined to be a free people. "Oh, freedom! Oh, freedom! Oh freedom o-ver me! an' be-fo' I'd be a slave, I'd be buried in my grave, an' go home to my Lord an' be free." This ending sets forth the belief that God was against slavery and if the Negro died in the effort to be free, the Lord would receive him in Heaven. The Negro's appreciation for freedom is vividly expressed in the spiritual:

"No more, no more, no more auction block for me, many thousand gone
No more peck o' corn for me,
No more driver's lash for me
No more pint o' salt for me
No more hundred lash for me
No more mistress for me."

"Lord, I want to be a Christian in my heart," "I'm going to lay down my life for my Lord," "I'm a-going to do all I can for my Lord," and "I want to live so God can use me" are convincing arguments to show that God transforms character. In the latter Spiritual God cannot use you unless you treat your sisters, brothers, children, and neighbors right. That is the condition under which God can use you. "Let us cheer the Weary Traveler along the Lonesome way" is a beautiful example of the fact that the spirits of many slaves could not be broken. John Work says:

" 'Aunt Ailsie' was a slave in Augusta County, Virginia..... Her disposition was wholly lovable until she angered, and then she was a lioness robbed of her cubs. 'Aunt Ailsie' had greatly provoked her master, who would have killed her had she not been too valuable. He decided to sell her South. The slave trader bought her, placed her in his 'gang' and went to Staunton on the first stage of the journey. They pitched camp on Sunny Hill, on the outskirts of the town. Uncle 'Chester Bowling,' her brother, heard the news and went out to Sunny Hill, and begged the trader to let him keep his sister in his cabin over night. The trader yielded, and that night the cabin was full of prayers and songs. Her slave friends came in and stayed all night. Not an eye closed that night. They sang and prayed for help and comfort for 'Aunt Ailsie,' and when the bright morn of nature broke upon the world, 'Aunt Ailsie' turned her way to the slave gang, bound for the South. The weary, heart-bowed slaves in weird voice, sang:

"Let us cheer the Weary Traveler,
. . . .
Along the Lonesome Way." [5]

Certainly "Joshua Fit De Battle Ob Jericho" is an assertion of the belief that fighting your battle with God's help will bring victory. One is not to sit and wait for God alone. Man does his part and God His part. The ideas of God in these Spirituals are not compensatory and they are not other-worldly.

B. Sermons and Utterances of Ministers from 1760 to 1860.

Richard Allen, father, founder, and first bishop of the African Methodist Church was born a slave in 1760. He had a kind master who allowed him to purchase his freedom. Allen was one of the Negroes worshipping in St. George's Church, Philadelphia, in 1787, when Absalom Jones was forced from his knees during prayer because he and the other Negroes did not sit in the segregated seats provided for them. The final result of this act of discrimination was the organization of the African Methodist Episcopal Church in 1816. Allen believed in the traditional views of God which were current in his day and in our own time. Many of his traditional ideas of God, as will be seen later, were developed along social and racial lines. He accepted the orthodox view of God relative to sin and salvation. He believed that sinners would be lost and that conversion was a miraculous act of God. God forgives and saves the repentant sinner. Speaking of his conversion, Allen says:

"My mother and father and four children of us were sold into Delaware State, near Dover; and I was a child and

---

[5] Work, John W., *Folk Song of the American Negro* (Nashville: Press of Fisk University, 1915), pp. 85, 86.

lived with them until I was upwards of twenty years of age, during which time I was awakened and brought to see myself, poor, wretched and undone, and without the mercy of God must be lost. Shortly after, I obtained mercy through the blood of Christ, and was constrained to exhort my old companions to seek the Lord. I went rejoicing several days and was happy in the Lord, in conversing with many old, experienced Christians. I was brought under doubts, and was tempted to believe I was deceived, and was constrained to seek the Lord afresh. I went with my head bowed down for many days. My sins were a heavy burden. I was tempted to believe there was no mercy for me. I cried to the Lord both night and day. One night I thought hell would be my portion. I cried unto Him who delighted to hear the prayers of a poor sinner, and all of a sudden my dungeon shook, my chains flew off, and glory to God, I cried. My soul was filled. I cried enough for me—Savior died. Now my confidence was strengthened that the Lord, for Christ's sake, had heard my prayers and pardoned all my sins." [6]

This passage shows that Allen was primarily concerned with the salvation of his soul. He sought that emotional security which comes to one who knows that his sins are forgiven and who firmly believes that Heaven awaits him on the other side. Allen held a firm belief in prayer. He believed that God answered his prayers as the following quotation shows:

"I used ofttimes to pray, sitting, standing or lying; and while my hands were employed to earn my bread, my heart was devoted to my dear Redeemer. Sometimes I would awake from my sleep, preaching and praying. I was after this employed in driving of a wagon in time of the Continental War, in drawing salt from Rehobar, Sussex County, in Delaware. I had my regular stops and preaching places on the road." [7]

In many of Allen's enterprises it appears that he was sustained because he believed that God was with him. When he,

---

[6] Allen, Richard, The Life, Experience and Gospel Labors (Philadelphia: A. M. E. Book Concern), p. 5.
[7] Ibid, p. 8.

Absalom Jones, and William White were requested to leave their seats in St. George's Church during prayer, Allen believed that they had the support of God when they withdrew and that He was with them as they set out to establish a Church free of discrimination. He writes:

> "We had not been long upon our knees before I heard considerable scuffling and low talking. I raised my head up and saw one of the trustees, H—M—, having hold of the Reverend Absalom Jones, pulling him up off of his knees, and saying, "You must get up—you must not kneel here." Mr. Jones replied, "Wait until prayer is over." Mr. H—M— said "No, you must get up now, or I will call for aid and force you away." Mr. Jones said, "Wait until prayer is over, and I will get up and trouble you no more." With that he beckoned to one of the other trustees, Mr. L—S— to come to his assistance. He came, and went to William White to pull him up. By this time prayer was over, and we all went out of the Church in a body, and they were no more plagued with us in the Church. This raised a great excitement and inquiry among the citizens, in so much that I believe they were ashamed of their conduct. But my dear Lord was with us, and we were filled with fresh vigor to get a house erected to worship God in." [8]

Allen expresses further the idea reflected here when they were being coerced to return to St. George's Church under the threat of their being disowned by the Methodist body. Speaking of the man who tried to persuade them not to solicit money for the new Church, Allen writes:

> "We told him we were willing to abide by the discipline of the Methodist Church, 'And if you will show us where we have violated any law of discipline of the Methodist Church, we will submit; and if there is no rule violated in the discipline we will proceed on.' He replied, 'we will read you all out.' We told him if he turned us out contrary to rule of discipline, we should seek further redress. We told him we were dragged off of our knees in St. George's Church, and treated worse than heathens; and we were determined to seek out for ourselves, the Lord being our

---

[8] Ibid, pp. 14, 15.

helper.....'And if you deny us your name, you cannot seal up the scriptures from us, and deny us a name in heaven. We believe heaven is free for all who worship in spirit and truth.' And he said, 'So you are determined to go on.' We told him 'Yes, God being our helper.' He then replied, 'We will disown you from the Methodist connection.' We believed if we put our trust in the Lord, he would stand by us..... I was confident that the great head of the Church would support us. My dear Lord was with us." [9]

Richard Allen was not bitter and radical in his attitude toward slavery and the slave holder. He even urged his people not to hold any malice or ill-will against their owners. Yet he believed that slavery was against the will of God as he reveals in his address entitled "To Those Who Keep Slaves and Approve the Practice":

"We believe if you would try the experiment of taking a few black children, and cultivate their minds with the same care and let them have the same prospect in view as to living in the world, as you would wish for your own children, you would find upon the trial, they were not inferior in mental endowments. I do not wish to make you angry, but excite your attention to consider how hateful slavery is in the sight of that God who hath destroyed kings and princes for their oppression of the poor slaves. Pharaoh and his princes, with the posterity of King Saul, were destroyed by the protector and avenger of slaves.....

"When you are pleaded with, do not you reply as Pharaoh did, "Wherefore do ye, Moses and Aaron, let the people from their work, behold the people of the land now are many, and you make them rest from their burden." We wish you to consider that God himself was the first pleader of the cause of slaves.....

"If you love your children, if you love your country, if you love the God of love, clear your hands from slaves." [10]

Allen's ideas of God are further revealed under the captions which follow.

---

[9] Ibid, pp. 16, 17.
[10] Ibid, pp. 52, 53.

God Himself Has Pleaded the Cause of the Slave.

"Will you, because you have reduced us to the unhappy condition our color is in, plead our incapacity for freedom, and our contented condition under oppression, as a sufficient cause for keeping us under the grievous yoke? I have shown the cause, I will also show why they appear contented as they can in your sight, but the dreadful insurrections they have made when opportunity has offered, is enough to convince a reasonable man that great uneasiness and not contentment is the inhabitant of their hearts. God himself hath pleaded their cause; He hath from time to time raised up instruments for that purpose, sometimes mean and contemptible in your sight, at other times He hath used such as it hath pleased him, with whom you have not thought it beneath your dignity to contend." [11]

God Will Open a Way for the Slave; Love Your Masters and Trust God; Failing Here God Has a Place Above.

In his address "To the People of Color," Allen seems to believe that being good obedient slaves and affectionate toward the masters—would promote the slave's freedom. He comes very close in this address to advising the slaves to wait on the Lord to free them, if they failed to get freedom here they would get it in the other world.

"Feeling an engagement of mind for your welfare, I address you with an affectionate sympathy, having been a slave, and as desirous of freedom as any of you; yet the bands of bondage were so strong that no way appeared for my release; yet at times a hope arose in my heart that a way would open for it; and when my mind was mercifully visited with the feeling of the love of God, then these hopes increased, and a confidence arose that He would make way for my enlargement, and as a patient waiting was necessary, I was sometimes favored with it, at other times I was very impatient.....

I mention experience to you, that your hearts may not sink at the discouraging prospects you may have, and that you may put your trust in God, who sees your condition, and as a merciful father pitieth his children, so doth God pity them that love Him; and as your hearts are inclined to

---

[11] Ibid, pp. 53, 54.

serve God, you will feel an affectionate regard towards your masters and mistresses, so called, and the whole family in which you live. This will be seen by them, and tend to promote your liberty, especially with such as have feeling masters; and if they are otherwise, you will have the favor and love of God dwelling in your hearts; which you will value more than anything else, which will be a consolation in the worst condition you can be in, and no master can deprive you of it; and as life is short and uncertain, and the chief end of our having a being in this world is to be prepared for a better, I wish you to think of this more than anything else; then you will have a view of that freedom which the sons of God enjoy; and if the trouble of your condition end with your lives, you will be admitted to the freedom which God hath prepared for those of all colors that love him. Here the power of the most cruel masters ends, and all sorrow and tears are wiped away." [12]

You Trespass Against God If You Hate Your Former Masters.

"To you who are favored with freedom, let your conduct manifest your gratitude toward the compassionate masters who have set you free; and let no rancour or ill-will lodge in your breast for any bad treatment you may have received from any. If you do, you transgress against God, who will not hold you guiltless. He would not suffer it even in his beloved people Israel; and you think He will allow it unto us? Many of the white people have been instruments in the hands of God for our good; even such as have held us in captivity, are now pleading our cause with earnestness and zeal." [13]

God Punishes Ministers and Teachers Who Fail to Warn Sinners.

Allen believed that it was the indispensable duty of ministers and teachers to warn sinners and interest them to turn from their sinful ways to righteousness. If they did not do this the sinner's blood would fall upon the shepherd's head. He says:

"Ye ministers that are called to preaching,
Teachers and exhorters too,
Awake! behold your harvest wasting;
Arise! there is no rest for you.

---

[12] Ibid, pp. 54, 55.
[13] Ibid, p. 55.

"To think upon that strict commandment
That God has on his teachers laid
The sinner's blood, who die unwarned,
Shall fall upon their shepherd's head." [14]

God Demands That We Be Charitable.

To be good in a negative sense is not enough. To lay up comfortable provisions for one's family is good but it doesn't go far enough. God's will is that we use what God has given us to help those less fortunate than we are. In his address, "To the People of Color," Allen makes this point clear.

"Our blessed Lord has not committed his goods to us as dead stock, to be hoarded up or to lie unprofitably in our own hands. He expects that we shall put them out to proper and beneficial uses, and raise them to an advanced value by doing good with them, as often as we have opportunity of laying them out upon the real interest and welfare of his poor children and subjects. By doing acts of mercy and charity, we acknowledge our dependence upon God, and His absolute right to whatever we possess through His bounty and goodness; we glorify Him in His creatures, and reverence Him by a due and cheerful obedience to His commands. By applying our substance to the pomps and vanities of this wicked world, or the gratification of the sinful lusts of the flesh, we deny God's right to what He hath thought fit to place in our hands; and disown Him as our master by laying out His substance in ways expressly contrary to His orders; we thereby gratify Satan, whom we renounced at our baptism, and most shamefully, dishonor our Maker by the abuse of His talents. When, therefore, we are called to reckoning at that awful tribunal before which the most wealthy and powerful upon earth shall appear as naked and friendless as the poorest beggar, and when nothing but the goodness of our cause, and the mercy of our judge, can afford us the least support if in that strict and solemn examination we have no better accounts to give in, than—so much laid out in luxury and extravagance, rapine and oppression; so much in a vexatious, litigious lawsuit, or other idle, useless diversions, but little

---
[14] Ibid, p. 57.

or nothing in charity. Shillings and pounds upon our vanity and folly, but scarce a few pence upon doing good! With what shame and confusion shall we hang down our heads, and wish for rocks and mountains to cover us, not only from the view of our justly offended master, but from the eyes of angels and men, all witnesses of our disgrace.

"Some may, perhaps, say, 'Well, I have refrained from debauchery, folly and idleness; I have earned my honest penny, and kept it, and laid up a comfortable provision for my family.' Be it so; this is laudable and praiseworthy and it were to be wished that many more in this country would do so much. But may not such a one be asked, have you been charitable withal? Have you been as industrious in laying up treasures in heaven, as you have been in hoarding up perishable riches of this world? Have you stretched out your hand, as you had opportunity, beyond the circle of your own house and to God, who blessed them, by doing good to any beside your own? Has the stranger, the widow or the fatherless ever tasted of your bounty?.....And consider further, that the real poor and needy are Christ's representatives. We cannot, surely, doubt of this, if we look into our Saviour's own account of the last judgment, 25 Chapter of St. Matthew's Gospel, which plainly shows us that the inquiry at that great and solemn day will be very particular about our works of mercy and charity." [15]

God Decrees That the Righteous Shall Live in Eternal Memory.

It is said that on Sunday, December 29, 1799 in the African Methodist Episcopal Church, Richard Allen gave an address on the death of George Washington praising him for the manumission of his slaves. Allen says in that address:

"We, my friends, have peculiar cause to bemoan our loss. To us he has been the sympathizing friend and tender father. He has watched over us, and viewed our degraded and afflicted state with compassion and pity. His heart was not insensible to our sufferings. He, whose wisdom the nation revered, thought we had a right to liberty. Unbiased by the popular opinion of the state in which is the memorable Mount Vernon, he dared to do his duty and

---

[15] Ibid, pp. 60-62.

wipe off the only stain with which man could ever reproach him.

"And it is now said by an authority on which I rely, that he who ventured his life in battles—whose 'head was covered' in that day, and whose shield the 'Lord of hosts' was, did not fight for that liberty which he desired to withhold from others. The bread of oppression was not sweet to his taste, and he 'let the oppressed go free,' he undid every burden; he provided lands and comfortable accomodations for them, when he kept this 'acceptable' fast to the Lord, that those who had been slaves might rejoice in the day of their deliverance.....

"The name of Washington will live when the sculptured marble and stature of bronze shall be crumbled into dust; for it is the decree of the eternal God that the 'righteous' shall be 'held' in everlasting remembrance, but the memorial of the wicked shall not."[16]

Ideas of God as Developed by Richard Allen.

One might expect Allen to adhere closely to the traditional views of God. He used these ideas, for the most part, to try to improve the quality of living and to urge social changes that would be to the advantage of the Negro. When Allen advised Negroes to trust God for their freedom, love their masters and be obedient, to the end that freedom might be the result, if not here, in the world to come, it can hardly be said that these ideas were developed along social lines. He comes closer here, than elsewhere to a compensatory conception of God. If the slave did not get freedom here, he would get it in Heaven. This view of God had in it the germ to make the slave contented with his lot, thus accepting slavery until God saw fit to abolish it. But Richard Allen presents other ideas of God that move definitely away from those ideas that are merely compensatory toward those that urge social change. His courage to walk out of St. George's Church and to erect a new one on the conviction that God was with him are facts to show how the idea of God was

---

[16] Address taken from a framed copy of the "Philadelphia Gazette," dated Tuesday, December 31st, 1799, according to the A. M. E. Church Review, Vol. VI, page 365.

developed to arouse him to act to free the race from discrimination in worship. The ideas that slavery is hateful to God and that God punishes those who oppress the slaves are meant to induce masters to free their slaves. The idea that the slave trespasses against God if he hates his master is meant to improve the slave's quality of life. His other worldly ideas of God are so connected with life and conduct here that they are almost void of the compensatory element, for the entrance of man into Heaven is conditioned not by negative goodness but by the charitable attitude he takes toward those in need. The idea that God approves of those, like George Washington, who see to it that their slaves are free is another use of the idea of God in the area of social reconstruction.

What Allen desires most is that the needs of the race be met. He wants the race emancipated; worship conducted without discrimination; love and good will between master and slave fostered; equal opportunity for the mental development of the race provided; souls saved; and a heavenly home secured after death. His ideas of God are developed so that one will strive to achieve these needs here in this life and in the end achieve salvation in the world to come, none of which can be obtained without God.

Daniel Coker was born in slavery in Frederick County, Maryland. He was the son of Edward Coker and Susan Coker, an English woman who was an indentured servant of the man to whom Coker was a slave. At an early age, Daniel Coker ran away and found freedom in New York. Later he returned to Baltimore, hiding around until he could arrange to purchase his freedom from his master. Having learned to read and write from his master's son, he began the first African School in Baltimore. Daniel Coker had great influence in the organization of the A. M. E. Church having been the first or one of the first bishops elected in 1816, although he declined the election. A few years later Coker left America as a missionary to Liberia. He went there in company with ninety other Negroes who were sent to Sherbro by the American Colonization Society for the purpose of colonization. He died in Africa and is recognized as the "first pioneer and martyr of the African Methodist Episcopal Church to the cause of missions."[17] He reveals interesting ideas of God.

God Is in This Venture of Ours; It Is God's Work.

Writing at sea, February 12, 1820, Coker says:

"This morning, I awoke, and found that the wind had greatly abated; the vessel had got under sail. Mr. Bacon called unto me, as I slept in the next berth, to know how my faith was, I told him it was not moved. He interrogated each of the agents to the same purpose. Mr. Bankson, spoke in language that shewed strong faith in the arrival of the vessel in Africa..... We had not been long under sail, before we espied a wreck, and the captain gave order to steer for it. We found it to be the ship *Elizabeth*, of Boston, the chief mate and two of the sailors got into the long-boat, and ventured to go to the windows to see if any of the crew were on board; but found none. No doubt but they are all drowned. O God! Why were we spared? Surely because this expedition is in the care of God, as it is the object of sincere prayer of thousands in America. My soul travails that we may be faithful. And should God spare us to arrive in Africa that we may be useful." [18]

At sea, February 16, 1820 Coker writes:

"This day, we have pleasant sailing and fair wind, the minds of our agents are turned toward the governor of Sherbro, in what manner to bring the expedition before him, they have, however, concluded to lay the objects of the colonizing society, and the United States fully before him, in all its bearings, and leave the event to that God whose work we believe this is." [19]

---

[17] Wesley, Charles, Richard Allen, Apostle of Freedom (Washington: Associated Publishers, Inc. 1935), p. 170.
[18] Journal of Daniel Coker (Baltimore: Edward J. Coale, Publisher, 1820) p. 12, A copy of the Journal is found in the Library of Congress.
[19] Ibid, p. 13.

On arrival in Africa, Coker exclaims again, "God is in this Work."

"We have just got in sight of Mr. Kezzel's, where we expect to stay during the rainy season. We can see Mr. Kezzel walking on the beach, waiting to receive us—O God! thy name be praised, that it is not a lion, a tiger, or company of slave traders, that we first see—which might have been the case. When we came to shore, we were gladly received. —Mr. Kezzel had erected some small homes or huts, in case we should come from America, and perhaps arrive in the rainy season, that we could stay in these until we could get land and build houses. It is very surprising that all this Mr. Kezzel had done, although he has never heard from America since the return of Messrs. Mills and Burgess. But God is in this work." [20]

Here we have a group of Negroes possessing a sense of divine mission going forth to Africa for the purpose of colonizing the free people of color of the United States. They believed it was God's will and that God was helping and protecting them in the enterprise. All through history we find people who have done great things because they believed in God. These people did more than fold their arms and pray. They ventured and did things under the conviction that it was God's bidding. Ideas of God used in this way are ideas that are developed along the line of social reconstruction.—God is used as a helpful instrument in colonizing in Africa the free Negroes of color in the United States.

Slavery Will Be Abolished; God So Decrees; He Has Made of One Blood All Nations.

The Reverend Nathaniel Paul, Pastor of the First African Baptist Society in the city of Albany, delivered an address, July 5, 1827, in celebration of the abolition of Slavery in New York. Paul speaks with unusual firmness and conviction. At times he appears angry. He hates slavery so much that he would deny the existence of God if he thought slavery would last forever. In that address Paul says:

---
[20] Ibid, p. 33.

"The progress of emancipation, though slow, is nevertheless certain: It is certain because that God who has made of one blood all nations of men, and who is said to be no respecter of persons, has so decreed; I therefore have no hesitation in declaring from this sacred place, that not only throughout the United States of America but throughout every part of the habitable world where slavery exists, it will be abolished..... Did I believe that it would always continue, and that man to the end of time would be permitted with impunity to usurp the same undue authority over his fellows, I would disallow any allegiance or obligation I was under to my fellow creatures, or any submission that I owed to the laws of my country; I would deny the superintending power of divine Providence in the affairs of this life; I would ridicule the religion of the Saviour of the World, and treat as the worst of men the ministers of the everlasting gospel; I would consider my bible as a book of false and delusive fables, and commit it to flame; Nay, I would still go further: I would at once confess myself an atheist, and deny the existence of a holy God." [21]

Heaven Is Against Slavery.

The Reverend Mr. Paul says also in this address:

"Slavery, with its concomitants and consequences, in the best attire in which it can possibly be presented, is but a hateful monster, the very demon of avarice and oppression, from its first introduction to the present time; it has been among all nations the scourge of heaven, and the curse of the earth. It is so contrary to the laws which the God of nature has laid down as the rule of action by which the conduct of man is to be regulated towards his fellow man, which binds him to love his neighbor as himself, that it ever has, and ever will meet the decided disapprobation of heaven." [22]

Slavery Stands in the Way of Divine Grace.

Paul says further: "Since affliction is but the common lot of men, this life, at best, is but a vapor that ariseth and soon passeth away. 'Man,' said the inspired sage, 'that is

---

[21] Paul, Nathaniel, An address on the celebration of the Abolition of Slavery in New York delivered in Albany, New York, July 5, 1827, pp. 15-16—See Library of Congress.

[22] Woodson, Carter G., Negro Orators and their Orations (Washington: The Associated Publishers, 1925), p. 65.

born of a woman, is of few days and full of trouble'; and in a certain sense, it is not material what our present situation may be, for short is the period that humbles all to the dust, and places the monarch and the beggar, the slave and the master, upon equal thrones. But although this life is short, and attended with one entire scene of anxious perplexity, and few and evil are the days of our pilgrimage; yet man is advancing to another state of existence, bounded only by the vast duration of eternity in which happiness or misery await us all. The great author of our existence has marked out the way that leads to the glories of the upper world, and through the redemption which is in Christ Jesus, salvation is offered to all. But slavery forbids even the approach of mercy; it stands as a barrier in the way to ward off the influence of divine grace; it shuts up the avenues of the soul, and prevents its receiving divine instruction; and scarcely does it permit its miserable captives to know that there is a God, a Heaven or a Hell!" [23]

Righteousness and Judgment Are the Habitation of God's Throne.

In this section of the address, the Reverend Mr. Paul is in a quandary. He does not even understand why God permits the evils of slavery to exist. He finally ends with the conviction that God can bring good out of evil and He is able to make the wrath of men praise Him. He questions the waters, the winds, the waves, and God as to their aid in permitting slavery and the traffic in slavery to go on. The exact quotation follows:

"Tell me, ye mighty waters, why did ye sustain the ponderous load of misery? Or speak, ye winds, and say why it was that ye executed your office to waft them onward to the still more dismal state; and ye proud waves, why did you refuse to lend your aid and to have overwhelmed them with your billows? Then should they have slept sweetly in the bosom of the great deep, and so have been hid from sorrow. And, oh thou immaculate God, be not angry with us, while we come into this thy sanctuary, and make the bold inquiry in this thy holy temple, why it was that thou didst look on with the calm indifference of an unconcerned spectator, when thy holy law was violated, thy divine authority

---

[23] Ibid, p. 67.

despised and a portion of thine own creatures reduced to a state of mere vassalage and misery? Hark! While he answers from on high: hear Him proclaiming from the skies— Be still, and know that I am God! Clouds and darkness are round about me; yet righteousness and judgment are the habitation of thy throne. I do my will and pleasure in the heavens above, and in the earth beneath; it is my sovereign prerogative to bring good out of evil, and cause the wrath of man to praise me, and the remainder of that wrath I will restrain." [24]

Ideas of God Are Developed Along Social Lines.

The ideas of God expressed by the Reverend Nathaniel Paul deal almost exclusively with the institution of slavery. They are used to show that slavery should be abolished. Slavery is the one outstanding sin and it cuts off divine grace. Heaven and God are against it. It cannot stand because God has made of one blood all the nations of the earth. The ideas of God are developed along the line of social reconstruction in two particulars: the author uses God to prove that slavery should and will be overthrown and he develops the idea to instill race pride and group self respect in the Negro. The Negro, therefore, has no right to sit complacently by and accept slavery as God ordained; he has no reason to believe that he is inferior to other people. The ideas are not compensatory. The author, though a firm believer in Heaven and the rewards that accrue to one there, thinks that Heaven can hardly be obtained without the abolition of slavery.

All Souls Belong to God and Are Equal.

The Reverend Mr. Joseph M. Corr, of the First African Episcopal Methodist Church of Philadelphia, delivered an address in 1834 before the Humane Mechanics' Society. The one great aim of the address is to show that there is one Creator who has not made any discrimination in His work. The Reverend Mr. Corr desires status for his race; and he uses God to prove

---

[24] Ibid, p. 69.

that the Negro is the equal of men of other groups. His ideas of God are developed along social lines in that they tend to abolish from the mind of the Negro the feeling of inferiority—to make him feel that he is "somebody"—that he is made in the image of God. His words are convincing:

"Then let me ask the important question, Why! O Why! should not the coloured American citizen be equal, in all the qualities of the heart, and the powers of the mind, with his white brother? Has nature made him inferior? Has his great Creator designed him to be less, in any respect? Has he at any time, or on any occasion, declared it? Can there be a prophet produced, a revelation quoted, an oracle consulted, to unfold such an idea, to resolve such a problem, or expound such a theory? Ask the standard of truth; let Heaven's own inspiration be heard, and God himself speak! 'All souls are mine,' is his express declaration, 'for my ways are equal,' saith the Lord God, 'and consequently all my works are founded on the same basis.' "

"The pages of history furnish us with abundant proofs, from the achievements of our ancestors, that heaven has designed us to be an equal race." [25]

God Approves of the Fight for Freedom.

The Reverend Highland Garnet might justly be called a radical. He is one of the few leaders of his time who advocated any means whereby freedom might be achieved even to the point of violence and bloodshed. He was born a slave, December 23, 1815. He escaped with his parents nine years later and settled in Pennsylvania. He graduated from Oneida Institute in 1840 and taught school in Troy, New York. He became a minister and served congregations in New York and the District of Columbia.[26] At the National Convention of Colored Citizens held in Buffalo, New York, in 1848, he offered an address to be sent to all slaves in the United States. Quotations containing his ideas of God are taken from this address.

---

[25] Corr, Joseph M., Address Delivered Before the Humane Mechanics' Society (Philadelphia: 1834), p. 9—Moorland Room, Howard University.
[26] Woodson, C. G., Negro Orators and their Orations (Washington: The Associated Publishers, 1925), p. 149.

"If a band of heathen men should attempt to enslave a race of Christians, and to place their children under the influence of some false religion, surely Heaven would frown upon the men who would not resist such aggression, even to death. If, on the other hand, a band of Christians should attempt to enslave a race of heathen men, and to entail slavery upon them, and to keep them in heathenism in the midst of Christianity, the God of heaven would smile upon every effort which the injured might make to disenthrall themselves. "Brethren, it is as wrong for your lordly oppressors to keep you in slavery as it was for the man thief to steal our ancestors from the coast of Africa. You should therefore now use the same manner of resistance as would have been just in our ancestors when the bloody foot-prints of the first remorseless soul-thief was placed upon the shores of our fatherland. The humblest peasant is as free in the sight of God as the proudest monarch that ever swayed a sceptre. Liberty is a spirit sent out from God and, like its great Author, is no respecter of persons.

Brethren, the time has come when you must act for yourselves. It is an old and true saying that, 'if hereditary bondmen would be free, they must themselves strike the blow'." [27]

Obey God Rather Than Masters.

"The divine commandments you are in duty bound to reverence and obey. If you do not obey them, you will surely meet with the displeasure of the Almighty. He requires you to love Him supremely, and your neighbor as yourself—to keep the Sabbath day holy—to search the Scriptures—and bring up your children with respect for His laws, and to worship no other God but Him. But slavery sets all these at naught, and hurls defiance in the face of Jehovah. The forlorn condition in which you are placed does not destroy your obligation to God. You are not certain of heaven, because you allow yourselves to remain in a state of slavery, where you cannot obey the commandments of the Sovereign of the universe." [28]

---

[27] Ibid, pp. 153–54.
[28] Ibid, p. 153.

The Slave too Is Made in the Image of God.

While pastor of the Fifteenth Street Presbyterian Church in Washington, D. C., the Reverend Mr. Garnet delivered an address in the Hall of the House of Representatives, at the request of the Chaplain, Reverend William H. Channing. The following is an excerpt from that address.

"Let us view this demon, which the people here worshipped as a God. Come forth, thou grim monster, that thou mayest be critically examined! There he stands. Behold him, one and all. His work is to chattelize man; to hold property in human beings. Great God! I would as soon attempt to enslave Gabriel or Michael as to enslave a man made in the image of God, and for whom Christ died. Slavery is snatching man from the high place to which he was lifted by the hand of God, and dragging him down to the level of the brute creation, where he is made to be the companion of the horse and the fellow of the ox..... Our poor and forlorn brother whom thou hast labelled 'slave,' is also a man. He may be unfortunate, weak, helpless, and despised, and hated nevertheless he is a man. His God and thine has stamped on his forehead his title to his inalienable rights in characters that can be read by intelligent beings. Pitiless storms of outrage may have beaten upon his defenseless head and he may have descended through ages of oppression, yet he is a man. God made him such, and his brother cannot unmake him." [29]

Garnet, like most of his predecessors since 1760, saw one outstanding need for his people—freedom from the curse and thraldom of slavery. He, along with others, felt that there could be no kind of status and no security for the race without complete release from bondage. Security and status in freedom were sought mainly in this world. Some of these men developed the idea of God to persuade the masters to free the slaves because slavery was against God, but others urged a more violent way of freeing slaves, arguing that God would smile upon the slaves' efforts if they would strike a blow for freedom. Garnet, somewhat like the zealots among the Jews, implies that if the

[29] Dunbar, Alice Moore, Masterpieces of Negro Eloquence (New York: The Bookery Publishing Company, 1914), p. 110 ff.

Negro slaves would start a revolution, they would succeed because God would help them. He urges that it is right and just to resist slavery and that God would sanction their efforts to obtain freedom. It is quite plain that the ideas of God in Garnet's address are developed along the lines of social reconstruction which, he thought, would come through violent revolution. The slaves, he believed, were not to wait for God to start the fight; they themselves must start and finish it. They are not to wait for freedom in Heaven but they are to fight to achieve it here and now.

Bishop Daniel A. Payne

Daniel A. Payne was born of free parents in Charleston, South Carolina, February 24, 1811. On May 7, 1852, he was elected bishop of the A. M. E. Church at the General Conference in New York City. As early as 1829, Payne opened a school in a house on Tradd Street in Charleston. Though beginning with only six pupils, after the first year Payne's School grew rapidly until April 1, 1835, when an anti-slavery teaching bill passed by both houses of the South Carolina Legislature, in December, 1834, became effective. A part of the bill reads as follows:

> "If any person shall hereafter teach any slave to read or write, or cause, or procure any slave to read or write, such person, if a free white person, upon conviction thereof shall for each and every offense against this Act be fined not exceeding one hundred dollars and imprisoned not more than six months; or, if a free person of color, shall be whipped not exceeding fifty lashes and fined not exceeding fifty dollars, at the discretion of the court of magistrates and freeholders before which such person of color is tried." [30]

Speaking of this Act and how it weighed upon him, Payne says that he could not sleep and that he dreaded the approach of night. He even prayed for sleep but there was no answer to his prayers. His reaction to the Act reveals some of his views of God.

---

[30] Payne, Daniel A., Recollection of Seventy Years (Nashville—Publishing House of the A. M. E. Sunday School Union, 1888), p. 27.

Questioning the Existence of God.

"Sometimes it seemed as though some wild beast had plunged his fangs into my heart, and was squeezing out its life-blood. Then I began to question the existence of God, and to say: 'If he does exist, is he just? If so, why does he suffer one race to oppress and enslave another, to rob them by unrighteous enactments of rights, which they hold most dear and sacred?' Sometimes I wished for the lawmakers what Nero wished—"that the Romans had but one neck." I would be the man to sever the head from its shoulders. Again said I: 'Is there no God?' But then there came into my mind those solemn words: 'With God one day is as a thousand years and a thousand years as one day. Trust in him, and he will bring slavery and all its outrages to an end.' These words from the spirit world acted on my troubled soul like water on a burning fire, and my aching heart was soothed and relieved from its burden of woes." [31]

The author of this quotation clamors for the emancipation of his race and for the liberty to teach and uplift them. It is the social situation which inclines him momentarily to doubt God's existence. His firm faith in God enabled him to express the conviction that God in time would bring slavery to an end; that God would preserve his soul "when foes unite, or waves of trouble roll"; that the "Good Lord" would give him strength and sustain his feeble mind; and that God would not permit his sighs to ascend to Him in vain.[32] The idea of God here expressed gives the author emotional peace and calm. It soothes his soul as he struggles against the odds that confront him and his race.

Payne Is Commissioned by God.

Payne was able to go on in his program of racial uplift and social change because he believed God was in it and that he had been commissioned by God to perform a great task. This statement is confirmed by Payne's own words. When he opened his school in 1829 he had six pupils, each paying him fifty cents

---
[31] Ibid, p. 28.
[32] Ibid, p. 29.

a month, a total of three dollars. Although he was discouraged at the end of the year and desired other employment he refused the offer of a wealthy slave-holder to take him to work in the West Indies where he would earn much more than his school paid him. The reason which Payne gives for refusing the offer is that if he abandoned the school room, he would be fleeing from the Cross which God had laid on him. So on January 1, 1830, he reopened his school.[33] The firm conviction that God had commissioned him to do a special job caused Payne to go North to help his people since the Act of 1834 prohibited his teaching in Charleston after April 1, 1835. He had a dream which he interpreted to be a divine revelation directing him to the North where he could continue his work. Commenting on the dream, Payne writes:

"The effect of this dream was to settle my mind on the determination to seek a field of usefulness as a teacher in the free North, where I believed I could teach without let or hindrance." [34]

Speaking further on this point, Payne says:

"I sailed from Charleston the 9th of May, 1835, about four o'clock Saturday, in search of a field of usefulness as a teacher of children and youth, for such was the work to which I was conscious God had been training and was still training me." [35]

The idea that he was divinely commissioned permeated Payne's life and was uppermost in his mind when important decisions had to be made. When about twenty-six years of age, Payne began his career as a pastor. Shortly after beginning his pastoral work, he was offered three hundred dollars a year and traveling expenses to lecture for the Anti-Slavery Society. This was a great temptation for him, but he believed that God had dedicated his life to the pulpit and that he could not afford to turn aside from a position so high and holy. He writes:

---
[33] Ibid, p. 20.
[34] Ibid, p. 34.
[35] Ibid, p. 41.

"When God has a work to be executed he also chooses the man to execute it. He also qualifies the workman for the work. Frederick Douglass was fitted for his specialty; Daniel Alexander Payne for his. Frederick Douglass could not do the work which was assigned to Daniel Alexander Payne, nor Daniel Alexander Payne the work assigned to Frederick Douglass. 'The hour for the man, and the man for the hour.' He who undertakes, through envy, jealousy, or any other motive or consideration, to reverse this divine law resists the purpose of the Almighty and brings misfortune, sometimes ruin, upon himself." [36]

Color Discrimination is UnGodly; Retributive Justice Follows.

Bishop Payne was consistent in his belief that discrimination on the basis of color was against God. He not only objected to white people discriminating against Negroes but he took a firm hand against Negroes erecting the color bar in the face of white people. Shortly after his election to the bishopric, Payne had to rule against color prejudice in Bethel A.M.E. Church. In 1853, a white woman opened a school in Philadelphia for Negro children. Being somewhat ostracised by the white people, she found association among the parents of the children who employed her and worshipped at Bethel. Later she joined one of the classes. Great opposition arose on the part of the female members of the Church. Payne says:

"At this time I was in New England. On my return a male member asked me if our discipline permitted white persons to join our Church. I answered that there was no prohibition, and that the A.M.E. Church like Christianity itself, ought to be open to all and for all. On learning that the women were determined to have her turned out, I visited the pastor, and finding that he had authorized the classleader and local preacher to receive her, I expressed the hope that he would defend her rights, which he promised to do, but did not. The opposition increased daily. She was insulted in class and elsewhere. Not satisfied with this, they threatened to withhold support from the pastor, and to starve me out if I maintained her rights. Upon this I re-

---

[36] Ibid, p. 68.

solved to let those evil minded ones know that I belonged to that class of Christian ministers who cannot be controlled by back nor belly. I hired two rooms, fitted them up, bought kitchen utensils, and commenced keeping bachelor's hall. I not only did my own cooking, but washed my own garments, that I might support the right and uphold the government of the Church. The pastor expelled the woman because she was white and because he was urged to such an unchristian act by his own color—that is, the women in Bethel. My sense of duty in this case led me to leave that pastor without an appointment at the next Annual Conference. This caused much excitement among his personal friends, and I was urged to change my purpose; but to all I firmly replied that I feared not the result..... I was asked by Bishop Nazrey if I would consent that Bishop Quinn or himself should employ him in their service. I replied that they might do whatever they thought proper in the case, but I believed that the pastor who would turn away from God's sanctuary any human being on account of color was not fit to have charge of a gang of dogs. He was stationed by Bishop Nazrey at Toronto.

"Eleven years passed away. Meanwhile this pastor became a member of the British M. E. Church; but having lost his standing in it, he came back irregularly to the General Conference of 1864. His seat was disputed, and four times did the General Conference reject him in the very church from which he had expelled the white woman. The judgment of God in this case reminds me of his judgment against a certain pro-slavery, caste-loving bishop of the Protestant Episcopal Church." [37]

Payne was also opposed to the color prejudice which white people direct against Negroes. He continues:

"Sometime between 1837 and 1840 a young man who had been classically trained, of fine person, so highly mixed that he was mistaken for a white man, was admitted into the General Theological Seminary of the Protestant Episcopal Church. When his African descent on one side was ascertained he was ordered out by this bishop. Time passed, and another gifted and scholarly man completed his course as a star of the first magnitude at Oneida Institute. He also

---

[37] Ibid., pp. 116–17.

applied for admission into the same theological school at New York, but was rejected by the same bishop on account of his color. Both of these young men were obliged to take private instruction in theology. A day of retribution came. This grand prelate was accused, tried and found guilty of conduct unbecoming a Christian gentleman, still more in a prelate of such towering pretensions. He was expelled from the episcopacy. Several efforts were made by his friends to restore him, but he died expelled from the bishopric.

"If 'he that oppresseth the poor reproacheth his maker,' how great must be the reproach cast upon the Infinite when one man oppresses another on account of the color which distinguishes him from his fellow-mortals!" [38]

Bishop Payne developed his ideas of God along the lines of social reconstruction. He developed them to fight discrimination in the house of worship. He used them as a weapon to be hurled against the institution of slavery. He utilized them to defend his position against unchristian and anti-social practices. He made use of them at times when a less believing person might have resigned to the inevitable and accepted things as they were. His convictions about God gave him poise in the midst of conflict. He developed his ideas of God to perfect social changes that were racial and universal in scope.

Slave Holders Are Accountable to God.

In behalf of emancipation, the Rev. J. W. C. Pennington, pastor of the Colored Presbyterian Church of New York, placed the Negro's case before the public opinion of England. Speaking to the Glasgow Y.M.C.A., and the St. George's Biblical, Literary and Scientific Institute of London, Pennington pleads the cause of his race and predicts a great destiny for it. He, too, is interested in the emancipation of the race. Referring to the Negro, he says:

"Yes, I have shown you a people who are practicing, more faithfully than any other, the true Christian law of

---

[38] Ibid, pp. 117–19.

moral power. I mean the law of forgiveness and endurance of wrong. There is no solitary case on record of a minority, with justice on its side, being crushed, while adhering to the law of forgiveness and endurance. It is not the nature of God's moral government to permit such a thing. On this grand basis the colored people of America are safe for their future destiny. The American oppressor may destroy himself, but destroy the colored man he never can—He that reproveth God by taking moral agents which he has made for himself, and reducing them to the perpetual drudgery of brutes, will surely have to answer for it." [39]

Beliefs of this kind are capable of developing great patience among the oppressed. In the midst of stifling conditions one can be strong and brave because the moral government of God will not let him be crushed. Justice is on the Negro's side, thus he cannot lose. Though these ideas of God are closely related to compensatory ideas they can hardly be classed with them. They are interpreted as socially constructive. Masters are encouraged to abolish slavery on the ground that God is holding them accountable for treating moral agents as brutes. The day of retribution is sure to come. The slave, like other people, is made for God. A conviction of this kind tends to give the group the feeling that it has status in God and eventually God will vindicate it. The ideas give the impression of urging the oppressed to "wait for God to take care of them." But they are also capable of helping the Negro to become superior to environmental conditions, never allowing himself to be beaten down by them. They give poise, serenity, hope, and courage to one who struggles and fights, and promote faith in God that some day the clouds will break.

All ministerial utterances between 1760 and 1860 did not deal with social problems. Some ministers were not moved by the horror of social evils and their sermons are heavily laden with discussions of celestial things. Little attention was paid in them to the vital necessities of this life. They, like many

---

[39] Pennington, J. W. C., Address delivered before the Glasgow Y. M. C. A., p. 20—Moorland Room, Howard University.

other utterances of the period, served as an opiate for the people, leading them to endure whatever condition they faced since a better day awaited them after death. Many of the sermons preached between 1834 and 1853 in the African Protestant Episcopal Church of Philadelphia are definitely unrelated to social problems, though uttered at a time when the contest over slavery was precipitating the Civil War. The following quotations sustain the point advanced:

Hope in God and Rejoice.

"There is no such thing as chance in the history of God's people. Every event of their life, however afflicted in its character, is a link in that golden chain, which is to raise them progressively from earth to heaven. Are you bowed down with the weight of years and their increasing infirmities? Hope in God and rejoice, that the time is so near at hand, when angels at the gate of Paradise, shall hail you as an immortal born; born "to an inheritance, incorruptible, undefiled and that fadeth not away, reserved in heaven for you, who are kept by the power of God through faith unto salvation, ready to be revealed in the last." [40]

The thought of the beyond and the end continues in the next quotation.

The Day of the Lord Comes as a Thief in the Night.

"A word of admonition and entreaty to that class of our hearers, whose hopes are all centered in this lower world. It is true my deluded friends, that this earth has its peculiar attractions. The innumerable multitude, that in every land, throng the "broad way that leadeth to destruction" is proof positive, that some strong enchantments are beguiling their devious pathway to the unknown future. But bear in mind, do not forget, in your silly chase after a phantom, that this planet, with all its fine furniture, is to be dissolved." The day of the Lord will come as a thief in the night, in which, the heavens shall pass away with a great noise, and the elements shall meet with fervent heat, the earth also and the works that are therein shall be

---

[40] Douglass, William, Sermons Preached in the African Protestant Episcopal Church, of St. Thomas, (Philadelphia: King and Baird, 1854,) p. 22.

burned up. Nevertheless, we according to his promise look for new heavens and a new earth, wherein dwelleth righteousness." [41]

The other-worldly ideas of God continue in the sermon entitled "Servants of God."

Servants of God Rest from Toils and Cares; Death to Them Is Sleep.

"The approach of death excites no terror in the bosom of the Christian, because he has the Lord Jehovah for his everlasting strength. It matters not under what circumstances he comes, whether at midnight or in the morning; whether in a slow measured pace, or as quick as the lightning's flash, he walks "through the valley and shadow of death," calm and collected, fearing "no evil," for the "rod and staff" of his divine master affords him unspeakable "comfort."....."Death to the pious may with great propriety be represented under the idea of sleep. Because they then rest from all the toils and cares inseparable from this probationary state. As when evening comes on the labourer takes his rest, and forgets the toils of the day when he lies down to sleep, so at death, the faithful servant of God finishes his course of service, retires from the field of labor and then goes to his rest in the Paradise of God." [42]

By every count the ideas of God revealed above are both traditional and compensatory. They are traditional in that they are supported by Orthodox Christianity and scriptural proof can be found for them. They adhere to compensatory patterns because they support an other-worldly view and are capable of attracting so much attention to the life beyond that life here is renounced. Many people with such ideas, more than likely, would accept life at a poor dying rate with apparent satisfaction because they consider life here only transitory. It is true that some ideas in the book of sermons call for repentance but repentance usually as a means of escaping the impending judgment. These ideas, too, fall in the category of the compensatory because they tend to produce negative goodness based wholly on a fear of the wrath of God in the next world. They

---

[41] Ibid, p. 23.
[42] Ibid, pp. 238–40.

make it easier for the adherents to escape social responsibility here, and they probably had this effect on many during the heated years between 1830 and 1850.

The Reverend N. C. Cannon in his book *The Rock of Wisdom*, published in 1833, is not concerned with social questions. His primary concern is to save souls for the next world.

Prepare to Live with God.

"Oh ye Sons of Ethiopia awake unto righteousness, for Jesus saith come unto me and if the ministers will not preach the word nor come to God, you all come and escape Hell's dark gates, for in that awful day this is their portion, the wicked is cast down into Hell, Psalm 9, 17v. and p. 11, 6v. Upon the wicked he shall rain fire and brimstone and a horrible tempest, this shall be the portion of their cup; two great wonders in heaven to see the poor and the outcast and the despised standing in white at the right hand of God, exalted to the throne of glory, crowned in endless bliss; the second wonder, those whom we condemned in our judgment for to go down to Hell; see! Oh see arrayed in white robes and palms in their hands going the great rounds of eternal bliss, these are the two great wonders in heaven; and now the third wonder is to see tens of thousands and hundreds of thousands whom we judged to be unworthy fight for the Kingdom, but in God's righteous judgment they will be condemned to blow the awful flames of Hell fire; Oh man, this is the great wonder man will see, and now is the time to seek for pardon and live with God while he is calling come, Oh come, and be liberated for there is a time coming when the great door of pardon will be closed forever and ever, Deut. 32c 22v. my anger shall burn the lowest Hell, Rev. 9c 6v. and in those days shall men seek death and shall not find it, and shall desire to die but death shall flee from them, Rev. 20c. 14v. death and hell were cast into the lake of fire, this is the second death, and whosoever was not found written in the book of life, was cast into the lake of fire, their punishment will be forever and ever." [43]

Come to God before Its too Late.

---

[43] Cannon, N. C., The Rock of Wisdom, 1933, p. 12 and 13—Moorland Library, Howard University.

"Now, Sinners, I warn you, as from the mouth of God, come and go with us, that you may escape the wrath of that great day. Come now and delay not, lest the spirit of God should cease to strive with you; like Noah's dove to take its flight and no more to return..... While the celestial Sun is yet shining, let us act our part like pure hearted men and fly unto Jesus and beg for Sinners for God to have mercy on them, for we see by the revelation of God, the earth will burn, the moon will bleed, the Sun will be turned into darkness, and behold! the comets will blaze through the sky, and then you will hear Jesus say unto his watchman, leave the Walls of Zion. The trumpet is to be blown no more: and he will say, come ye blessed, enter into the Kingdom which I have prepared for you..... while entering, O hear the shouts, the loud hallelujah of the church militant—Now to the wicked look back o my soul and wonder, could it be possible that an intelligent man or woman, could neglect their soul's salvation, while the gospel trumpet was sounding unto them to awake and fly to Jesus, for there is no other help found, nor no other name given whereby man can have salvation:" [44]

Through the *Rock of Wisdom* the author pictures the spectacular and miraculous with respect to God, sin, salvation, Heaven, and Hell. His sermons are highly other-worldly. They give the impression that man's primary object is to save his soul from Hell. In them the power of motivation is fear, and there seems to be no relation between social salvation here and individual salvation in Heaven.

One more quotation illustrating ideas of God that are exceptionally compensatory prior to the Civil War will suffice. Timothy Mather Cooley records some of the sermons of the Reverend Lemuel Haynes. His sermons deal mostly with individual salvation which is to be achieved after death. A negative ethical goodness is the main requirement for salvation in the world to come. He says:

"As God's rewarding the Saints will humble them, so it will tend to fit them for the world of everlasting adoration.

---

[44] Ibid, pp. 51-52.

One great design of the day of judgment will be to exhibit the riches of divine grace, which will excite endless songs of joy to the saints..... The scars and signals of sufferings in the cause of God, that his people will carry with them, will procure more illustrious monuments than pillars of marble; they will possess that kingdom prepared for them, and be made Kings and priests unto God." [45]

Two of the areas of development with respect to the idea of God are found in the "mass" literature between 1760 and 1860 The compensatory ideas are prominent, but in the literature examined, they are less conspicuous than the ideas developed to support a growing sense of social rehabilitation. It is conceivable that the literature of the period would be laden with other-worldliness and ideas of God that serve as an opiate to deaden one's sensitivity to slavery and other social problems. As strange as it may seem this is not the case. The Negro ministers of the first period were keenly aware of social questions and they used God to support their claim that social righteousness should be established. Though adhering strictly to traditional views of God they made the most of those ideas that could be used to advance the cause of the race. Many of these early Negro writers were truly abolitionists and deserve a place along with Garrison, Harriet Beecher Stowe, and others. The ideas of God developed in this period are inherent in the Christian religion but the forms they take and the ways in which they are used are conditioned by the social life of the time. Since God is just, slave holders will be punished. Since all men are made in the image of God, slavery is wrong and it is against God. Since God is against slavery, it cannot last. God is love; therefore, the slave must be kindly disposed toward his master. God is no respecter of person, and to discriminate on the basis of color is ungodly. God is to be obeyed above all others; it is, therefore, all right for slaves not to obey their masters, particularly since slavery stands in the way of divine grace. Com-

---

[45] Cooley, Timothy Mather, Sketches of the Life and Character of the Rev. Lemuel Haynes (New York: Harper and Brothers, 1837), p. 192 ff.

pensatory ideas are likewise developed at the point of social crisis. When people are defeated, tired, and weary of this life, rather than suffer defeat they often project a heaven above and renounce life on the earth.

C. "Mass" Literature between 1860 and 1914

Prior to 1860 the ideas of God in "mass" literature were developed in connection with social changes that involved the abolition of slavery. It will be interesting to note the dominant social issues after emancipation and to see how the ideas of God are related to them.

The Hand of God in Colonization.

On May 14, 1863, the Rev. Alexander Crummell preached a sermon in Trinity Church, Monrovia, West Africa. He sees God at work in the colonization of Africa:

> "All human events have their place in that grand moral economy of God, in which He himself is an ever-present, ever-active agent; they are all elements and instruments in His hand, for the accomplishment of the august objects of His will.....So indeed has it been in all the world's history of colonization. The great, vital, permeating power, propelling, guiding, checking, ordering it, has been the spirit of God, resting upon, entering into the hearts of men, owning and governing them, albeit oft-times unknown to themselves; even as we read in the Divine work that "the spirit of God moved upon the face of the water." We see every where God's hand in history; we feel that its anointing spirit is the breath of God. In all the movements of society, or the colonization of peoples, we see the clear, distinct, "finger of God," ordering, controlling, directing the footsteps of men, of families, and of races......
> "And what does this suggest but the immediate remembrance of that signal parallel of history, so painful and so personal to ourselves; viz; the forced and cruel migration of our race from this continent, and the wondrous providence of God, by which the sons of Africa by hundreds and by thousands, trained, civilized, and enlightened, are coming

hither again, bringing large gifts, for Christ and his Church, and their heathen kin." [46]

God Prepared the Negro in America for Service in Africa.

"The day of preparation for our race is well nigh ended; the day of duty and responsibility on our part, to suffering, benighted, Africa, is at hand. In much sorrow, pain, and deepest anguish, God has been preparing the race, in foreign lands, for a great work of grace on this continent. The hand of God is on the black man, in all the lands of his sojourn for the good of Africa." [47]

Here the ideas of God are used to encourage Negroes in their efforts to colonize Africa for the Negro race. Seeing in it the hand of God they were able to work, suffer, and endure hardships. There is hardly any greater stimulus to sustained effort in difficult undertakings than the conviction that what we do is the will of God and that in the final analysis, we cannot lose. Whether the ideas result in socially desirable or socially undesirable ends, it cannot always be proved. But great social changes have been accomplished by people who were urged on by a belief that God sanctioned and blessed what they did.

Prior to emancipation the outstanding need was freedom; God was used in the argument to bring about the overthrow of slavery. After emancipation, during reconstruction and subsequently, the emphasis shifts from the argument for physical freedom to the argument for those rights and privileges which emancipation gave theoretically and which the constitution of the United States guarantees. The ideas of God that had been developed to get the Negro emancipated were then used to get the Negro accepted as full participant in the affairs of society. The quotation which follows gives evidence of this new emphasis in the use of the idea of God. It is taken from a speech entitled "The Race Problem Stated" delivered by the Rev. J. C. Price, brilliant Negro orator, who was born in North Carolina in 1854

---

[46] Crummell, Alexander, Sermon preached in Trinity Church, Monrovia, W. Africa, (Boston: Press of T. R. Marion and Son, 1865) pp. 8–ff.
[47] Ibid, p. 14.

and who completed his college and theological training in Lincoln University (Pa.) in 1879 and 1881:

Rights Are God-given.

"The southern question is simply this,—How long can we deny to men their inalienable and constitutional rights, the denial of which they most keenly feel, even when no complaint is made, without a serious conflict involving not only the section and races immediately concerned, but the nation as well?

"It is seriously asked,—"Can such a condition continue with impunity?" The question is not, whether the races can live side by side in peace, but whether the two races can live together in harmony, with the one denying the natural and constitutional rights of the other. Can the one persist in not recognizing the political and civil privileges,—privileges conceded by the highest tribunal of the land,—of the other, with no ultimate harm to both?..... Will the South ever concede to the Negro his unrestricted privileges as a citizen, and thereby solve this problem?.....

"The South is, providentially, the home of the Negro as a mass in this country, and he is willing and ready to live in peace with his white brethren under any conditions save those which violate the very instinct of his being and imply the surrender of his manhood and God-given rights." [48]

The address shows throughout that Price wants for the race the same rights and privileges enjoyed by members of the white race. He objects to discrimination on lines of public travel such as railroad and steamboat. He opposes the lack of eating accommodations on the trains. He calls for unrestricted privileges in the use of the ballot and in the participation in government. He points out that the said rights denied Negroes are God-given and for that reason they should not be denied him. The idea is an instrument to perfect social changes that would bring justice and equality of privilege to the Negro race.

The same argument for social and political rights, on the ground that they are given by God, was advanced on the floor

---

[48] Woodson, C. G., Negro Orators and Their Orations (Washington: The Associated Publishers, 1925), p. 495.

of Congress by the Reverend Richard H. Cain. He was a clergyman, missionary, and politician. He was born in Virginia, educated at Wilberforce, elected the fourteenth bishop of the A. M. E. church, and was a member of the 43rd and 45th Congresses. He died in Washington in 1887. Speaking on the Civil Rights Bill on the floor of Congress, Cain says:

"And for what, Mr. Speaker, and gentlemen, was the great War made? The gentleman from North Carolina (Mr. Vance) announced before he sat down, in answer to an interrogatory by a gentleman on this side of the House, that they went into the War conscientiously before God. So be it. Then we simply come and plead conscientiously before God that these are our rights, and we want them. We plead conscientiously before God, believing that these are our rights by inheritance, and by the inexorable decree of Almighty God."

"We believe in the Declaration of Independence, that all men are born free and equal, and are endowed by their Creator with certain inalienable rights, among which are life, liberty, and the pursuit of happiness." [49]

Hiram R. Revels, was born in North Carolina in 1822 and died in Mississippi in 1901. He, too, was a politician and minister. In 1870, he was elected to fill an unexpired term in the United States Senate. He, like other Negro Congressmen, was trying to secure the enactment of legislation that would "protect the freedmen in the enjoyment of their rights so easily jeopardized" at that time throughout the South. Pleading on the floor of the Senate, he says:

"Mr. President, I maintain that the past record of my race is a true index of the feelings which animate them. They bear toward their former masters no revengeful thoughts, no hatred, no animosities. They aim not to elevate themselves by sacrificing one single interest of their White fellow-citizens. They ask but the rights which are theirs by God's universal law." [50]

---

[49] Cain, Richard J., The Civil Rights Bill, (Congressional Record, Volume II, Part I, 43rd Congress, 1st Session, pp. 565–567.
[50] Revels, Hiram R., The Georgia Bill (Congressional Globe, Part 3, 2nd Session, 41st Congress), pp. 1986 ff.

The needs of the race are specifically stated by the post-emancipation orators. They pleaded for economic security and political status in America. They fought for social security to assure protection from discrimination—in brief, full American citizenship rights. The idea of God reflected in these speeches is developed to show the reasons why these privileges should not be withheld. It helped to gain for the Negro fuller participation in American life.

In a sermon preached by C. T. Walker around 1902, he says:

"God was against slavery, and in His own time and way He removed the foul blot from the national escutcheon..... God has wrought wonderfully among us. God is still opening the way for greater progress." [51]

The idea of God in the quotation above adheres to traditional, compensatory patterns. It may encourage one to believe that God changes affairs without the aid of man, that God has His time set when He is to perfect social change. There seems little for man to do except wait on the Lord. In the next quotation, however, it is clear that man is not to wait wholly on God; it is strongly implied that God expects man to do his share.

" 'Go forward'—there is time to pray, and the time to act, to move. God seemed to say, 'you have prayed—now obey orders, go forward.' The leaders moved off to the edge of the sea; the mighty waters divided.—The Eternal God cut a pathway for the moving caravan.—The Eternal God fully protects His people.—God stopped the sun and the moon; Israel did the fighting." [52]

It is not stated just what it is that one, in our day, is expected to do when he obeys God since the Red Sea story and the Joshua narrative of the sun standing still can hardly be duplicated in modern time. The significant point is that though God is all powerful and protects His people, it is not enough for man to pray. After prayer, he must work and fight for the things he

---

[51] Floyd, S. X., Life of Charles T. Walker (Nashville: National Baptist Publishing Board, 1902), p. 127.
[52] Ibid, p. 131.

needs. As the Israelites fought for economic, civic, and political security in getting possession of the Promised Land, it is implied that after the Negro prays, he must rise and go after the things he needs such as economic, politic, and civic necessities. The idea of God is interpreted here to mean that God requires man to rise, work, and fight for the necessities of life. It is developed to mean, or it is strongly implied to mean, that God is opposed to a life of complacency.

D. Ideas of God in the "Mass" Literature after 1914

God's Trombones

Since the ideas of God in *God's Trombones* are representative of those reflected in many modern sermons and since Johnson received the stimulus to write them after hearing a sermon in Kansas City not many years ago, it is quite fitting to begin the modern period of "mass" literature with the sermons recorded in *God's Trombones*.

The ideas of God as reflected in *God's Trombones* may be briefly summarized as follows: God is in every particular a personal God, possessing all the human characteristics of man—He is loving, kind, revengeful, and just to the point of cruelty; nevertheless omnipotent, omniscient, and omnipresent. He is a Warrior. A typical illustration of God's human characteristics may be gleaned from the following quotation taken from "The Creation":

"Then God walked around,
    And God looked around
On all that he had made.
He looked at his sun,
And he looked at his moon,
And he looked at his little stars;
He looked on his world
With all its living things,
And God said: I'm lonely still.

"Then God sat down—
On the side of a hill where he could think;
By a deep, wide river he sat down;
With his head in his hands,
God thought and thought,
Till he thought: I'll make a man:

"Up from the bed of the river
God scooped the clay;
And by the bank of the river
He kneeled him down;
And there the great God Almighty
Who lit the sun and fixed it in the sky,
Who flung the stars to the most far corner of the night,

Who rounded the earth in the middle of his hand;
This great God,
Like a mammy bending over her baby,
Kneeled down in the dust
Toiling over a lump of clay
Till he shaped it in his own image;
Then into it he blew the breath of life,
And man became a living soul.
Amen. Amen.[53]

In the seven sermons set forth in *God's Trombones* two ideas of God are dominant. One is that of a God who fights the battles of His chosen people and brings them out victors in every conflict. This idea is well portrayed in the sermon, "Let My People Go." The closing part of the sermon follows:

"But Moses said:
Stand still! stand still!
And see the Lord's salvation.
For the Lord God of Israel
Will not forsake His people.
The Lord will break the chariots,
The Lord will break the horsemen,
He'll break great Egypt's sword and shield,
The battle bows and arrows;
This day He'll make proud Pharaoh know
Who is the God of Israel...............

---

[53] Johnson, James Weldon, God's Trombones (New York: The Viking Press, 1927), pp. 19, 20.

"And Moses lifted up his rod
Over the Red Sea;
And God with a blast of His nostrils
Blew the water apart,
And the waves rolled back and stood up in a pile,
And left a path through the middle of the sea
Dry as the sands of the desert.
And the children of Israel all crossed over
On to the other side.

"When Pharaoh saw them crossing dry,
He dashed on in behind them—
Old Pharaoh got about half way across,
And the waves rushed back together,
And Pharaoh and all his army got lost,
And all his host drowned.
And Moses sang and Miriam danced,
And the people shouted for joy,
And God led the Hebrew Children on
Till they reached the promised land.

"Listen!—Listen!
All you sons of Pharaoh.
Who do you think can hold God's people
When the Lord God Himself has said
Let my people go?" [54]

The other idea is other-worldly. According to it, God provides a home in Heaven for those who have labored in His vineyard. This idea is dramatized in the sermon, "Go Down Death," from which the following quotation is taken:

"Weep not, weep not,
She is not dead;
She is resting in the bosom of Jesus.
Heart-broken husband—weep no more;
Left-lonesome daughter—weep no more;
She's only just gone home.

"Day before yesterday morning,
God was looking down from his great, high heaven,
Looking down on all his children,

---

[54] Ibid, pp. 51, 52.

> And his eye fell on Sister Caroline,
> Tossing on her bed of pain.
> And God's big heart was touched with pity,
> With the everlasting pity...............
>
> "And God said: Go down, Death, go down,
> Go down to Savannah, Georgia,
> Down in Yamacraw,
> And find Sister Caroline.
> She's borne the burden and heat of the day,
> She's labored long in my vineyard,
> And she's tired—
> She's weary—
> Go down, Death, and bring her to Me." [55]

The ideas of God in *God's Trombones* are virtually the same as those discovered in the Spirituals. They are traditional and compensatory. The human qualities of God are more prevalent in *God's Trombones*. Otherwise, there is no difference in the ideas of God set forth in the two sections.

The Ideas of God in Modern Sermons

One of the arguments advanced to justify the use of the Spirituals and *God's Trombones* as representative of the ideas of God held by many Negroes today is the fact that sermons collected in 1930 and 1931 in the study of the Negro Church in sixteen centers in the United States, present ideas of God quite similar to those found in the Spirituals and in *God's Trombones*. Of one hundred sermons, stenographically reported, fifty-four, slightly more than half, are distinctly other-worldly in character and contain what some might call naive conceptions of God. As a few examples will show, the ideas of God reflected in the one hundred sermons are not radically different from those reflected in the Spirituals and *God's Trombones*. The ideas of God are traditional and compensatory, for example:

> "Seems like to me the day is a fine time to praise God, no use putting off until the evening of life. We went through

---
[55] Ibid, pp. 27 ff.

one of the hardest winters we have had in our lives. God wouldn't let them put us out of doors and we were fed at soup houses. God took care of us." [56]

It was God who kept those in power from putting the unfortunate out of doors. It was He who caused them to be fed from soup kitchens. God is to be praised for what He does for man.

Clearly there is a yearning for shelter and food—physical security is the end sought. It would not be fair to say emphatically that these ideas of God lead one to sit and wait for food and shelter to be brought to him—that would be an exaggeration; but the ideas certainly do support that view and they do not encourage one to exert himself to actualize his fundamental needs. The ideas savor of the belief that although times are hard God will take care of us. In some way, God will supply the food and shelter. Man's task is to praise Him. These ideas tend to encourage people to take a *laissez-faire* attitude toward their poverty. They help to keep the people free from worry. They, too, adhere to compensatory patterns. Especially is this true when the ideas just analyzed are viewed in connection with those in the same sermon that are highly other-worldly. For instance:

Going to Shout, Sing, and Pray.

"You cannot help but cry. Oh, sinner, my God is bothered about you. You ran away. My God, my God, and they try to make us hold our peace by limiting my preaching. No man can limit me to preach God's word. God called me to preach and it would be woe unto me if I did not preach. When I come up to the judgment I want my God to say, 'Well done, well done.' When I lay down to die and when I shall go back to Him, I shall not be afraid. When I shall look over that mystic river and see my Savior on the shore I want to wait until I hear His voice and see the print of the nails in His hands. I am going to shout and sing and pray until I get to glory. When the war is over,

---

[56]Mays & Nicholson, The Negro's Church (New York: Institute of Social and Religious Research, 1933), p. 74.

when the war is over, I shall stack up my hymn book and Bible. In the morning, in the morning when the war is over, and when the saints go marching in, I mean to be in that number. Oh, church, do you remember when your dungeon shook and your chain fell off? [57]

The definite things that are to be achieved in Heaven are not stated. It is clear that the author plans to sing, pray, and shout in order to get to Heaven with the inferences that all desires will be satisfied there. It is also clear that the minister considers Heaven to be his true home. There is little to show that the idea of God helps one to adjust to the realities of the objective world. As in most of the Spirituals, the ideas of God in the sermons (some of them) encourage one to look altogether beyond this world for salvation. The present world is to be tolerated and not enjoyed.

Since fifty-four of the one hundred sermons are dominantly other-worldly, more examples of the other-worldly sermons should be given. Two ideas of God stand out preeminently: the idea that God fights your battles for you and the idea that He saves you after death. This sermon is expressive of the desire for security and also the desire for new experiences. The sermon in part follows:

Going Home.

"Oh, glory! the waves rolled back on both sides and the children of Israel walked across and as they journeyed they sang 'Glory to His Name.' God said, 'Go on down, Pharaoh cannot pass.' I don't care where you are my God will find you sure enough. I don't know where I will be next year but I know I will be standing in line marching somewhere. He will fight your battle for you. You should serve the same God that brought the children of Israel out of bondage for He will take care of you. The same God that drowned Pharaoh is the same God today. After a while, bye and bye, when the war is over, the church will be there. I will be there.....I imagine when the war is over that Gabriel will step out with one foot planted on the land and the

---

[57] Ibid, p. 75.

other planted on the sea and time will be no more. I want to know what the trumpet of God will say......

"As they go on their march, the people will ask what place is this? The children of God will cry 'what place is this?' But they will say 'heaven is farther still, farther still to go,' and the church will march on. The people will cry again 'what place is this?' But the answer comes 'heaven is still farther.' Still another time 'Angel of God, what place is this?' But the march still goes on. Then those in heaven will look down and see that it is the church people who are God's people that are on board and they will ask, 'who are those coming up from the lower world?' Jesus will say, 'these are they who carried their burdens in the heat of the day.' " [58]

The traditional, compensatory character of the ideas of God here portrayed is more marked than in the preceding sermon and is as dominant as the ideas set forth in the Spirituals and *God's Trombones*. Security, new experience, and recognition are all to be experienced outside the process of history.

In another sermon we find the following:

"If death comes to you, it comes because God permits it, and if God permits it you ought to take a Christian view of the situation. If God permits it to come to you just say, 'I am no better than anybody else.' We ought not to set ourselves against God and say God has not done justice by us."[59]

The implication here seems to be that God permits everything to happen that does happen and there is nothing man can do about it. Things could not happen if God did not permit them to happen. This belief is deeply rooted in the minds of many orthodox christians. It goes a long way in helping people to adjust themselves to the inevitable. However painful and heart rending the death of mother may be, the load is perhaps easier

---

[58] Ibid, p. 81.
[59] Where sermon references are not given, they are quoted from the sermons not quoted in the Negro's Church. These sermons are on file in the office of the Institute of Social and Religious Research.

to carry if that person believes that it was God's will. Even though the idea may be false, it has great value for the person who believes it. It is perhaps this idea that accounts in part for the attitude which many people hold toward doctors. It is the view of some that it is useless to call a doctor because when God gets ready for you all the doctors in the world cannot save you; if your time has not come, you will not die regardless of the seriousness of the case. This idea of God adheres closely to traditional, compensatory patterns, not only because it is expressive of orthodox Christianity and lessens the grief sustained by death, but also because it has the tendency to lead one to take a complacent, *laissez-faire* attitude toward life in that the person sees the will of God in all that happens. In the following quotation there is expressed a desire to be saved from disease, poverty, and enemies:

> "We have many hardships. They are made hard upon us when we do our best; even then we are yet criticised. It takes a very strong person sometimes to stand up..... Many times there are faults found, and when you come to rectify them there are still faults found. But when a man's ways please God, He will make his enemies be at peace with him. There are many enemies. Sickness is an enemy, an enemy to health; poverty is an enemy to finance..... But if a man's ways please God, God will make his enemies to be at peace with him."

In another sermon, this idea is continued:

> "God gives us health and life and He spares and protects us during the storms of life and from our enemies. 'The Lord is my Shepherd.'"

The ideas of God are clear. God is a helper, the source of all life and He will help and protect us if our ways are pleasing to Him. He protects one from sickness, poverty, and enemies. The quest for security is dominant in these two sermons. It is God who gives us security from sickness and poverty; the requirement on man's part is almost nil. How a man's ways please God is not explained. The belief that God protects man during the storms of life is a source of consolation to him. It makes him happier and healthier to believe what he does.

He Sees All You Do.

"Today my friends, everywhere you look the eye of Jesus is looking at you. So often we fail to look up. Somebody told the story of the father who went with his little boy to steal something and the father told the little boy to watch and let him know if he saw anybody watching them. The little boy looked around and he said, 'Father, look, God is looking at us.' The father dropped what he was stealing and went away. When you think nobody sees you, God is looking. The boy knew that rogues cannot enter the portals of heaven."

Though based on fear, the idea that God is everywhere and sees all that one does has a restraining influence upon conduct. It makes a difference in one's life for it promotes goodness that lacks positive action. This idea of God is also compensatory in its effect because its restraining influence is based on the traditional idea that God is to be feared and that the end sought is other-worldly. The next quotation sets forth the belief that God punishes those who are not in harmony with Him.

"We have so many folks today to whom God is speaking, trying to get them to repent, to listen, but they are stubborn. The Christian world is not in harmony with God and God is pleading for them to come back to Him, but the folks won't hear God. So God causes calamity to come unto them.

"You are too busy with things of the world to stop and confer with God. You are compassed about with things of the world and saying that it is impossible for you to find time to work for God. God will lay such persons on the bed of affliction—too busy to serve Him." [60]

In this quotation, it is not clear to what end God wants man to repent and it is not clear what man is to do when he repents or works for God. "Working for God" and "coming back to

---

[60] Mays and Nicholson, The Negro's Church (New York: Institute of Social and Religious Research, 1933) p. 87.

God" seem to indicate something quite different from things of earth. "Working for God" hardly implies working to create a world where justice and mutual goodwill prevail. It seems to mean that the way to serve God is by shouting, singing, and praying for the purpose of being protected from a burning hell and the eternal wrath of God. It is an idea of God that encourages fear and produces a kind of "negative goodness." It is in line with the revengeful, wrathful ideas of God that are so prevalent in the Old Testament. The way God protects His own is clearly revealed in what follows:

God Fights Your Battles and Solves Your Problems.

> "If you know how to stay in touch with God, you can win any battle. David stayed in touch with God and won his battle..... I fear prayer has no charm for us. Mothers and fathers haven't got time to pray and yet they expect God to help them. Go back to the knee way. The hard times that are coming, the misunderstanding, they come because of a lack of prayer. Go back to prayer and God will fight your battle."
>
> "If a man's ways please God, he can awake at the hour of midnight with a smile on his face and solve the problems and he will defeat those who try to retard his progress. He simply kneels down and tells God about his problems and God will solve them." [61]

Here the ideas of God are: that He fights your battles, that He solves your problems, that He hears and answers prayers, that He helps those who pray, and that He allows calamity and hard times to befall those who do not pray. He is a Sovereign God and does what He pleases. The person seeks security from the stress and strain of life. It is emotional security that is sought.

No ideas of God thus far given adhere more closely to traditional compensatory patterns than those contained in the quotations just given. Man's chief task is done when he prays. God is to do the rest. Here again the idea of God soothes the

---

[61] Ibid, pp. 87–88.

individual; it blinds him to the reality and gravity of his plight; it is likely to cut the nerve to action that might eliminate hard times; it may lead him to pray and to sit with folded hands expecting God to do it; the idea may also enable the individual to be at peace and calm when conditions are stifling and all but unbearable. It serves as an opiate for the people. The partial character of God is evident as set forth below:

The Lord Saved Him.

> "I knew a family during the World War that had four sons. They had a faithful father and a praying mother. After these boys had sailed and were fighting in the War, this mother came to my house and said to my mother, 'the Lord told me that none of my sons will perish in Flanders Field.' She said this in the heat of the War. She said the Lord said none of them would perish. When the War was over those boys came back and threw their arms around her and said, 'Mother, we have come home.' The Lord saved them, they did not perish." [62]

The casualty list of the World War was approximately ten millions and it is safe to assert that each one of the ten millions had some devout, sincere mother, father, brother, sister, or sweetheart praying for him.

The idea that God answers prayers and will give to those who ask of Him had great influence upon the behavior of this mother. It caused her to pray for the safety of her four boys, the thing which she desired most. The idea did more than that, it helped the mother to feel better. She worried less than she would have worried had she not believed that God was protecting her boys. She was able to enjoy a more peaceful rest at night because of her belief that God was answering her prayers. Her behavior was greatly modified by her belief and for her the idea had great value. There is substantiation here of traditional, orthodox views that God hears and answers prayers.

---

[62] Ibid, p. 90.

God Is Source of All Being.

"We are indebted to God for creation. You may describe creation from the evolutionary point of view but we are indebted to God for creating us; not only that, but we are indebted to God for saving us, when we were lost in sin, before Moses cried from the bulrushes; and in due time Jesus came bearing the Cross and brought salvation into the world. We are indebted to God for giving His Son, also for the day and night, for permitting us to rise and face a new day each morning. There is nothing that we can do without God. We see by this time that we have quite a large account for which we are indebted. The next question is how much do we owe? If you will look about you, you will see that we have different talents. God wants us to use these to benefit humanity. Some of us have one talent and some of us have many talents. I want you to put them into use to benefit humanity. How are we to pay God? Let us consecrate to God our minds, thoughts, strength, and our time. These are the things God has given us with which we can pay Him back." [63]

In that part of the sermon which is not quoted in the Negro's Church, the author states further:

"We are to use our talents to help bring the more abundant life to all people: justice, mercy, and an opportunity for all races and groups to enjoy the rights and privileges which God intends for them."

According to the author, God is omnipotent, omniscient, and omnipresent. All that there is comes from God. Salvation and security are sought in God. He makes exacting demands upon man because man owes Him everything and man's debt to Him is to be paid by serving humanity in definite, tangible ways here in this life. Serving humanity includes doing one's bit to make life more livable and working to bring larger opportunities to groups and races that are denied them. God makes urgent social demands upon man for the debt he owes Him.

It is true that the ideas of God just cited are mainly traditional in character. But there is an effort here to reinterpret them along social lines to show that God lays upon man the

---

[63] Ibid, pp. 88–89.

responsibility for the improvement of life in deficient areas, which is a thing desirable and acceptable in His sight. It is the will of God that this be done. These ideas of God are not compensatory; they are potentially constructive because they tend to impel man to search in order to realize needs that are necessary for the development of an abundant life. Man labors under the impression that he is carrying out the mandates of God when he seeks to achieve larger opportunities for all peoples. In the next quotation there is also a move away from the compensatory pattern, and an effort is made to reinterpret the idea of God along ethical and social lines that transcend race.

God Demands Clean Hearts.

"The sermon is not the chief thing in our worship; it is a clean heart before God, worshipping God in the beauty of His Holiness. Our hearts should be clean when we worship. We should cut out envy, hate, and malice. We should possess that peace which St. Paul speaks of as passing all understanding. Jesus Christ brought it from heaven with Him and gave it to all the world. But we cannot be at peace if we are at anger, one with the other, and if we exploit men and disregard their right to achieve an abundant life. So we must have our hearts cleared of these things before we come to prayer. We should forgive those who have done us wrong; strive to give justice to all men for we cannot worship in His beautiful Holiness with envy, hatred, and malice in our hearts."

A similar idea is expressed in the next quotation:

"The church where God's spirit dwells—that is God's home. Family life makes the man a loving father, it makes him a man the people will trust, a man the bank will trust— a man who will not be dishonest and work the life out of people and steal their blood and bread. That is what God's Holy Spirit will do."

The ideas of God are clearly stated in the preceding quotations. God demands clean hearts—hearts free of envy, hate, and malice. God requires that one man must not exploit another and that the rights of each must be respected. God is so exacting on the points indicated that worship is ineffective without purity of heart. It is implied that God requires that we forgive one another and that even those who have wronged us should be forgiven. To worship God with purity of heart includes striving on one's part to give and secure justice for all men. God's Spirit does something definite to man when it enters his heart. It makes him a loving father, a man the community can trust, and a man who will not rob the poor of their earnings.

Here we find in the modern sermons the third expression of ideas of God that are distinctly not compensatory. The development takes a significant turn in that the authors use the traditional ideas of God to support a growing consciousness of the necessity of social adjustment. This, you will note, is one of the main emphases in the study. It is the will of God that one becomes reconciled here with the view of enhancing life on the earth. The ideas of God are so interpreted that one is not only to seek reconciliation but he is to seek to maintain mutual goodwill and fellowship.

Strangely enough, in neither of these sermons did the ministers say anything about Heaven or Hell, nor of reward or punishment. The fruits of the Christian life were emphasized along with the idea that one is in harmony with God when he is in harmony with man.

The next extract, more than any thus far presented, sets forth the idea that God is a God of social righteousness.

The Meaning of the Kingdom.

"Habitually and obviously without thought, we pray 'Thy Kingdom Come.' But in reality, we do not want the Kingdom to come. If I understand what is meant by the Kingdom, it means the existence of that state of society in which human values are the supreme values. It means the creation of a world in which every individual born into it would be given an opportunity to grow physically, to develop mentally, and progress spiritually without the imposition of artificial obstructions from without. Everything in the environment would be conducive to developing to the nth degree the individual's innate powers. At the center of our social, religious, political, and economic life, there would be not a selfish profit motive, not a prostituted conception of nationalism, and not a distorted notion of race superiority. Whatever we did, the chief aim would be to protect life and improve it.

"Let us see for a moment, what would happen if such a Kingdom as this should come to the world. As an individual, I would not wish any good thing for myself that I would not wish for every other man on God's earth. And if the thing I want, though beneficial to me, would be damaging to my neighbor of whatever color or class, I would not want that thing. I would not and I could not pile up my millions if I had to do it at the expense of long hours and low wages on the part of those who produce the wealth.

"If this kind of Kingdom should come to the earth, no race would want to keep another race down. Our military forces would not be in Nicaragua; they would not be in Haiti. We would gladly help the Philippines to independence and without condescension and without patronage. India would be free and Africa would not be exploited. All forms of segregation and discrimination such as those that exist in the United States in the expenditure of public funds, in travel, in politics, and those that operate against us in social and economic areas would all disappear if the Kingdom of God should come." [64]

Clearly the outstanding idea of God is that He is a God of social righteousness. He is a God who is interested in the welfare and development of every child regardless of class or race. God is no respecter of person.

The desires sought are equally obvious. There is the desire for peace; the desire for political and civic security; the desire and yearning for the physical, mental, and spiritual growth of every child; and the desire that each person should enjoy economic security and status. The idea is developed along social lines that are universal in character, transcending the narrow confines of race. Although the idea of God here pictured opposes all national and racial views of superiority and presup-

[64] Mays & Nicholson, The Negro's Church (New York: Institute of Social and Religious Research, 1933) pp. 64-65.

poses a community or brotherhood that is world-wide in its scope, the idea is also used to support the author's contention that the Negro is entitled to all the rights and privileges that other racial groups enjoy. This idea of God, therefore, deviates from the compensatory pattern. It does not encourage one to wait for justice in the other world. It does not dissipate itself in mere feeling. On the other hand, it tends to give one poise and balance to struggle for social righteousness here on the earth.

God Liberates Human Personality.

It is interesting to note how the author of the sermon, "God Liberates Human Personality," which is constructed upon a traditional text appropriate for attributing to God all the other-worldly functions, confines his remarks to this life and has an idea of God which liberates human personality for the purpose of transforming the social order. The text is: "Who shall roll us away the stone from the door of the Sepulchre?" A few excerpts follow:

"The large sealed stone in the entrance to the tomb offered a real problem to those despairing pilgrims of the way. The situation is thought-provoking. Not only who will roll away the stone from that tomb, that massive piece of granite, but who will roll away the stone of despair from their discouraged souls? The question merits wider application; consequently we find ourselves face to face on this Easter morning with the problem of sealed lives, both individual and social.

"Many are the human souls in this world with the capacity for the expression of the abundant life, if only the stone of remorse could be rolled away from the doorway of their hearts. Others there are whose lives would be gems of abiding influence if the stone of conceit could be rolled away. Whole communities could be electrified, changed, transformed if stones of shallowness, indifference, indolence, could be rolled back, so that the entombed life might come forth with glorified power and revolutionize the social order..... This rolling back of human repressions is absolutely essential to the peace and happiness of the world.

"A wailing, whining, complaining disposition may overthrow the finest possibilities. How many souls are driven to their graves by those thoughtless, ever diligent messengers of woe, who never have enough sense to apply genius to drive away the stones of winter in a friendly sort of way. The truism is obvious. Summer can never come, my friends, until the signs of winter have been driven away. For sunshine to come into your soul or into mine, we must have an opening to receive its warm and happy rays.

"Then again, preoccupied souls lose sight of the big things in life; overlook the value of co-operation; refuse to dim their light in the way of friendliness and contact. We retard substantial progress. We give ourselves to the task of building more barns, which are transitory things. We do these things instead of building our characters—that immortal, everlasting thing. This leads us naturally to a question. Who shall roll us away the stone from the door of the Sepulchre? Or better still: who shall roll away the sealed stone of remorse, conceit, shallowness, indifference, from human hearts? There is only one answer. The power of God through the Spirit of the risen Christ. If in the human heart there is a capacity imprisoned, that human heart through the Spirit of the risen Christ can be released to a broader life.

"Who shall roll away the stones which seal the possibilities of social progress within the sepulchre of inertia and retrogression? There is only one answer. You and I liberated from the tomb of fruitless decay..... Liberated personality is God's most successful force, by which whole communities may be elevated from spiritual lethargy and transformed into resplendent life." [65]

According to the sermon, the Spirit of God in the life of the individual transforms that life. It removes conceit, remorse, indolence, shallowness, indifference, and despair. It leads to an abundant life; it stimulates one to work to transform communities, it places one under obligation to live a life of co-operation, friendliness, peace, and happiness; and it challenges one to strive to revolutionize the social order. We are not told how the power or Spirit of God does these things. But it is clear that God

---

[65] Ibid, pp. 59–61.

makes a difference in the life of the individual and this difference expresses itself in behavior that has community value. Perhaps it is not too much to say that from the ideas of God presented in this sermon, God may be defined as the power or force in man and in the world that impels man to seek to transform life in the interest of a healthier and a more resplendent life for mankind individually and generally. The ideas are not other-worldly. They place one under obligation to adjust himself to a life of peace where all may enjoy the fruits necessary for resplendent living. They go far beyond the limits of race, but the needs of the race are met in the universality of the ideas of God presented. They are far removed from traditional, compensatory patterns. They are constructively developed in terms of social reconstruction that is universal.

The Negro Is a Chosen Race and God Is on His Side.

In the sermon which follows the author is teaching Negroes to be satisfied with their race, urging them to cease imitating the worst in other races, and to cease trying to escape from their own race. He preaches from the text, "Princes shall come out of Egypt; Ethiopia shall soon stretch out her hands unto God."

"It would do you good to know something about the background of the Ethiopian people so that you would stop trying to get away from your race. Nothing disgusts me more than those who want to be taken for members of any other race than their own. We will never amount to anything as long as we let our young people know that we think it is wrong to be anything but what we are.

"We must stop imitating the worse in other races. A white woman comes on the stage with no clothes on and after that every woman that comes to church has got no clothes on. It is a sin before God. God wants the Negro woman to lift up a standard that other women may know that they are walking before God.

"They have always tried to kill us out. : . . . If we had not been a chosen race of the Almighty God, we would have been gone long ago. Out on X Avenue where Negroes live, they won't put in sewers and give them the same protection as in white neighborhoods that are farther out. They call out race riots and shoot us, yet they expect us to be as good in every respect as they are. It makes me angry; on the other hand, it makes me have confidence in God. God is on our side." [66]

Here is reflected an idea of God which leads the Negro to believe that God is on his side and that God has chosen the Negro as His own in some special way. The desires sought are physical security from race riots, civic protection, and race pride. It is implied here that God gives physical protection; otherwise, the fact of the Negro's survival could not be explained.

The author takes the traditional idea of a "chosen race" and uses it to instill group self-respect in the Negro.

E. *The God-Idea in Prayers.*

This section is a brief analysis of the development of the ideas of God as found in an analysis of fifty-one prayers stenographically reported—twenty-seven recently recorded, and twenty-four recorded in connection with the study of the Negro's Church—prayers taken from prayer meetings, the opening and closing of Church School services, and prayers taken from regular eleven o'clock preaching services.

Summary of Ideas of God in Prayers.

The ideas of God might be briefly summarized: God is in heaven. He is all powerful—the source of all things even to allowing us to go to bed and to rise in the morning. In allowing us to do this, He displays mercy. God is a rock in a weary land and a shelter in a mighty storm. All that happens is God's will. God is a partial God who is to be feared and appeased. He does things arbitrarily, apparently for no other reason than the fact that He is all powerful and can do what He pleases.

---

[66] Ibid, pp. 69–70.

God is Partial and Arbitrary.

"Oh, Father, you are a good God, because some are lying on their beds of affliction, some are behind prison bars, some are in the hospital, and some are sleeping in their graves; yet, we have been wonderfully blessed with health."[67]

"I thank Thee for this opportunity which we now enjoy. There are thousands of people who would be glad to be here today. There are some in the graveyard, some on their bed of affliction, but, O Lord, You have spared us and given us another chance to work out our salvation and redemption.

"When I awoke this morning I was glad to know that my blood was still running warm in my veins and that I was still able to rise from my bed and go forth to see another day in this New Year, a day that I had not seen before in my life. Nine days ago was the beginning of this year. And my Lord, as I thought of Thy goodness to us.... Thou has left us here for a little while longer and now we are able to meet again at an appointed place to serve You and praise Thy Holy Name."

In these three selections the desire for security is uppermost. There seems to run through all three an element of fear, a fear of disease and a fear of death. Health, life, and security from disease and death come from God. It is taken for granted that God extends life and gives health at will. Those who are fortunate to be the recipients of these from God are under obligation to thank God for them. Nothing seems to be required of the individual except to praise and thank God. Here is laid upon him no obligation to exert himself in his own behalf. The idea encourages one to fold his hands and let God do it. The implication of this idea is that God will protect you if you pray.

God Fights for Those Who Ask; He Guides, Protects, and Counsels.

Three or four illustrations follow:

"Oh, Lord, come down here and bless our souls..... You know we down here are sometimes down and sometimes up; sometimes standing wringing our hands wondering what we must do. Oh Lord, have mercy on us, I pray. Lord, You remembered Daniel in the Lion's Den, You saved the three Hebrew children, and I know You have heard me pray day after day and I know You will hear me today if I pray

---

[67] Where prayers are quoted without reference, they are quoted from unprinted stenographic reports.

right.....Oh Lord, have mercy upon us. You know we need You down here. We need You wherever we go to lead us, down here where men and women are so sinful."

"We ask Thee, oh Father, to come and fight our battles for us. We pray that Thou will be by our sides each and every hour. Be with us when we leave our homes in the morning for we know not whether we will see our families alive again, but we pray Thy blessings upon them and that Thou be with us and stand by us. Fight our battle for us and lead us to the rock of salvation."

"Oh, Lord, here we are down here in a world of trouble, where we are troubled; down here in a world of sorrow. We ask You to have mercy right now."

"Father, we are thankful for our blessings and we do thank Thee and give praise to Thy name. We know You know the secrets of our hearts and that You know sometimes what we need better than we know ourselves. You know sometimes the way gets dark and troubles get heavy upon us and we have heavy burdens to bear. Sometimes we are called everything but a child of God; but in the midst of all of our trouble, we pray and expect to fight until the war is ended. Have mercy upon me, oh Lord, and hear my cries. You promised You would be with me in the midst of my affliction and that You would not forsake me.....Talk with us, walk with us, help us to come closer together and to find more grace, and in the end, prepare for Thy servants a place in Thy Kingdom where we can live and praise Thee world without end."

The desire for response and the desire for emotional security are both represented here. One desire is to be protected from bodily harm, trouble, and enemies. The present world is considered a world of trouble and sorrow. There is the desire for strength to endure them, not necessarily strength to eliminate the source of the sorrow and the trouble. In this section the idea persists that God will fight your battles, that He will protect you from danger, that He will help you carry your burdens, that He will enable you to endure to the end, and, we infer, that He will afford you perfect security in Heaven.

The idea that God is with you and that He protects you as you go forth from your home in the morning is quite consoling to the person who believes it. In the midst of stifling and frightening circumstances the idea stabilizes one's behavior and helps him to carry through the work of the day. To believe that God is with you in the midst of your affliction makes the affliction easier to bear and gives emotional calm and peace. The idea is likely to serve as an anodyne for the people.

Of the fifty-one prayers, thirty-five, or more than sixty-nine per cent, end with a plea to God to save us to eternal life when death comes. Three or four endings will suffice to show the character of the thirty-five.

Save Us When We Come to Die.

"You know in this land of sorrow, we need Thee today our Father, and we ask You to guide us through this weary land. Have mercy right now and we ask You to remember the world at large as far as men and women are concerned and when our days are over and we go over yonder where our loved ones have gone; over yonder where my mother has gone; where there is no more sickness and no pain and sorrow; where they are crying "hallelujah," we pray that Thou would still lead us. Oh Lord, have mercy right now this day our Heavenly Father and in the end, give me a lasting resting place in that city where we can praise Thy Name forever, Amen."

"We ask Thee to bless the sick and afflicted, we ask Thee to bless us all one by one, for we need Thy blessings. I ask You to have mercy on sinners and turn them around before it is too late. And Lord, we ask Thee to bless the little children, take them in Thy hands and guide them in the way Thou would have them to go. Oh, Lord, put your strong arm around the people and bring them into the fold. Bless me and strengthen me where I am weak. When I am through fighting, I ask for mercy and a home in Thy Kingdom where I can sit down and praise Thee forever. Amen."

"Bless also our homes we pray Thee and all the sick and afflicted, and oh, Lord, when we are through here, through going from one prayer meeting to another, and when we have gone our last journey, we pray our Father that Thou will be with us in the last dying hours, and may our grace be sufficient to carry us safely over, and our last wish shall be for a home in heaven with the loved ones who went on before. Oh, Lord hear this prayer of Thy humble servant and bless us as we pray. Amen."

"Heavenly Father in heaven, today we once more meet again before Thee in Thy sight and in Thy Holy place and we, your servants, are down on bended knees trying to return to Thee and to Thy blessings..... Some of us our Father, don't know whether we will be able to go until the end, but we are trying to make it through 1934, but if oh, Lord, You don't see fit to spare us, oh, Lord, we are packing up getting ready to go. Oh, Lord, come on down and bless those who are in trouble and bless those who are burdened down and bless those, my Father, who are weeping, bless the poor, bless the old and the blind, I pray, my Father...... You know we are a long way from home and sometime we feel like we haven't a friend in the world. We sometimes, our Father, wring our hands wondering whether we will ever get to heaven or not, but, oh, Lord, we are coming on. You said You were a rock in a weary land, and a shelter in a mighty storm. Oh Lord, hear us down here today..... And when we are through praying and praising Thee on this earth, give us a home in Glory."

Summary Statement of the Other-Worldly Prayers.

According to the ideas expressed in the thirty-five other-worldly prayers, this world is a land of sorrow and trouble, not of joy. Life here is accepted as a temporary affair; the real home is on the other side, for frequent reference is made to "packing up to leave." Journeying through this life is wearisome and we need the guidance of God in order to get through. It is not only a weary journey and a world of trouble, but it is a friendless world. Such expressions as "I am a long way from home" and "I feel like I haven't a friend in the world" show loneliness and the desire for intimate response as expressed in the songs, "I must tell Jesus," and "Sometimes I feel like a motherless child." Expressions such as "Thou art a rock in a weary land and shelter in a mighty storm" show the desire for security. This desire for security crops out also in the prayers requesting God to be with them at the dying hour; it also shows a fear of death. The people pray earnestly for God to bring sinners into the fold in order that their souls might be saved.

This life is almost completely denied and refuge is sought in Heaven. Even the fulfilling of the desire for intimate response in Jesus or God is a means of endurance to the end, so that Heaven may be gained. It is not a response which sends one out buoyantly to achieve. God is to give complete security and adequate response but these are to be experienced in Heaven. Like the ideas of God expressed in the Spirituals, *God's Trombones*, and in the other-worldly sermons, the ideas of God in the prayers adhere to traditional, compensatory patterns in that they support and sustain compensatory beliefs with respect to God.

F. *The Idea of God in Church School Literature.*

This section is the result of the analysis of the Church School literature of three Negro denominations which the author prefers not to name. The foot notes to this literature are also withheld. It covers the literature of all grades including a time span of fifteen months for one denomination, nine months for another and a period of three months for the third. The only point in considering this literature at all is the fact that, in a survey of this kind, the field should be covered as completely as possible. It is quite obvious, as will soon be seen, that the ideas set forth in this literature conform perfectly to the God-patterns already given. The literature follows the traditional set up of uniform, ungraded lessons. The underlying assumption of it is that the Bible, like a loaf of bread, is composed of material, all parts of which are equally good. This statement is based on the fact that there is little discrimination used in the selection of Biblical material. The selection may be a passage where God punishes Israel because David took the census or it may be the Sermon on the Mount.

Nowhere in this literature is there any attempt to draw the line between the God of the Old Testament and that of the New Testament, such as is represented in Jesus. Every statement about God is accepted. And so God is omnipotent, omniscient, and omnipresent. He possesses all the characteristics of human beings. He is represented as cruel, revengeful, and capricious. He is set forth as one who exacts praise and is influenced by it. But he is also revealed as kind, loving, merciful, and forgiving. The chief idea of God reflected in the literature is that of a God who protects those who are good, guarantees victory for them in their struggles, and punishes those who do not conform to His ways. These ideas are best seen in the points stressed in the explanatory notes of the lessons and the illustrations that are drawn from the Biblical text.

The fact that the Bible is accepted as a loaf of bread, all parts of which are equally good, is clearly set forth in the primary quarterly of one of the denominations for 1934—first series. The lessons proper are taken from the New Testament. At the end of each lesson are quotations taken from the Old Testament. At the end of the lesson on the Parable of the Kingdom (Matthew 13: 31-33, 44-52) the following questions are asked at the end, based on the Old Testament:

1. "What did they do? The woman ate the forbidden fruit and gave it to the man, who likewise ate."
2. "What did they become then? Sinners."
3. "What then happened to them? God was displeased with them and drove them from the garden."
4. "For what reason were they driven from the garden? That they might not eat of the tree of life and live forever."
5. "Was any curse put upon them? Yes; that they should work hard all their lives."
6. "Did the curse extend any further? Yes; that they should have sickness, pain and death."

These questions and answers are from the primary quarterly designed for children from six to eight years of age. For the most part the examples in the Church School material are taken from those quarterlies which include the children whose ages range from six to seventeen. It is here that the comments from the lesson texts reflect most vividly the ideas of God. This literature is also significant because it reveals the religious ideas that are being taught to the very young in these Church Schools. The idea that God punishes may instill abnormal fear in the children, which if effective at all, may produce negative goodness based on fear of punishment.

God Is Influenced by Praise.

"Bound hard and fast in stocks, Paul and Silas prayed unto the Lord and sang songs that were touching and far-reaching, and rejoiced in the mercy of God. It was at midnight, and so pleasing were their praises to God, that in answer to their prayers, an earthquake came and shook off the stocks from their feet and freed all other prisoners in the jail. Not one of the prisoners tried to escape, however, from the grounds of the prison."

The idea of God reflected here is likely to encourage children to believe that all they have to do is to sing praise to God and ask Him for what they want. An idea of God that leads one to believe that his chief task is done when he prays is compensatory, even though the holding of the idea may produce a fervent prayer life and a feeling of satisfaction in the one who prays.

God Protects the Righteous.

Under the captions "Tacks to Drive" and "Important Questions for Juniors" we read that "righteousness commands the favor of God, and makes sure His protection."

"When God's people believe in Him their lives are safe and secure. He who walks with God, makes sure his footsteps are upon solid ground."

Success is guaranteed to the Juniors who "read, meditate, and pray upon the things that be of God." "The steps of the good man are ordered by the Lord."

The things desired are success and security. The way to get them is probably too simple: read, meditate, and pray.

God Is Good—He Fights Our Battles.

"The grateful child is always intelligently appreciative of his Father's goodness; and hence he is more obedient and faithful to Him than ever. This is the spirit that God wants; after helping us and fighting our battles, then we should realize and be conscious of His goodness, and hence be more faithful and loyal to Him and His cause."

God Rewards the Good and Destroys the Evil.

"Our Lord will reward the good and destroy the evil one day. Lost souls shall be turned into a lake that burns with fire and brimstone, a place of endless misery and frenzied despair.
"If life is to be saved by doing something on the Lord's Day, there is no sin. But if I am trying to please myself and have fun it is a great sin which God will punish."

God Knows What We Need and He Will Provide It.

Commenting on the lesson "Putting God's Kingdom First," the author of the Adult Sunday School lesson writes:

"God our Heavenly Father knows what is necessary for you and will provide it.
"It is God who provides the necessities of life anyway, and why not give Him the glory, and put more faith in Him and stop worrying about such matters.....He knew that most people are more concerned over eating and drinking and dressing than anything else, especially spiritual things, and He is showing how foolish it is, for God will take care of them, for it is God who cares for them after all and there is no need to worry and fret over such matters."

All Things Work Together for Good for Those Who Love the Lord.

"Let us never lose faith in God when things do not please us. God never forgets those who love Him. He makes everything work together for good. John was put into prison for telling the truth. Help us to know God wants us to do right even though we must suffer for doing right. If we love Jesus we need never be afraid. He never forgets His people."

God Does What Man Cannot Do.

"Just a word about Ananias. God used him as His great agent to lead Saul to the light, God always has used some person to do His work. God will do all that human beings cannot do, then He turns the balance over to men. God did for Saul what Ananias could not do. Then He turned Saul over to Ananias who acted as His agent and started Saul on the most remarkable career of any man in human history. God can use us if we put ourselves in position. If we have talents and gifts and graces, all we have to do is to ask God as Saul did: 'Lord, What Wilt Thou Have Me to Do?'"

Let us summarize this section of the Sunday School literature. It should be noted that far less stress is placed on salvation outside of the process of history than is the case in the fifty-four sermons, prayers, the Spirituals, and *God's Trombones*. The things most desired in this portion are: protection from danger as illustrated in the quotation about Paul and Silas, which gives the idea of an all-powerful God who produces the security; security through life as set forth in the section where God guarantees success to the righteous, which indicates a God who cares although He is partial; assurance that we will win out in the conflicts of life, as shown in the emphasis on giving thanks to God for fighting our battles—again indicating an omnipotent God who protects His own; security in the belief that God provides everything for us, as revealed in the quotation which represents a God of authority and power; and finally, security when things go wrong, as reflected in the belief that all things work together for good for those who love the Lord.

In this section, there is little effort at a constructive rehabilitation of the God-idea. The idea that God does things for His people rather than stimulate them to co-operate with Him or do for themselves permeates the section. The ideas are developed along compensatory lines because they are likely to lead one to pray and worship, but beyond that they may not lead. Though not other-worldly, the ideas are capable of ending in prayer, worship, and mere feeling.

Ideas of God in Quarterlies for Young People and Adults.

For the most part, the Sunday School literature so far dealt with has had to do with that prepared for young people between the ages of six and seventeen. Attention will now be given to the ideas of God reflected in adult literature. Only those ideas will be presented that seem to set forth a conception of God different from that already given. In the practical application of the lesson "John Prepares the Way for Jesus" we find the idea that God sends special representatives into the world in time of crisis. For instance:

"The birth of John the Baptist is another evidence that God sends great souls into the world in the time of crises to lead people to something higher and better."

The idea has developed in the Christian tradition that God always has a special person to send into the world in time of crisis. The author makes use of this traditional idea.

In another connection the author says:

"In this time of financial depression Christ is asking christians, 'Why are you so fearful?' The same God that was with us in the days of prosperity will walk with us through the night of adversity. Then, let us not be dismayed for whatever befalls us, Christ will take care of His own."

The idea of God in both quotations previous to this one tends, if followed, to make one fold his hands. This one helps to give emotional security during hours of adversity, and stimulates the endurance of pain and suffering.

Commenting on the lesson entitled "Solomon," the author writes:

"Solomon built the splendid temple at Jerusalem and dedicated it in great pomp to the service of Almighty God. Twenty-two thousand oxen and one-hundred twenty thousand sheep were sacrificed at the dedicatorial service. Representatives were there from all parts of the civilized world. The Ark of the Covenant was brought up and set in the central place in the temple. The people shouted the praise of Jehovah......No church or home is complete that does not have the Ark of the Lord in it; the presence and blessing of the Lord upon it. The glory of the Lord filled the temple while Solomon and all Israel lifted holy hands in prayer. Wherever men dedicate themselves to God, God opens the windows of heaven and pours out blessings upon them."

A dedication which offers sacrifices to God and sings praises to Him influences Him so much that He pours out His blessing upon them. The people who sacrifice to God do not necessarily have to have clean hearts and hands. The dedication is not necessarily one which places a person under obligation to serve his fellows. The sole object is to move God so that God will pour out His blessings. A different note is sounded in the following quotation:

"Our Father in Heaven, we thank Thee for Thy bountiful mercies; and are grateful for the forgiveness of our sins. And we pray that Thou wouldst so fix our hearts that we will work together with Thee, and so live that we may become worthy factors in bringing in that peace which the world so much needs, and which Thou didst send Thy Son and our Saviour to bring with our assistance. We are asking these things in the name of our Saviour, Christ Jesus. Amen."

"The world's crave for peace is one which her present condition will not permit her to enjoy. This peace cannot abound where hate, mobocracy and false justice reign. This peace will come only to men born of God's Spirit and washed in His Son's blood.....Real peace, therefore, cannot be received until old hearts of hate and envy are done away."

God is merciful; He forgives sin; He sent His Son into the world to bring peace; and God's Spirit frees us of envy and hate. The desire is for peace, justice, and a co-operating society. God obligates man to work and to free his heart of hate and envy in order to obtain peace. The idea of God pictured here is used to support views of ethics and social righteousness as held by the author just quoted. The next quotation reveals the idea that God is the source of all life and that we are under obligation to Him.

"No man giveth himself life; no man can give himself the things that make for life, nor sustain life. If a man lives he lives not of himself nor for himself. He is obligated in life both to his Life Giver and to others who are in fellowship within the same gifts. There is a divine value in human life and every recipient is under obligation to God to respect that value, for all human life is precious unto Him. .... We are bound to Him, while we live, to be just to every human creature, even to our own lives. Committing suicide does not relieve us of our obligations to God, for every man must stand before Him to render his account for the divine treasure of life, both of himself and that of others over whom he had influence. Since God alone gives life, we have no right to rob God of that which is His, neither in manslaughter nor in suicide. We are further obligated in life to our fellowman in the same sense that Jesus felt His obligation to die to better the conditions of human life..... If we adopt the Christ ideal of life we will feel a loving urge for our brother's welfare that will restrain us from voting for the return of the system or kingdom of liquor to our land, lest it may contribute to his downfall rather than his salvation..... Thus man is eternally obligated to God, not only as his life-giver, but to his fellowman who is possessor of the same life and interest to God as that which he himself has."

Here, God is the author of all life. All human life is precious in God's sight. He expects us to respect life. He holds man accountable for what he does. God and man are inextricably woven together because there is a divine value in human life and because each life is rooted in God. This anchorage in God challenges man to be just, to work in order to better conditions, and to improve life. According to the idea of God given above, life is so constructed in God that the destiny of each individual or group is interwoven with that of other individuals or groups. The traditional idea that "God is the source of all life" is reinterpreted in terms of God's requirements in the area of social welfare and ethical righteousness.

Summary of Chapter Two.

Almost uniformly, the ideas of God in the Spirituals, in *God's Trombones,* in the fifty-four other-worldly sermons, in the stenographically reported prayers, and in the church literature for pupils between the ages of six and seventeen, conform to the traditional, compensatory pattern which we have already described. Very often the need for security, and the like, is to be experienced outside the process of history. In many instances, the ideas serve as an opiate for the people, enabling them to suffer and endure conditions which they should strive to change. In most of the "mass" literature before and after 1860, in the this-worldly sermons, and in the Sunday School literature for adults and young people, we find a significant change—the ideas do not develop along compensatory lines. They are interpreted in social terms, an attempt being made to show what God requires of man in the area of social and economic reconstruction. Prior to 1860, reconstruction means the abolition of slavery. During the reconstruction period, and subsequently, it means social reconstruction to gain for the Negro the rights and privileges enjoyed by white Americans.

The ideas of God containing these two widely opposite trends, the compensatory and those which move along the line of social rehabilitation, developed simultaneously in the same period; particularly is this true of the ideas in prayers, in sermons and in Sunday School literature. On the one hand, the social and economic emphases that have developed among Negroes since the days of Booker Washington have done little to stimulate a new interpretation of God along social lines. The masses, on the whole, see no connection between God and social and economic reconstruction. On the other hand, it seems clear that some ministers and a few Sunday School writers have been definitely influenced by those forces that aim to perfect some kind of social change. But for the most part, the social, educational, and economic upheaval resulting from the World War and its aftermath has not produced a similar upheaval in the thinking of the masses of Negroes with respect to the idea of God. The period prior to the Civil War seems to be less compensatory with respect to God than the modern period since 1914.

CHAPTER III

Ideas of God in "Classical" Literature

1760–1860

"Classical" Negro literature begins, as far as we know, with Jupiter Hammon, who is the author of the first poem produced by a Negro in the United States. His poem, "An Evening Thought: Salvation by Christ," appeared in 1761. He was born probably between 1720 and 1730, and died around 1800. He was the slave of Henry Lloyd of Long Island, New York.

Though Hammon did not believe that slavery was necessarily ordained of God, he did believe that it was for the best interest of Negroes that they be good, obedient slaves. Hammon was a favored servant and his life was "one of comparative ease." He himself was quite willing to remain a slave; he wished, however, that the younger Negroes might some day be free. In his address to the Negroes of the state of New York, he shows clearly what he thinks of God and his relationship to slavery. He wants freedom for the younger Negroes, but he firmly believes that there is nothing they can do to get it except obey their masters and wait patiently on the Lord. His ideas of God follow:

Be Content with Slavery; Obey Your Masters; God Will Free You If He So Designs:

"My brethren, when I think of you, which is very often, and of the poor, despised, and miserable state you are in, as to the things of this world; and when I think of your ignorance and stupidity, and the great wickedness of most of you, I am pained to the heart. It is at times, almost too much for human nature to bear; and I am obliged to turn my thoughts from the subject....I have wanted exceedingly to say something to you, to call upon you with the tenderness of a father and friend, and to give you the last, and I may say, dying advice of an old man who wishes your best good in this world, and in the world to come. But while I have had such desires, a sense of my own ignorance, and unfitness to teach others, has frequently discouraged me from attempting to say anything to you; yet, when I thought of your situation, I could not rest easy....I think you will be more likely to listen to what is said, when you know it comes from a Negro, one of your own Nation and colour; and therefore can have no interest in deceiving you, or saying anything to you, but what he really thinks is your interest and duty to comply with. My age, I think, gives me some right to speak to you, and reason to expect you will hearken to my advice. I am now upwards of seventy years old, and cannot expect, though I am well and able to do almost any kind of business, to live much longer. I have passed the common bounds set for man, and must soon go the way of all the earth. I have had more experience in the world than most of you, and I have seen a great deal of the vanity and wickedness of it. I have had great reason to be thankful that my lot has been so much better than most slaves have had. I suppose I have had more advantages and privileges than most of you, who are slaves, have ever known and I believe more than many white people have enjoyed....I do not, my dear friends, say these things about myself to make you think that I am wiser and better than others; but that you might hearken, without prejudice, to what I have to say to you on the following particulars.

"1st. Respecting obedience to masters. Now, whether it is right and lawful, in the sight of God, for them to make slaves of us or not, I am certain that while we are slaves, it is our duty to obey our masters in all their lawful commands, and mind them unless we are bid to do that which we know to be sin, or forbidden in God's word....It may seem hard for us, if we think our masters wrong in holding us slaves, to obey in all things!...As we depend upon our masters for what we eat, and drink, and wear,...we cannot be happy unless we obey them. Good servants frequently make good masters.

"Now I acknowledge that liberty is a great thing, and worth seeking for, if we can get it honestly; and by our good conduct, prevail on our masters to set us free: though for my own part I do not wish to be free, yet I should be glad if others, especially the young Negroes, were to be free; for many of us who are grown up slaves, and have always had masters to take care of us, should hardly know how to take care of ourselves; and it may be more for our own comfort to remain as we are. That liberty is a great thing we may know from our own feelings, and we may likewise judge so from the conduct of the white people in the late war. How much money has been spent, and how many lives have been lost to defend their liberty. I must say that I have hoped that God would open their eyes, when they were so much engaged for liberty, to think of the state of the poor blacks, and to pity us.... Let me beg of you, my dear African brethren, to think very little of your bondage in this life; for your thinking of it will do you no good. If God designs to set us free, he will do it in his own time and way; but think of your bondage to sin and Satan, and do not rest until you are delivered from it.... I will conclude what I have to say with a few words to those Negroes who have their liberty.

"What I have said to those who are slaves, may be of use to you; but you have more advantages, on some accounts, if you will improve your freedom, as you may do, than they. You have more time to read God's holy word, and to take care of the salvation of your souls.

"One great reason that is given by some for not freeing us, I understand, is, that we should not know how to take care of ourselves, and should take to bad courses; that we should be lazy and idle, and get drunk and steal.

"Let me beg of you then, for the sake of your own good and happiness, in time, and for eternity, and for the sake of your poor brethren, who are still in bondage...." [1]

Since God does not sanction slavery, Hammon's advice to Negroes is to "wait on the Lord." If God wants them to be free, He will free them. It is far more important for Negroes to think of their bondage to sin and Satan and their soul's salvation than it is for them to worry about physical freedom. Hammon's ideas of God are clearly compensatory and they serve as an opiate for the people. Having received good treat-

---

[1] Hammon, Jupiter, An Address to Negroes in State of New York (New York: Carroll & Patterson, 1787).

ment as a slave, his attitude toward slavery is colored by that fact. His advice, if followed, would lead, and perhaps it did encourage, Negroes to be satisfied with their lot and to look to Heaven for freedom if God did not see fit to give it to them here.

Any idea of God that encourages one to sit complacently, expecting God alone to improve his lot fits into the category of a compensatory idea.

Hammon perpetuates this conception of God in his poetical works. The "Dialogue Between the Master and Slave" is illustrative. It contains the words of a kind master and of a dutiful servant. They talk of grace, salvation, Heaven, saints, and angels; but not of freedom for the slave. The poem shows contentment and satisfaction. It evidently indicates the good relationship that must have existed between Hammon and his master. The words follow:

Master
1. "Come my servant, follow me,
   According to thy place;
   And surely God will be with thee,
   And send thee heav'nly grace.

Servant.
2. "Dear Master, I will follow thee,
   According to thy word,
   And pray that God may be with me,
   And save thee in the Lord.

Master.
3. "My Servant, lovely is the Lord,
   And blest those servants be,
   That truly love his holy word,
   And thus will follow me.

Servant.
4. "Dear Master, that's my whole delight,
   Thy pleasure for to do;
   As for grace and truth's in sight,
   Thus far I'll surely go.

Master.
5. "My Servant, grace proceeds from God,
      And truth should be with thee;
   Whence e'er you find it in his word,
      Thus far come follow me.

Servant.
6. "Dear Master, now without controul,
      I quickly follow thee;
   And pray that God would bless thy soul,
      His heav'nly place to see.

Master.
7. "My Servant, Heaven is high above,
      Yea, higher than the sky:
   I pray that God would grant his love,
      Come follow me thereby.

Servant.
8. "Dear Master, now I'll follow thee,
      And trust upon the Lord;
   The only safety that I see,
      Is Jesus's holy word.

Master.
9. "My Servant, follow Jesus now,
      Our great victorious King;
   Who governs all both high and low,
      And searches things within.

Servant.
10. "Dear Master, I will follow thee,
       When praying to our King;
    It is the Lamb I plainly see,
       Invites the sinner in.

Master.
11. "My Servant, we are sinners all,
       But follow after grace;
    I pray that God would bless thy soul,
       And fill thy heart with grace.

Servant
12. "Dear Master I shall follow then,
    The voice of my great King;
    As standing on some distant land,
    Inviting sinners in.

Master.
13. "My servant we must all appear,
    And follow then our King;
    For sure he'll stand where sinners are,
    To take true converts in.

Servant.
14. "Dear Master, now if Jesus calls,
    And sends his summons in;
    We'll follow saints and angels all,
    And come unto our King.

Master.
15. "My servant now come pray to God,
    Consider well his call;
    Strive to obey his holy word,
    That Christ may love us all." [2]

In this dialogue between the master and the slave, there is no correlation between earth and Heaven. There is nothing inherent in slavery that would cause the door of Heaven to be shut in the face of the slaveholder nor the slave. Both can be good christians and both can inherit the Kingdom of God.

Hammon's first poem, "An Evening Thought: Salvation by Christ," illustrates further the fact that he was more interested in salvation in Heaven than he was in any form of social reconstruction. The closing lines of this poem suffice to show the other-worldly-compensatory character of his ideas of God:

"Come, holy spirit, Heavenly Dove,
The object of our care;
Salvation doth increase our Love;
Our Hearts hath felt thy fear.

---

[2] Wegelin, Oscar, Jupiter Hammon, American Negro Poet (New York: Printed for Charles Fred Heartman, 1915), p. 41–46.

"Now Glory be to God on High,
Salvation high and low;
And thus the Soul on Christ rely,
To Heaven surely go.

"Come, Blessed Jesus, Heavenly Dove,
Accept Repentance here;
Salvation give, with tender Love;
Let us with Angels share. Finis." [3]

Phillis Wheatley will now claim our attention. Having been born in Africa, she was brought to the United States in 1761 and sold as a slave. She was between seven and eight years of age when she arrived. It was fortunate for Miss Wheatley that she was sold to Mr. John Wheatley, a respectable citizen of Boston. Almost immediately she won the affection and goodwill of her mistress. She was never assigned to menial occupation, as it was first intended; "nor was she allowed to associate with the other domestics of the family, who were of her own color and condition, but was kept constantly about the person of her mistress."[4] She was to Mrs. Wheatley as a daughter. It seems that Miss Wheatley never received any formal manumission, but she hardly needed one since she was exceptionally well treated in the Wheatley home. The Wheatleys even sent her to Europe in the interest of her health. While there, she was widely acclaimed. Miss Wheatley joined the church at sixteen and throughout her life showed signs of having good religion. She suffered much after the death of her mistress and died at thirty-one.

In a letter which Phillis Wheatley wrote to Obour Tanner, who was probably one of the girls brought over with her, she expressed her thanks to God for bringing her to America. The letter is dated May 19, 1772.

"Dear Sister.—I received your favour of February 6th, for which I give you my sincere thanks.... Happy were it

---
[3] Ibid, p. 31.
[4] Wheatley, Phillis, Memoir & Poems, (Boston: Published by Oscar Knapp, 1839), p. 12.

for us if we could arrive to that evangelical repentance, and the true holiness of heart which you mention. Inexpressibly happy should we be, could we have a due sense of the beauties and excellence of the crucified Saviour. In his Crucifixion may be seen marvellous displays of Grace and Love, sufficient to draw and invite us to the rich and endless treasures of his mercy; let us rejoice in and adore the wonders of God's infinite Love in bringing us from a land semblant of darkness itself, and where the divine light of revelation (being obscured) is in darkness. Here the knowledge of the true God and eternal life are made manifest; but there profound ignorance overshadows the land. Your observation is true, namely, that there was nothing in us to recommend us to God. Many of our fellow creatures were passed by, when the bowels of divine love expanded towards us. May this goodness and long suffering of God lead us to unfeigned repentance.

"It gives me great pleasure to hear of so many of my nation seeking with eagerness the way to true felicity. O may we all meet at length in that happy mansion.... Till we meet in the region of consummate blessedness, let us endeavor, by the assistance of divine grace, to live the life, and we shall die the death of the righteous." [5]

It is said that Saint Augustine and Martin Luther never ceased to thank God for saving their souls. Luther was always a buoyant, jubilant christian. It seems that Phillis Wheatley was equally thankful that God had brought her from ignorant and benighted Africa to enlightened, "civilized" America. Her attitude toward life and slavery, like Jupiter Hammon's, was greatly influenced by the kind treatment she received at the hands of the Wheatleys. Speaking of the death of her mistress, Miss Wheatley writes thus to Miss Tanner:

"I have lately met with a great trial in the death of my mistress; let us imagine the loss of a parent, sister or brother, the tenderness of all these were united in her. I was a poor little outcast and a stranger when she took me in; not only into her house, but I presently became a sharer in her most tender affections." [6]

---

[5] Renfro, Herbert G., Life and Works of Phillis Wheatley (Washington: Published by Robert L. Pendleton, 1916), p. 27.
[6] Ibid, p. 29.

Hammon, therefore, could advise Negroes to obey their masters and Phillis Wheatley could write almost ignoring the fact of slavery—certainly showing no progressive, militant attitude toward its abolition. The ideas of God expressed in the letter are to be classified as compensatory. The belief that God had a hand in bringing her to America and placing her in such fine hands made her ever grateful. It made her feel jubilant and happy; but she does not interpret the ideas of God in terms of social change. Her views of God brought her contentment and satisfaction. Her firm conviction of eternal salvation after death added to the contentment.

The other-worldly character of her thoughts is set forth in another letter to Obour Tanner under date of July 19, 1772.

Prepare for Eternal Judgment.

"How happy that man who is prepar'd for that night wherein no man can work!...O! who can think without horrors of the snares of the Devil. Let us by frequent meditation on the eternal Judgment prepare for it. May the Lord bless to us these thoughts, and teach us by His spirit to live to Him alone, and when we leave this world may we be His." [7]

She continues the Heavenly emphasis in a beautiful statement written to the Honorable T. H., Esq., on the death of his daughter. A part of the discourse follows:

"She unreluctant flies to see no more her dear—
Lov'd parents on earth's dusky shore;
Impatient heav'n's resplendent goal to gain,
She with swift progress cuts the azure plain,
Where grief subsides, where changes are no more,
And life's tumultous billows cease to roar;
She leaves her earthly mansion for the skies,
Where new creations feast her wond'ring eyes.
To heavn's high mandate cheerfully resign'd she mounts,
And leaves the rolling globe behind;

---

[7] Ibid, p. 28.

> She, who late wish'd Leonard might return,
> Has ceas'd to languish, and forgot to mourn;
> To the same high empyreal mansions come,
> She joins her spouse, and smiles upon the tomb." [8]

In the same other-worldly strain, Phillis Wheatley writes a poem to console a gentleman and lady on the death of the lady's brother and sister, and a child named Avis, aged six. She says in part:

> "But madam, let your grief be laid aside,
> And let the fountain of your tears be dry'd.
> In vain they flow to wet the dusty plain,
> Your sighs are wafted to the skies in vain,
> Your pains they witness, but they can no more,
> While death reigns tyrant o'er this mortal shore.
> The glowing stars and silver queen of light
> At last must perish in the gloom of night:
> Resign thy friends to that Almighty hand,
> Which gave them life, and bow to his command:
> Thine Avis give without a murm'ring heart,
> Though half thy soul be fated to depart.
> To shining guards consign thine infant care
> To waft triumph through the seats of air:
> Her soul enlarg'd to heav'nly pleasure springs,
> She feeds on truth and uncreated things.
> Methinks I hear her in the realms above,
> And leaning forward with a filial love,
> Invite you there to share immortal bliss
> Unknown, untasted in a state like this.
> With Tow'ring hopes, and growing grace arise,
> And seek beatitude beyond the skies." [9]

Miss Wheatley's religion is one of sweetness and affection. Her ideas of God help one to endure suffering and to bear up under it. They are capable of lending sweetness to life, giving it an elegant tone. They have the power to produce poise and balance in the midst of situations that otherwise might be emotionally stifling. She is hardly concerned about transforming society. She is more interested in the individual and his

---
[8] Ibid, p. 95.
[9] Ibid, p. 87.

soul's salvation. The next character presents a striking contrast.

Benjamin Banneker, astronomer and mathematician, was born in Baltimore County, November 9, 1731. He was a man of extraordinary powers and well deserves the titles of astronomer and mathematician. One of the earliest pleas for universal peace comes from him.

It is to be noted that when Benjamin Banneker was arguing for universal peace and for the appointment of a Secretary of Peace in the United States, there was considerable strife in the world. About that time, 1793, the United States and the American Indians were having wars. There was strife between the British nation and Tuppoo Saib. The planters of St. Domingo and other African slaves were fighting. And the French nation was fighting the Emperor of Germany.

Concerning his peace plan, Banneker argues that only God has "the power to take away the life of a human being."

War Is Against the Laws of God.

"Let a power be given to this secretary to establish and maintain free schools in every city, village, and township of the United States; and let him be made responsible for the talents, principles, and morals of all his schoolmasters. Let the youth of our country be carefully instructed in reading, writing, and arithmetic, and in the doctrines of a religion of some kind; the Christian religion should be preferred to all others; for it belongs to this religion exclusively to teach us not only to cultivate peace with all men, but to forgive, nay more—to love our very enemies. It belongs to it further to teach us that the supreme Being alone possesses a power to take away human life, and that we rebel against his laws whenever we undertake to execute death in any way whatever upon any of his creatures." [10]

There Is One Universal Father.

Banneker not only believed that to kill is contrary to the commandments of God, but he also believed in the Fatherhood

---

[10] Phillips, Philip Lee, The Negro, Benjamin Banneker, (Astronomer and Mathematician, Plea for Universal Peace), p. 17, Reprint from Recorder of the Columbia Historical Society, Vol. 20, 1917.

of God. His views on this point are set forth in a letter written to the Secretary of State, August 19, 1791:

> "It is a truth too well attested, to need proof here, that we are a race of beings, who have long laboured under the abuse and censure of the world; that we have long been looked upon with an eye of contempt; and considered rather as brutish than human, and scarcely capable of mental endowments.
>
> "I hope I may safely admit, in consequence of the report which has reached me, that you are a man far less inflexible in sentiments of this nature, than many others; that you are measurably friendly, and well disposed toward us; and that you are willing to lend your aid and assistance for our relief from those many distresses, and numerous calamities, to which we are reduced.
>
> "If this is founded in truth, I apprehend you will embrace every opportunity to eradicate that train of absurd and false ideas and opinions, which so generally prevail with respect to us: and that your sentiments are concurrent with mine, which are, that one universal Father hath given being to us all; that He hath not only made us all of one flesh but that He hath also, without partiality, afforded us all the same sensations, and endowed us all with the same faculties; and that, however variable we may be in society or religion, however diversified in situation or in colour, we are all the same family, and stand in the same relation to Him." [11]

The author wants peace on earth. He wants slavery abolished. He wants status, recognition, and justice for his race. He uses his ideas of God to support the view that wars are wrong. He develops them to show that the Negro race is not inferior, that he should be free, that he possesses all the faculties of other races, and that he should be delivered from injustices of every description.

These ideas of God are not compensatory. They are developed along the line of social reconstruction that is universal

---

[11] Copy of a letter from Benjamin Banneker, To the Secretary of State (Philadelphia: Printed and Sold by Daniel Lawrence, Vol. 33, 1792).

in scope. Unlike Hammon and Wheatley, Banneker is little concerned with heavenly salvation. The same is true of the next writer, Gustavus Vassa (Olaudah Equiano).

He was born in 1745, in Benin, a country west of the lower Niger, forming part of Southern Nigeria. Strictly speaking he was not an American Negro. He served considerable time in this country in bondage and his book was frequently reprinted in the United States. These facts make it legitimate to treat him in this connection. At eleven he was seized by kidnappers and after many adventures he was placed on a ship to be taken to America. He served on a plantation in Virginia and worked with a British Naval officer, who helped him to get an education. He worked on vessels en route to the West Indies as the property of a Philadelphia merchant who helped him to save the money with which he purchased his freedom. He traveled widely as a ship steward and finally settled in England to engage in anti-slavery work. It is said that in 1790 he presented to Parliament a petition for the suppression of the African slave trade. Vassa died in 1801.[12] His idea of God is revealed below.

Dominion of One Man over Another Never Intended by God.

"For I will not suppose that the dealers in slaves are born worse than other men—No! such is the fatality of his mistaken avarice, that it corrupts the milk of human kindness and turns it into gall. And, had the pursuits of those men been different, they might have been as generous, as tender-hearted and just, as they are unfeeling, rapacious, and cruel. Surely this traffic cannot be good, which spreads like a pestilence, and taints what it touches: which violates that first natural right of mankind, equality and independency, and gives one man a dominion over his fellows which God could never intend! For it raises the owner to a state as far above man as it depresses the slave below it; and with all the presumption of human pride, sets a dis-

---

[12] Brawley, Benjamin, Early Negro American Writers (Chapel Hill: The University of North Carolina Press, 1935), p. 56.

tinction between them, unmeasurable in extent and endless in duration." [13]

Equality, independence, justice, and freedom are the things which Gustavus Vassa (Olaudah Equiano) craved. He interpreted God in relation to these and used God as the basic point in the argument against slavery and the slave traffic. His conception of God serves as a stimulus to arouse one to act against slavery and comes under the head of ideas that are developed in the interest of social reconstruction.

It is interesting to note how early Negroes themselves began to cry out against the wrongs of slavery. Carter Woodson points out that the first protests against slavery came from the Negro himself. At first their protests were not heard because it took considerable time for the freedmen to "acquire the means of expressing their thought forcefully." The Negro was aided in his efforts, however, by the struggle for the rights of man which was developing during the last quarter of the eighteenth century. The Negro profited by this wave of new liberalism and availed himself of the opportunities offered for education. Many of the able Negroes had to write under assumed names. Such was the case of "Othello" who was identified as a Negro by Abbé Grégorie in his *De la Litterature des Negres*.[14] "Othello" writes with force and bitterness on Negro slavery as the following quotations show:

Assert the Cause of God and Exterminate Slavery.
"Amidst the infinite variety of moral and political subjects proper for public condemnation, it is truly surprising that one of the most important and affecting should be so generally neglected.... To what cause are we to impute this frigid silence—this torpid indifference—this cold inanimated conduct of the otherwise warm and generous Americans? Why do they remain inactive amidst the groans of injured humanity, the shrill and distressing complaints of expiring justice and the keen remorse of polluted

---
[13] Life of Gustavus Vassa, The African (Boston: Isaac Knapp Publisher, 1837), p. 126—Library of Congress.
[14] Woodson, Carter G., Negro Orators and their Orations (Washington: Associated Publishers, 1925), p. 13–14.

IDEAS OF GOD IN "CLASSICAL" LITERATURE

integrity? Why do they not rise up to assert the cause of God and the world, to drive the fiend Injustice into remote and distant regions, and to exterminate oppression from the face of the fair fields of America?" [15]

Slavery an Outrage Against Providence.

Continuing "Othello" says:

"Slavery, in whatever point of light it is considered, is repugnant to the feelings of nature, and inconsistent with the original rights of man. It ought, therefore, to be stigmatized for being unnatural; and detested for being unjust. 'Tis an outrage to Providence and an affront offered to divine majesty, who has given to man His own peculiar image.—That the Americans after considering the subject in this light—after making the most manly of all possible exertions in defense of liberty—after publishing to the world the principle upon which they contended, viz., "that all men are by nature and of right ought to be free," should still retain in subjection a numerous tribe of the human race merely for their own private use and emolument, is, of all things, the strongest inconsistency, the deepest reflection on our conduct, and the most abandoned apostasy that ever took place since the Almighty fiat spoke into existence this habitable world. So flagitious a violation can never escape the notice of a just Creator, whose vengeance may be now on the wing, to disseminate and hurl the arrows of destruction." [16]

Like Gustavus Vassa, "Othello" wants slavery abolished. He believes that it is the cause of God to rise up against it and that since it is an affront to God it can never escape the wrath of God. His ideas of God are inherently militant and tend to create in one a divine discontent with slavery. They do not encourage one to sit and wait for God to abolish slavery but they rather encourage the people to go out in the name of God and change the social order by eradicating slavery from American soil. It seems clear to "Othello" that he who goes out to aid in eradicating slavery, goes out in the name of God.

---

[15] Ibid, p. 14.
[16] Ibid, p. 15.

James Forten, a Philadelphian, argues for status, recognition, and security for the Negro. God has made the white man and the Negro the same; therefore, they should exercise the same liberty and be protected by the same law. He objects to any law that restricts the Negro's privileges and circumscribes him as less than human. He develops his ideas of God in terms of social change when he argues against certain restrictions of the Negro made in a bill that was before the State Senate of Pennsylvania in 1813. The bill before the Senate of Pennsylvania was to prevent the emigration of people of color into that state. Forten argues:

God Made the Negro and the White Man From Same Species.

"Those patriotic citizens, who, after resting from the toils of an arduous war, which achieved our independence and laid the foundation of the only reasonable republic upon earth, associate together, and for the protection of those inestimable rights for the establishment of which they had exhausted their blood and treasure, framed the constitution of Pennsylvania, have by the ninth article declared, that "all men are born equally free and independent, and have certain inherent and indefeasible rights, among which are those of enjoying life and liberty. Under the restraint of wise and well administered laws, we cordially unite in the above glorious sentiment, but by the bill upon which we have been remarking, it appears as if the committee who drew it up mistook the sentiment expressed in this article, and do not consider us as men, or that those enlightened statesmen who formed the constitution upon the basis of experience, intended to exclude us from its blessings and protections. If the former, why are we not to be considered as men? Has God who made the white man and the black left any record declaring us a different species? Are we not sustained by the same power, supported by the same food, hurt by the same wounds, wounded by the same wrongs, pleased with the same delights, and propagated by the same means? And should we not then enjoy the same liberty, and be protected by the same laws?" [17]

---

[17] Ibid, p. 44.

The use of the ideas of God to oppose anti-social legislation is clearly set forth by Robert Purvis. In 1838, there was a proposal before the legislature of Pennsylvania to disfranchise the free people of color. Robert Purvis was chairman of the "Appeal of forty thousand citizens threatened with disfranchisement to the people of Pennsylvania." The appeal against the proposal is made in the name of God "who has no respect of person."

"We entreat you to make our case your own—imagine your own wives and children to be trembling at the approach of every stranger lest their husbands and fathers should be dragged into slavery worse than Algerine—worse than death. Fellow citizens, if there is one of us who had abused the right of suffrage, let him be tried and punished according to law. But in the name of humanity, in the name of justice, in the name of the God you profess to worship, who has no respect of persons, do not turn into gall and wormwood the friendship we bear to yourselves by ratifying a constitution which tears from us a privilege dearly earned and inestimably prized.... Firm upon our old Pennsylvania Bill of Rights, and trusting in a God of Truth and Justice, we lay our claim before you, with the warning that no amendments of the present Constitution can compensate for the loss of its foundation principal of equal rights, nor for the conversion into enemies of forty thousand friends." [18]

As strange as it may seem, many of these Negroes who were most violent in their attack upon slavery were most insistent upon moral persuasion as the best means of obtaining their objectives. They believed in peace. Reference has already been made to Benjamin Banneker. The ideas of God are used to persuade those in power to do what God requires. Though the ideas are developed to secure freedom, rights and privileges denied, they are seldom developed to encourage the acquisition of these by revolutionary means. The Negro in American history has used legal means, organized pressure, and Christian God-

---

[18] Ibid, pp. 102-103.

concepts to achieve his place rather than resort to violence to achieve it. William Whipper of Columbia, Pennsylvania, was a noted anti-slavery worker and an agent of the underground railroad. At the same time he was a great advocate of peace. Whipper insists that:

> "We must be prepared at all times to meet the scoffs and scorns of the vulgar and indecent—the contemptible frowns of haughty tyrants and the blighting mildew of a popular and sinful prejudice. If amid these difficulties we can but possess our souls in patience we shall finally triumph over our enemies. But among the various duties that devolve on us, not the least is that which relates to ourselves. We must learn on all occasions to rebuke the spirit of violence, both in sentiment and practice. God has said, "vengeance is mine, and I will repay it.". . . Whoever for any cause inflicts a single blow on a fellow being violates the laws of God and of his country and has no just claim to being regarded as a Christian or a good citizen." [19]

These authors desire peace—universal, national and local. They want complete citizenship rights for the Negro race. And they develop the idea of God to support their claim for these. The fight is on to attain these privileges here and it is not an other-worldly postponement. In the same connection Whipper argues:

> "Therefore let us, like them," speaking of the abolitionists, "obliterate from our minds the idea of revenge, and from our hearts all wicked intentions toward each other and the world, and we shall be able through the blessing of Almighty God to do much to establish the principles of universal peace." [20]

Here and there, the ideas of God are developed to support social reconstruction that is universal in scope. Both Whipper and Banneker developed their ideas on a universal plane, though not neglecting the social changes that were needed in areas pertaining to the Negro.

---

[19] Ibid, p. 113.
[20] Ibid, p. 117.

Charles Lenox Remond, reputed to be the most famous Negro in America prior to the rise of Douglass, continues the development of the idea of God in terms of desired social changes. Speaking on "Slavery As It Concerns the British" Remond declares that if he had to choose between the alternative of being the oppressed slave or the oppressor, he would choose to be the slave when they appear before the bar of God. He says further in his speech on "Slavery and the Irish" that "God has announced from Sinai that one cannot attempt the bondage of his fellowman without being guilty of a deadly crime."[21] Slavery is against God and Remond uses the idea to put fear in the hearts of the masters to the end that they might free their slaves. In the same speech, he argues for freedom on the ground "that God has made of one blood the nations of men to dwell on all the face of the earth." No one has the authority to doubt the truthfulness of that statement.

David Walker is another interesting character of the pre-Civil War era. He was born in Wilmington, North Carolina, September 28, 1785. His mother was free, but his father had been a slave. Young Walker hated slavery and decided not to live in the South. He made his way to Boston and after learning to read and write he dedicated his life to the cause of humanity. His home in Boston became a shelter for the poor and needy. In 1829, Walker wrote the *Appeal*. The book excited the slaveholders of the South so much that the governors of Virginia and North Carolina sent messages to their legislatures about it. The governor of Georgia urged the mayor of Boston to suppress the *Appeal*. Finally, a reward of one thousand dollars was offered for Walker's head and ten times that amount was offered if he was captured alive.[22]

Thankful to God for Our Color.

David Walker argues that the Negro is not ashamed of his color. He writes:

---

[21] The Liberator, July 7, 1841.
[22] Brawley, Benjamin, Early Negro American Writers (Chapel Hill: The University of North Carolina, 1935), p. 123.

"And those enemies who have for hundreds of years stolen our rights, and kept us ignorant of Him and His divine worship, He will remove. Millions of whom, are this day, so ignorant and avaricious, that they cannot conceive how God can have an attribute of justice, and show mercy to us because it pleased Him to make us black—which colour, Mr. Jefferson calls unfortunate!!!! As though we are not as thankful to our God, for having made us as it pleased himself, as they, (the whites) are for having made them white. They think because they hold us in their infernal chains of slavery, that we wish to be white, or of their color—but they are dreadfully deceived—we wish to be just as it pleased our Creator to have us, and no avaricious and unmerciful wretches, have any business to make slaves of, or hold us in slavery. How would they like for us to make slaves of, and hold them in cruel slavery, and murder them as they do us?—But is Mr. Jefferson's assertions true? Viz. "that it is unfortunate for us that our Creator has been pleased to make us black." We will not take his say so, for the fact." [23]

The idea of God expressed here helps the Negro to accept himself. It helps him to free himself of the inferiority complex, thus enabling him to make the necessary psychological adjustment. The ideas fall within the area of those that are socially developed.

God Is on Our Side.

Walker writes again in the *Appeal*:

"Fear not the number and education of our enemies, against whom we shall have to contend for our lawful right; guaranteed to us by our Maker; for why should we be afraid, when God is, and will continue, (if we continue humble) to be on our side?

"The man who would not fight under our Lord and Master Jesus Christ, in the glorious and heavenly cause of freedom and of God—to be delivered from the most wretched, abject and servile slavery, that ever a people was afflicted with since the foundation of the world, to the

---

[23] Walker David, Appeal (Boston: Revised and Published by David Walker, 1830), pp. 14–15.

present day—ought to be kept with all of his children or family, in slavery, or in chains, to be butchered by his cruel enemies." [24]

The idea of God in this quotation is developed along social lines—to make the Negro discontent with his servile condition and to arouse him to fight against slavery in the cause of freedom and God. Freedom is the watchword and God is used as an instrument to bring it about. Walker has a firm militant faith in God, yet it is sobered by the conviction that in due time God will bring about the emancipation of the race. "Our sufferings will come to an end, in spite of all the Americans this side of eternity."[25] If the Americans escape the wrath of Almighty God, He is not a God of justice. God is just; therefore, God Almighty will, in time, pour out his vengeance upon Americans for the way they treat the slaves. The idea of God in this connection is used to perfect social change by attempting to instill fear in the masters. Perpetuating this idea further Walker says:

"Know this, my dear sirs, that although you treat us and our children now, as you do your domestic beast—yet the final results of all future events are known but to God Almighty alone, who rules in the armies of heaven and among the inhabitants of the earth, and who dethrones one earthly king and sits up another, as it seemeth good in his holy sight. We may attribute these vicissitudes to what we please, but the God of armies and of justices rules in heaven and in earth, and the whole American people shall see and know it yet, to their satisfaction." [26]

Using the idea of God to bring about social reform in the abolition of slavery, Walker declares that destruction is at hand. He says:

"Can anything be a greater mockery of religion than the way in which it is conducted by the Americans? It appears as though they are bent only on daring God Almighty to do His best—they chain and handcuff us and our children and drive us around the country like brutes, and

---

[24] Ibid, p. 15.
[25] Ibid, p. 18.
[26] Ibid, p. 45.

go into the house of the God of justice to return Him thanks for having aided them in their infernal cruelties inflicted upon us. Will the Lord suffer this people to go on much longer, taking His holy name in vain? Will He not stop them, preachers and all? O Americans! Americans! I call God—I call angels—I call men, to witness, that your destruction is at hand, and will be speedily consummated unless you repent." [27]

In his argument against Henry Clay, Walker continues to prophesy that the judgment of God will fall upon those who love and indorse slavery. He continues:

"How astonishing it is, for a man who knows so much about God and His ways, as Mr. Clay, to ask such frivolous questions? Does he believe that a man of his talents and standing in the midst of a people, will get along unnoticed by the penetrating and all Seeing Eye of God, who is continually taking cognizance of the hearts of men? Is not God against him, for advocating the murderous course of slavery? If God is against him, what can the Americans, together with the whole world do for him? Can they save him from the hand of the Lord Jesus Christ?" [28]

The next writer, Miss Frances Ellen Watkins (Mrs. Frances Watkins Harper), might be justly called an abolitionist.

Miss Watkins was born in Baltimore in 1825, not of slave parentage. In 1853, or there about, Maryland had enacted a law which prohibited free people of color from the North from entering into the State on pain of being sold into slavery or imprisoned. A free man violated this statute and was sold into slavery. He soon escaped from Georgia, hiding himself behind the wheelhouse of a boat bound northward. Before reaching the North, he was discovered and remanded to slavery. It is said that he died soon after from the effects of exposure. Writing to a friend Mrs. Harper referred to this outrage setting forth her view of God.

---

[27] Ibid, p. 45.
[28] Ibid, p. 57.

Commissioned by God to Work for Freedom.

"Upon that grave I pledged myself to the anti-slavery cause." In a subsequent letter she wrote: "It may be that God himself has written upon both my heart and my brain a commission to use time, talent and energy in the cause of freedom." [29]

She connected herself with the Underground Railroad and devoted her life to the Anti-slavery Movement. Mrs. Harper's ideas of God are clearly developed along social lines. She feels commissioned by God to fight slavery and she goes out bravely to do so.

The Way to Get Close to the Heart of God.

One of the finest and the most beautiful ideas of God is expressed in this letter in which Mrs. Harper makes inquiries of the fugitives.

"How fared the girl who came robed in male attire? Do write me every time you write how many come to your house; and, my dear friend, if you have that much in hand of mine from my books, will you please pay the Vigilance Committee two or three dollars for one to help carry on the glorious enterprise—now, please do not write back that you are not going to do any such thing. Let me explain a few matters to you. In the first place, I am able to give something, I am willing to do so—oh, life is fading away, and we have but an hour of time! Should we not, therefore, endeavor to let its history gladden the earth? The nearer we ally ourselves to the wants and woes of humanity in the Spirit of Christ, the closer we get to the great heart of God; the nearer we stand by the beating pulse of universal love." [30]

God means definite social action in her case. The ideas of God which she entertains are dynamic ideas which send one out to perfect the social change desired. They are socially developed. She hates slavery with a perfect hatred. She writes of it:

---

[29] Still, William, The Underground Railroad (Philadelphia: Peoples Publishing Company, 1879), p. 759.
[30] Ibid, p. 763.

"Make me a grave where'er you will,
In a lowly plain, or a lofty hill,
Make it among earth's humblest graves,
But not in a land where men are slaves." [31]

Around 1864, she wrote a poem "To the Union Lovers of Cleveland" in which she condemns the act of returning a slave girl from Cleveland, Ohio, under the Fugitive Slave Law.

God's Judgment Will Come.

"There is blood upon your city,
Dark and dismal is the stain;
And your hands would fail to cleanse it,
Though Lake Erie ye should drain.

"There's a curse upon your union,
Fearful sounds are in the air;
As if thunderbolt were framing
Answers to the bondman's prayer.

"Ye may offer human victims,
Like the heathen priests of old;
And may barter manly honor
For the union and for gold.

"But ye cannot stay the whirlwind,
When the storm begins to break;
And our God doth rise in judgment,
For the poor and needy's sake.

And, your sin-cursed, guilty union,
Shall be shaken to its base,
Till he learn that simple justice
Is the right of every race." [32]

Mrs. Harper's ideas of God are further used in connection with the social changes desired when she sees in the Civil War God's way of protecting the oppressed.

God Allowed No Victory with Slavery.

"I am not uneasy about the result of this War. We may look upon it as God's controversy with the Nation; His

---
[31] Ibid, p. 763.
[32] Ibid, p. 764.

Ideas of God in "Classical" Literature 121

arising to plead by fire and blood the cause of His poor and needy people." [33]

After the Emancipation Proclamation she says in a speech in Columbus, Ohio:

"In the crucible of disaster and defeat God has stirred the nation, and permitted no permanent victory to crown her banners while she kept her hand upon the trembling slave and held him back from freedom." [34]

The ideas of God as developed by Mrs. Harper are thoroughly interwoven with social reconstruction—and to her the reconstruction most desired is the abolition of slavery. Against this background she developed her ideas revealing further evidence that some of the most outstanding abolitionists were Negroes.

Frederick Douglass was the most pronounced Negro abolitionist. It will be interesting to record what he thought of God.

Douglass was born in 1817 in Talbot County, Eastern Shore, Maryland. Up to the time of Booker T. Washington, he was the most prominent Negro in American history. The fact that Douglass escaped from slavery, that he rose to the position of one of America's greatest orators, and that he became an eminent statesman, made him outstanding among the abolitionists of the world. What he has to say about God is a revelation.

Puzzled about God.

When but a child Douglass began to raise questions about slavery and God. He wanted to know why he was a slave, why some people were slaves and others masters, whether there was ever a time when slavery did not exist, and how it began. "By some means I learned from these inquiries, that God, up in the sky, made everybody; and that He made white people to be masters and mistresses, and black people to be slaves. This did not satisfy me, nor lessen my interest in the subject. I was told, too, that God was good, and that He knew what was best for me and best for everybody. This was less satisfactory

---
[33] Ibid, p. 765.
[34] Ibid, p. 766.

than the first statement; because it came, point blank, against all my notions of goodness. It was not good to let old master cut the flesh off Esther, and make her cry so. Besides, how did people know that God made blacks to be slaves?.....It was some relief to my hard notions of the goodness of God that, although He made white men to be slaveholders, He did not make them to be bad slaveholders, and that, in due time, He would punish the bad slaveholders; that He would, when they died, send them to the bad place, where they would be "burnt up." [35]

Slavery Caused by Man, not God.

The author is in a quandary. But he is almost convinced that God did not intend for any people to be slaves. He began early to yearn for freedom and just as early he began to develop the idea that God was against slavery. "Once, however, engaged in the inquiry, I was not very long in finding out the true solution of the matter. It was not color, but crime, not God, but man, that afforded the true explanation of the existence of slavery." [36]

Equals at the Bar of God.

Douglass was not long in developing the idea that in Heaven there could be no distinctions except those based on obedience and disobedience. He rebelled against inequalities and against the idea of "superior" and "inferior." He says:

"One of the most heart-saddening and humiliating scenes I ever witnessed, was the whipping of old Barney, by Col. Lloyd himself. Here were two men, both advanced in years; there were the silvery locks of Col. Lloyd, and there was the bald and toilworn brow of Old Barney; Master and slave; superior and inferior here, but equal at the bar of God; and, in the Common Counsel of events, they must both soon meet in another world, in a world where all distinction, except those based on obedience and disobedience, are blotted out forever. "Uncover your

---

[35] Douglass, Frederick, My Bondage and My Freedom (New York: Miller, Orton & Mulligan, 1855), p. 90.
[36] Ibid, p. 90.

head!" said the imperious master; he was obeyed. "Take off your jacket, you old rascal!" and off came Barney's jacket. "Down on your knees!" Down knelt the old man, his shoulders bare, his bald head glistening in the sun, and his aged knees on the cold, damp ground. In this humble and debasing attitude, the master—that master to whom he had given the best years and the best strength of his life—came forward, and laid on thirty lashes, with his horse whip."[37]

God is Father, Slavery is a Crime.

"I was just as well aware of the unjust, unnatural and murderous character of slavery, when nine years old, as I am now. Without any appeal to books, to laws, or to authorities of any kind, it was enough to accept God as a Father, to regard slavery as a crime." [38]

The Almighty Did Not Will My Enslavement.

Developing his ideas of God to show that slavery should not exist, Douglass declares that it is a delusion to believe that God requires one to submit to slavery. Commenting on the result of some of his reading, he says:

"If I ever wavered under the consideration, that the Almighty, in some way, ordained slavery, and willed my enslavement for His own glory, I wavered no longer. I had now penetrated the secret of all slavery and oppression, and had ascertained their true foundation to be in the pride, the power, and avarice of man. The dialogue and the speeches were all redolent of the principles of liberty, and poured floods of light on the nature and character of slavery. With a book of this kind in my hand, my own human nature, and the facts of my experience to help me, I was equal to a contest with the religious advocates of slavery, whether among the whites or among the colored people, for blindness in this matter, is not confined to the former. I have met many religious colored people, at the South, who are under the delusion that God requires them to submit to slavery, and to wear their chains with meekness and humility. I could entertain no such nonsense as this; and I almost lost my patience when I found any colored man weak enough to believe such stuff." [39]

---

[37] Ibid, p. 114.
[38] Ibid, p. 134.
[39] Ibid, pp. 158–9.

The ideas of God are developed socially to convince white people that God did not will slavery, and to free the Negro's mind of the belief that God ordained it. The effort is to rob slavery of its religious sanction and at the same time to help the Negro to create within his mind a genuine integrity with respect to himself and a desire for freedom. The ideas are not compensatory.

Slaveholders Responsible to God at the Judgment.

So convinced was Douglass that slavery was wrong that there was no doubt in his mind that in the judgment slaveholders would receive their just rewards at the hands of a just God. He says in that connection:

> "Slaveholders have made it almost impossible for the slave to commit any crime, known either to the laws of God or to the laws of man. If he steals he takes his own; if he kills his master, he imitates only the heroes of the revolution. Slaveholders I hold to be individually and collectively responsible for all the evils which grow out of the horrid relation, and I believe they will be so held at the judgment, in the sight of a just God. Make a man a slave and you rob him of moral responsibility." [40]

Under Divine Mission to Work for Emancipation.

Douglass developed clearly his ideas of God in terms of social reconstruction. When his interest in the emancipation of the race became so strong that he believed that he was called of God to his task, he said:

> "I have felt it to be a part of my mission—under a gracious Providence—to impress my sable brothers in this country with the conviction that, not withstanding the ten thousand discouragements and the powerful hindrances, which beset their existence in this country—notwithstanding the blood—written history of Africa, and her children, from whom we have descended, or the clouds and darkness,..... now overshadowing them—progress is yet possible, and bright skies shall yet shine upon their pathway; and that "Ethiopia shall yet reach forth her hands unto God."

---

[40] Ibid., p. 191.

"Believing that one of the best means of emancipating the slaves of the South is to improve and elevate the character of the free colored people of the North, I shall labor in the future, as I have labored in the past, to promote the moral, social, religious, and intellectual elevation of the free colored people; never forgetting my own humble origin, nor refusing, while Heaven lends me ability, to use my voice, my pen, or my vote, to advocate the great and primary work of the universal and unconditional emancipation of my entire race." [41]

One more quotation from Douglass' utterances prior to the Civil War will suffice to show how completely his ideas of God are developed in an effort to perfect social change by abolishing the institution of slavery. He declared that the popular church, popular worship, and the popular religion are to be pronounced an abomination in the sight of God. In denouncing the religion of the popular church he affirms the belief that God is the Father of the race, that He is no respecter of person and that all men are brothers.

Relation of Master and Slave not Ordained of God.

"But the church of this country is not only indifferent to the wrongs of the slave, it actually takes sides with the oppressors. It has made itself the bulwark of American slavery, and the shield of American slave-hunters. Many of its most eloquent Divines, who stand as the very light of the church, have shamelessly given the sanction of religion and the Bible to the whole slave system. They have taught that man may, properly, be a slave; that the relation of master and slave is ordained of God; that to send back an escaped bondman to his master is clearly the duty of all followers of the Lord Jesus Christ; and this horrible blasphemy is palmed off upon the world for Christianity.

"For my part, I would say, welcome infidelity! Welcome anything! in preference to the gospel, as preached by those Divines! They convert the very name of religion into an engine of tyranny and barbarous cruelty, and serve to confirm more infidels, in this age, than all the infidel writings of Thomas Paine, Voltaire, and Bolingbroke put to-

---

[41] Ibid, p. 406.

gether have done!—It is a religion for oppressors, man-stealers and thugs. It is not that "pure and undefiled religion" which is from above, and which is "first pure, then peaceable, easy to be entreated, full of mercy and good fruits, without partiality, and without hypocrisy." But a religion which favors the rich against the poor; which exalts the proud above the humble; which divides mankind into two classes, tyrants and slaves.....it makes God a respecter of persons, denies His Fatherhood of the race, and tramps in the dust the great truth of the brotherhood of man." [42]

Summation.

As strange as it may seem, there is little other-worldliness in the literature between 1760 and 1860. Excepting the Spirituals (and they belong to either of the periods), this is true of the "mass" literature and it is true of the "classical" literature. One finds in both, ideas of God that are compensatory; but for the most part they are developed along the lines of social reconstruction. The one outstanding need is freedom and the ideas of God are developed to support that need. It is not surprising that the "mass" literature is no more compensatory and other-worldly than the "classical" literature. This is true because in the early period the majority of leaders were ministers and they were on the whole, the best trained men of the race.

The Negroes' ideas of God in this period are those of traditional Christianity, but they are the most lofty of the traditional ideas. The dominant ones are: God is just; He is love; He is no respecter of person; He is a God of peace; from one blood or species God made all mankind; God is on the side of the righteous and the oppressed; and God will eventually bring to judgment those who continue to violate His laws. It is clear, therefore, that these early Negro writers exercised a keen sense of selectivity and chose those ideas of God that supported their claim for social justice and complete emancipation. This unique sense of selectivity was developed out of the social situation in which

[42] Ibid, p. 215.

the Negro found himself. It was natural that he would select those ideas of God that would further his desires. They are ideas of God that are peculiar to oppressed people. Probably the most compensatory ideas of this period, excepting those of the Reverend Mr. Cannon, come from Jupiter Hammon and Phillis Wheatley. Both of these slaves were especially favored by their masters. The great revelation is that so few Negro writers were compensatory and other worldly in their emphases. One might expect the Negro writers, during these times, to use God as an escape from reality, as a means to make the Negro complacent under the stern realities of slavery by looking away to the rewards that awaited him in Heaven. Much of this did take place and the reasons for it have already been given. But most of them were prophets of social righteousness and they developed their ideas of God in keeping with the social needs of their time.

CHAPTER IV

Ideas of God in "Classical" Literature
1865–1914

Lincoln's emancipation proclamation did not solve all the Negro's problems. Immediately after freedom was declared new problems arose. Proscriptions and discriminations of varying characters developed. It is natural that men like Frederick Douglass who developed their ideas of God to assist in the overthrow of slavery would use them after emancipation to perfect social reconstruction in those areas where the Negro was circumscribed and where legal rights were denied him. Many years after the Civil War, as was the case before the War, Douglass was one of the most commanding figures on the American platform. We leave him after citing one post-Civil War reference. Speaking on the subject "Why is the Negro Lynched," Douglass used his idea of God to oppose lynching. He says:

"But call this problem what you may or will, the all-important question is: How can it be solved? How can the peace and tranquility of the South and of the country be secured and established?

"There is nothing occult or mysterious about the answer to this question. Some things are to be kept in the mind when dealing with this subject and should never be forgotten. It should be remembered that, in the order of Divine Providence, the "man, who puts one end of a chain around the ankle of his fellow man, will find the other end around his own neck." And it is the same with a nation. Confirmation of this truth is as strong as proofs of holy writ. As we sow we shall reap, is a lesson that will be learned here as elsewhere. We tolerated slavery and it has cost us a million graves, and it may be that lawless murder now raging, if permitted to go on, may yet bring the red hand of vengeance, not only on the reverend head of age, and upon the heads of helpless women, but upon even the innocent babes in the cradle."[1]

The next person to receive consideration is Richard T. Greener. He was born in Philadelphia and was the first Negro to receive the A.B. degree from Harvard. He was graduated from that institution in 1870. He taught school in Philadelphia and the District of Columbia. For a brief while, he held a position in the office of the United States Attorney for the District of Columbia. He served as Professor of Metaphysics and Logic in the University of South Carolina until the Hampton Legislature closed the University. Subsequently, he taught Law in Howard University and later was elected Dean of the Law School.[2]

Around 1874 there was a great exodus of colored people from the southern states. Mr. Greener, September 12, 1874, not only favored the exodus, but he expressed the belief that it was the hand of God operating to get the Negroes to a section where conditions were better. He argued that the exodus would continue.

It Came from God.

"The little rill has started on its course toward the great sea of humanity. It moves slowly on by virtue of the eternal law of gravitation, which leads people and individuals toward peace, protection and happiness. Today it is a slender thread and makes way with difficulty amid the rocks and tangled growth; but it has already burst through serious impediments, showing itself possessed of a mighty current. It started in Mississippi, but it is even now being rapidly fed by other rills and streams from the territory through which it flows. Believing that it comes from God, and feeling convinced that it bears only blessings in its course for that race so long tossed, so ill-treated, so sadly misunderstood, I greet its tiny line, and almost see in the

---

[1] Douglass, Frederick, Why is the Negro Lynched (Bridgewater: Printed by John Whitby & Sons, 1885)—To be found in *"Addresses of Douglass,"* Moorland Room, Howard University.
[2] Woodson, Carter G. Negro Orators and Their Orations (Washington: Associated Publishers, 1925), p. 473-4.

near future its magnificent broad bosom, heaving proudly onward, until at last, like the travel-worn and battle-scarred Greeks of old, there bursts upon its sight the sea, the broad sea of universal freedom and protection." [3]

Greener uses the idea of God to encourage Negroes to seek a land where conditions are better. The idea is developed to arouse Negroes to seek a solution to their ills by running away from the stifling circumstances which they confront from day to day. As will be seen from this point on, the ideas remain almost constant. The social emphasis shifts to a clamor for social and civic privileges denied the Negro in the post-Civil War period.

Paul Laurence Dunbar arrived on the scene in the early nineties. His writings are fruitful sources for a study of the idea of God.

No effort is made to quote all the poems that contain Dunbar's ideas of God. A summary of his ideas is given and selections are quoted to illustrate the way his ideas of God are used.

They are developed along two extreme lines. Some ideas are clearly compensatory and adhere strictly to traditional patterns, while others are interpreted along social lines. As strange as this may seem, it is not wholly inexplicable. It is perhaps difficult for any one to possess ideas of God that are wholly constructive in character. Certainly is this likely to be true in the case of Dunbar—one whose life was an embodiment of struggle, disappointment, defeat, sickness, and finally, success and fame. The paradox existed in his own life. Perhaps the compensatory ideas were worshipful to him and sustained his faith sufficiently to keep up the militant struggle for existence. A summary of his ideas of God follows:

God soothes, comforts, and consoles weary travelers. During the storm and stress of life he gives protection. It is implied that God is the ideal toward which the race struggles. God is all powerful. He is concerned with human needs, helping humanity to rise. God is not interested in creeds and dogmas. He is merci-

---

[3] Ibid., p. 487.

ful. He is on the side of right guaranteeing the victory. God has a plan though we cannot always fathom it out. God is sovereign because His will seems to prevail arbitrarily. He gives strength for the battle of life. He approves war and He gives the Negro friends.

Closely associated with his ideas of God, and inseparable from them, are the wants and desires stated and implied in his poetry. Dunbar wants comfort when lonely, strength when weak, and companionship when the battle of life is fierce. He wishes to be free of sorrow and vexation. He wants protection from harm when the skies are dark. He yearns for righteousness to prevail. He wants grief and poverty eliminated. He desires security from temptation which comes to one who has won renown. It is implied that he wants security of existence after death. He craves for strength to face bravely the struggles of life and strength to fight. He yearns for clear vision. He wants status, privileges, and friends for the Negro. He desires a complete life and he wants a Heaven on the earth. Some of the poems that follow illustrate vividly the points advanced here.

A Hymn

"Lead gently, Lord, and slow,
For oh, my steps are weak,
And ever as I go,
Some soothing sentence speak;

"That I may turn my face,
Through doubt's obscurity,
Towards thine abiding place,
E'en tho' I cannot see.

"For lo, the way is dark,
Through mist and cloud I grope,
Save for that fitful spark,
The little flame of hope.

"Lead gently, Lord, and slow,
For fear that I may fall;
I know not where to go,
Unless I hear Thy call.

> "My fainting soul doth yearn
> For Thy green hills afar;
> So let Thy mercy burn—
> My greater, guiding star." [4]

It is the belief of the poet that God in hours of trial sustains man, speaks soothing words to him, and keeps him from failing. God is an ever-present companion when one is lonely, tired, and when he is approaching the end of life's journey. This idea of God makes endurance easier and an intolerable life a bit more tolerable. It helps one to look away from his troubles and afflictions and causes his mind to be focused on the goodness and blessings of God. The view of God expressed here lends support to the orthodox, traditional idea that God never leaves us alone. In another hymn, Dunbar expresses a similar idea of God supporting the traditional, compensatory pattern.

> "When storms arise
> And dark'ning skies
> About me threat'ning lower,
> To Thee, O Lord, I raise mine eyes
> To Thee my tortured spirit flies
> For solace in that hour.
>
> "Thy mighty arm
> Will let no harm
> Come near me nor befall me;
> Thy voice shall quiet my alarm,
> When life's great battle waxeth warm—
> No foeman shall appall me.
>
> "Upon Thy breast
> Secure I rest
> From sorrow and vexation;
> No more by sinful care oppressed,
> But in Thy presence ever blest,
> O God of my salvation." [5]

It is strongly implied that final security, rest from toil, freedom from sorrow and vexation, and protection from sin and

---

[4] Wiggins, Lida Keck, *The Life and Works of Paul Laurence Dunbar* (Washington: Mulliken-Jenkins Co.), p. 204.
[5] Ibid, pp. 178–179.

harm are to be achieved in God and in another world. It seems clear that God is an instrument of escape from the hard, unpleasant realities of this life. Such an idea may serve as an opiate to one as he journeys through life. It may dull reason, ease pain, and lead one to feel that all is well regardless of circumstances. It consoles and soothes. It tends to be other-worldly in character. It strengthens one to endure hardship, looking to the beyond for complete release from the cares of life.

A Prayer

>"O Lord, the hard-won miles
>Have worn my stumbling feet;
>Oh, soothe me with Thy smiles,
>And make my life complete.
>
>"The thorns were thick and keen,
>Where'er I trembling trod;
>The way was long between
>My wounded feet and God.
>
>"Where healing waters flow
>Do Thou my footsteps lead,
>My heart is aching so;
>Thy gracious balm I need." [6]

This is a prayer of a tired, lonely person—it is a yearning for companionship, sympathetic understanding, and emotional peace. The idea of God is not motivating; it is not a spur to constructive action; it gives a soothing, delightful feeling to the believer. Like the ideas in the two hymns, it adheres to the traditional view that complete security can be found in God. In essence the idea is compensatory.

Resignation

>"Long had I grieved at what I deemed abuse,
>But now I am a grain within the mill;
>If so be Thou must crush me for Thy use;
>Grind on, O potent God, and do Thy will." [7]

---
[6] Ibid, p. 142.
[7] Ibid, p. 209.

The implication is that whatever happens, it happens at the will of a potent God; that it is useless to grieve and worry about abuses and maladjustment; that God's will moves on and it is irrevocable. It is suggested that the thing for man to do is to resign himself to the inevitable, irretrievable will of God. The idea set forth here may be as hard and cold as the Stoic philosophy which taught that one should submit himself to the rigid terms of universal law. This view of God sustains the philosophy, prevalent among some people, that it is useless to be vexed and worried over the tragedies of life because man cannot change what God has already decreed. It may also help him to keep himself calm in the midst of chaotic circumstances, but the idea is not interpreted in terms of social rehabilitation. It would hardly lead one to constructive activity in the area of perfecting social change.

There are in Dunbar's writings, however, ideas that move definitely away from the compensatory into the area where the idea of God and that of social welfare are inseparable. Quotations containing these ideas are given below. It is said that at one time Dunbar was strongly contemplating the ministry as a life's profession. When he finally decided not to enter the ministry, he wrote the following poem entitled "Religion":

"I am no priest of crooks nor creeds,
  For human wants and human needs
Are more to me than prophets' deeds;
  And human tears and human cares
Affect me more than human prayers.

"Go, cease your wail, lugubrious saint;
  You fret high Heaven with your plaint,
Is this the "Christian's joy" you paint?
  Is this the Christian's boasted bliss?
Avails your faith no more than this?

"Take up your arms, come out with me,
  Let Heav'n alone; humanity
Needs more and Heaven less from thee,
  With pity for mankind look 'round;
Help them rise—and Heaven is found."

---

[8] Ibid, p. 160.

Though not typical of Dunbar, the idea of God in this poem is not given, but strongly implied. The qualities of God are: His social justice, His sympathy for those whose cares are heavy, His disinterest in creed, and His inclination to be moved more by actual human needs than by prayers. The thing Dunbar craves for is the elimination of barriers that keep humanity down. The idea of God implied in this poem lays upon the one who believes in this kind of God the obligation to do his share to help mankind to rise to a higher level. The human family is a unit and in helping humanity to rise, one would be under obligation to use his powers in behalf of all groups and particularly those whose cares and burdens are heaviest. The idea of God is so used as to make it a vital force in man's efforts to perfect some kind of social change. It is traditional in that it has a basis both in Jesus and the prophets. Though traditional, it is interlaced and interwoven with human needs so much so that the idea of God and that of social welfare are inseparable. This view of God goes beyond the narrow confines of race and challenges one to be interested in social and economic values for all groups, including those of the Negro.

In the following poem, "The Warrior's Prayer," Dunbar reveals an idea of God wherein God gives man power to face life with a courage that leads to action:

> "Long since, in sore distress, I heard one pray,
> "Lord, who prevailest with resistless might,
> Ever from war and strife keep me away,
> My battles fight!"
>
> "I know not if I play the Pharisee,
> And if my brother after all be right;
> But mine shall be the warrior's plea to Thee—
> Strength for the fight.
>
> "I do not ask that Thou shalt front the fray,
> And drive the warring foeman from my sight;
> I only ask, O Lord, by night, by day,
> Strength for the fight!

"When foes upon me press, let me not quail
Nor think to turn me into coward flight,
I only ask, to make mine arms prevail,
Strength for the fight!

"Still let mine eyes look ever on the foe,
Still let mine armor case me strong and bright;
And grant me, as I deal each righteous blow,
Strength for the fight!

"And when, at eventide, the fray is done,
My soul to death's bed chamber do Thou light,
And give me, be the field or lost or won,
Rest from the fight." [9]

In this passage, it is clear that the idea of complete reliance on God in anticipation of His doing man's task does not exist. It is assumed that God expects man to perform his own task. The idea does exist, however, that God gives man strength for the battle. The nature of the battle is not stated except in one section where strength is asked for when righteous blows are being administered. The author pleads for protection from enemies, but only in the sense that he wants God to give him strength to deal adequately with them. If it may be assumed that the battle applies to the struggle of life, clearly the idea of God is tied up with militancy and it gives man courage and zeal to go forth and contend for the things that improve life and make for righteousness. There is no implication that the struggle for righteousness is racial. It seems to be a battle for righteousness that is universal in scope, transcending race. The idea that God gives one strength to do the task is also expressed in Dunbar's poem, "The Unsung Heroes."

In Dunbar's memorial poem to Douglass, it is implied that God is sympathetic toward the Negro in his effort to rise. It is implied that God assures him victory; but it is a victory not without struggle. It is a victory that is won in the heat of the battle. It is an idea that encourages one to fight on; not to live

---

[9] Ibid, pp. 225–6.

a life of complacency, but to struggle in the faith of Douglass that God aids man in his efforts to achieve the right. The end of the poem follows:

> "Oh, Douglass, thou has passed beyond the shore,
> But still thy voice is ringing o'er the gale;
> Thou'st taught thy race how high her hopes may soar,
> And bade her seek the heights, nor faint, nor fail,
> She will not fail, she heeds thy stirring cry,
> She knows thy guardian spirit will be nigh,
> And, rising from beneath the chastn'ing rod,
> She stretches out her bleeding hands to God." [10]

The next and final poem from Dunbar is related in spirit to the one just cited and embodies more than any other quotation from him the idea that God stimulates one to make a constructive effort to rise toward higher things. Its title, "By Rugged Ways," is suggestive:

> "By rugged ways and thro' the night
> We struggle blindly towards the light,
> And groping, stumbling, ever pray,
> For sight of long delaying day.
> The cruel thorns beside the road
> Stretch eager points our steps to goad,
> And from the thickets all about
> Detaining hands reach threatening out.
>
> "Deliver us, oh, Lord," we cry
> Our hands uplifted to the sky.
> No answer save the thunder's peal,
> And onward, onward, still we reel.
> "Oh, give us now Thy guiding light;"
> Our sole reply, the lightning's blight,
> "Vain, vain," cries one, "in vain we call;"
> But faith serene is over all.
>
> "Beside our way the streams are dried,
> And famine mates us side by side.
> Discouraged and reproachful eyes
> Seek once again the frowning skies.

---

[10] Ibid, p. 140.

> Yet shall there come, spite storm and shock,
> A Moses who shall smite the rock,
> Call Manna from the Giver's hand,
> And lead us to the promised land!
>
> "The way is dark and cold and steep,
> And shapes of horror murder sleep,
> And hard the unrelenting years;
> But 'twixt our sighs and moans and tears,
> We still can smile, we still can sing,
> Despite the arduous journeying.
> For faith and hope their courage lend,
> And rest and light are at the end." [11]

In the poem just cited, the Negro race is seeking light and deliverance from that which binds and impedes it in its effort to rise to a place of prominence in America. It seeks strength to endure to the end of the journey. It is implied that God in His good time will deliver the race, will send a Moses to lead the group to the promised land.

At first glance the poem savors of an idea of God that is wholly compensatory—an idea which enables the race to sit and wait for God to send a Moses to champion its cause and to lead it to a land of better things. But the content of the poem reveals the fact that Dunbar represents the race as struggling toward something and is convinced as it struggles for the light that despite every crippling restriction, it will win through to a better day. Though without tangible proof, it is the belief that God himself is in harmony with the Negro's upward struggle and is in it, guaranteeing the victory. It is an idea that the race has the approval of God in its determination to gain status in American society. Though slightly related to a compensatory idea, it does not put one to sleep. It does not compensate by looking to the other world for relief. It enables one to suffer hardship and to feel good only in the confidence that the needs for which the race strives will be achieved. Certainly the idea gives one poise and emotional security, but it is a kind of poise

---

[11] Ibid, p. 291.

and security that the race needs in its upward march toward the light. Viewed in this light, the idea expressed here moves tangibly away from the compensatory and becomes an inseparable part of the race's social struggle.

Booker T. Washington

As in the case of Dunbar, the author does not intend to present all the passages in Washington's writings which embody his ideas of God; if this were done, it would mean useless repetition of the same ideas. In the section that follows, his ideas of God are summarized, the desires sought are given, quotations containing various ideas are given, and the ideas are appraised in the light of compensatory patterns, or patterns that are socially constructive. As is the case in Dunbar's writings, the ideas of God in Washington's speeches are developed in both the compensatory and the socially constructive areas.

According to the various writings of Washington, God is just, and being just, He punishes men for what they do. It was God who raised up antislavery voices. God disciplined the Negro in slavery and prepared him for freedom. God has ordained a specific work for each person. The results of our efforts must be left to God, our task is to strive. God answers prayers. He has one standard by which all races and individuals are judged. God transforms the life of those who accept Him. He requires that we treat each other as we would like to be treated. He gives strength and love which enable an individual to become free of hate. Finally, God demands that religious people take on His qualities and attributes.

The things Washington desired are: an opportunity for the American Negro to gain complete economic status; freedom and privileges for the Negro in proportion to the degree to which he proves himself worthy; the abolition of injustice, ignorance, poverty, and crime; and the desire to rise above any form of hatred or prejudice in his own heart. Further clarification of Washington's ideas of God is to be noted in the quotations that follow:

140   THE NEGRO'S GOD

God Prepared the Negro for Freedom.

"God for two hundred and fifty years, in my opinion, prepared the way for the redemption of the Negro through industrial development." [12]

If God designed the institution of slavery for the express purpose of preparing the Negro for emancipation, it is just as logical to conclude that God has a reason for allowing the Negro to carry the burdens and restrictions that he has carried since emancipation. Therefore, the Negro need not be unduly alarmed or excited about his condition. He should develop patience and the ability to suffer because God has a plan and in time He will reveal it. The institution of slavery, according to Washington, cannot be explained on any other basis except that God planned it. The Negro had to be prepared for emancipation, thus God chose slavery as the best method of getting him ready for it. The idea adheres to the traditional, Biblical patterns about God and its total effect is apt to be compensatory. Equally consoling and possibly compensatory is the idea that God raised up anti-slavery advocates. Speaking of the Church under which George Whitefield was buried, Washington says:

"Thus in the very spot where the life's work of a great advocate of slavery ended, God in His providence raised up a greater, more zealous advocate of anti-slavery, to rouse the people from the lethargy into which Whitefield and his disciples wooed them." [13]

God Punishes.

"From the results of the war with Spain, let us learn this, that God has been teaching the Spanish nation a terrible lesson..... God has been teaching Spain that for every one of her subjects that she has left in ignorance, poverty and crime the price must be paid; and, if it has not been paid with the very heart of the nation, it must be paid with

---
[12] Washington, Booker T., The Future of the American Negro (Boston: Small, Maynard & Co., 1899), p. 53.
[13] Washington, B. T., A New Negro for a New Century (Chicago: American Publishing House, date about 1900), p. 240.

the proudest and bluest blood of her sons and with treasure that is beyond computation. From this spectacle I pray God that America will learn a lesson in respect to the ten million Negroes in this country." [14]

It is clear that Washington is pleading to white Americans in the hope that they might take a determined stand to abolish ignorance, poverty, and crime that exist among the Negroes in this country. He uses one of the most traditional of the God-ideas to chasten the white man and to urge him to get in line. Pointing to Spain as an object lesson, he uses the idea of God to support the belief that the status of ten million Negroes should be improved. It is one of the clearest cases thus far presented to show how a traditional idea of God is reinterpreted to support a growing consciousness of social adjustment needed. His reinterpretation of the idea "that God punishes," in order to swing it in line with social change which Washington wanted to see perfected, does not mean that Washington was insincere. It was, perhaps, this belief in God that stimulated him to urge and to warn the dominant group in America to change its attitude and actions with respect to the Negro. Thus he developed an idea of God along social lines that adhere strictly to the needs of the race. It is to be noted that the relief which Washington desires is sought not in Heaven, but here.

Furthermore, he implies, as the following quotation shows, that retribution comes in the very nature of things when conditions exist that are against God. The idea that God punishes is also expressed in the following:

"They denounced in vehement and scathing language a barbarous custom which tore the infant from its mother's yearning breast that the one might be sold and the other left; scattering families, severing husbands and wives never to meet again, until they met at the bar of a just God as common accusers of an inhuman master." [15]

The traditional pattern is still adhered to, and the ultimate effect of the idea upon conduct is likely to be compensatory.

---
[14] Washington, B. T., Future of American Negro, p. 177.
[15] Washington, B. T., A New Negro for a New Century, p. 165.

The idea is developed, however, to show inhuman masters that they must cease being cruel to their slaves because at the judgment God punishes unjust masters. It is developed here to support Washington's idea of the kind of relationship that the whites should exercise toward Negroes. This idea of God is again carried forward in Washington's next utterance, including the belief that slavery was God's will.

"From the time the first mutterings of rebellion were heard, and the war cloud no longer than a man's hand appeared on our country's horizon, the Negro believed, with an unswerving faith, that slavery was the one cause of war; that God was now ready to punish the despoiler and let the oppressed go free." [16]

God Has One Standard.

"The mere fiat of law cannot make an ignorant voter an intelligent voter; cannot make a dependent man an independent man; cannot make one citizen respect another. These results will come to the Negro, as to all races, by beginning at the bottom and gradually working up to the highest possibilities of his nature. In the economy of God there is but one standard by which an individual can succeed; there is but one for the race." [17]

God has ordained that all races must begin at the bottom and work their way to the top in the light of their possibilities. The Negro, therefore, must have patience and work out his salvation according to the way God has planned it. God has not been partial in demanding this of the Negro because it is the requirement that He has set for all races. There is an adjustment here which the Negro needs to make. In his effort to rise in the social and economic life of America, he must form the right attitude toward his present position. He must start at the bottom and work patiently toward the top in the light of his highest possibilities. The idea of God is constructively developed to support an attitude which Washington believes should characterize the race.

---

[16] Ibid, p. 260.
[17] Washington, B. T., Story of His Life and Work (Booker T. Washington Copyright 1901—J. L. Nichols and Company, 1915), p. 291.

God Saves a Man From Hate.

"With God's help, I believe that I have completely rid myself of any ill feeling toward the southern white man for any wrong he may have inflicted upon my race." [18]

The idea here stated calls upon the individual to be reconciled to people of other races. It cleanses the heart from hatred and leads to mutual fellowship. Racial adjustment is the thing desired and the idea of God is developed to support racial adjustment constructed on the basis of mutual fellowship. The following quotation is in harmony with the one just expressed and shows how an idea is developed to substantiate the claim that religion makes exacting ethical demands upon those who profess it.

"To live the real religious life is in some measure to share the character of God. The word "atonement" which occurs in the Bible again and again, means literally at-one-ment. To be at one with God is to be like God. Our real religious striving, then should be to become one with God, sharing with Him in our poor human way His qualities and attributes. To do this we must get the inner life, the heart right, and we shall then become strong where we have been weak, wise where we have been foolish." [19]

Strength, wisdom, and God-like character are the things desired. The qualities and attributes of God are not given, but it is pointed out that we are at one with God when our hearts are right. The implication is that God demands right hearts. It is probably not too much to say that the idea of a right heart implies that the person is to hold the right attitude toward God and man. Sharing God's qualities and attributes must also mean maintaining and seeking to maintain the proper relationship with men. As the previous and subsequent quotations indicate, Washington thought that being one with God is not a mystical union in which one loses himself in the absolute but rather a reconciliation between God and man, based on a pure

---

[18] Washington, B. T., *Up From Slavery* (New York: Association Press, 1900–1904), p. 165.
[19] Ibid, p. 214.

heart. This idea of God has the potentiality to lead one to seek reconciliation and mutual goodwill among his fellows and it is capable of universal application. It is developed to promote the kind of ethical life that religion at its best demands.

God Answers Prayers.

Just before the Atlanta speech which made Washington famous, he writes that he asked God's blessing upon his effort.

"The next morning, before day, I went carefully over what I intended to say. I also kneeled down and asked God's blessings upon my effort. Right here, perhaps, I ought to add that I make it a rule never to go before an audience, on any occasion, without asking the blessing of God upon what I want to say." [20]

The idea that God answers prayers is traditional and apparently exercised great influence on Washington's life. It made a difference in his behavior in that it made him pray before speaking to an audience. It not only led Washington to pray, but it helped him psychologically, giving him confidence and enthusiasm. The belief that God answers prayers consoled him and made him feel better. If the idea did no more it would have been compensatory. But it is apparent that the prayer led to subsequent action in the interest of the things Washington desired. The idea, therefore, not only caused him to pray, but the belief that God answered his prayers gave him poise and emotional stability as he pleaded to white America for interracial justice and worked to improve the social and economic status of his people. An idea that strengthens and gives one courage in his effort to achieve larger economic opportunities for the group is an idea that has constructive social value.

The idea that God answers prayer is further revealed in another quotation. Speaking before the faculty and Theological Department of Vanderbilt University and the ministers of Nashville, Washington says:

---

[20] By Booker T. Washington c. 1900, 1929, reprinted with permission from Doubleday, Doran and Co., Inc., p. 214.

"If you want to know how to solve the race problem, place your hands upon your hearts and then, with a prayer to God, ask him how you to-day, were you placed in the position that the black man occupies, how you would desire the white man to treat you, and whenever you have answered that question in the sight of God and man, this problem in a large degree will have been solved." [21]

It seems clear that Washington believed that God would transform a man's attitude and his whole life, in the area of race relations, if the person in sincerity asked God to direct him in the right path. The idea of God set forth in the quotation is the belief that God through prayer can so transform the life of white men that they will desire to have the Negro treated as themselves, which means that they would strive to have the Negro enjoy and exercise larger opportunities in every phase of American life. God reveals to one what his responsibilities are and obligates him to seek solution to his problems in the light of the revelation received from Him through prayer.

The social adjustment the author desires is clear. He wants white people and Negroes to live in harmony with the Golden Rule. The interpretation which he places upon the idea of God's ability to transform life is wholly along the lines of social rehabilitation. He develops the traditional idea that God answers prayers to give added weight to the argument that the Negro should have a square deal in American society.

If God helps white men to form the right attitude toward Negroes, He must also help Negroes to create the proper attitude toward white people. The idea would also stimulate the Negro to find out his duties toward the white man and discovering them through answer to prayer, the Negro would seek the solution to his problems in the light of the revelation obtained from God. Social change would be sought by both races in the light of the will of God revealed in prayer. It is clear that prayer is not the end of the activity; it is an instrument for discovering what God requires one to do.

---

[21] From Selected Speeches of Booker T. Washington, by E. D. Washington. Copyright 1932 by Doubleday, Doran & Company, Inc., p. 189.

Speaking against the compensatory, other-worldly aspects of Christianity, Washington says:

"Sentimental Christianity, which banks everything in the future and nothing in the present, is the curse of the race." [22]

He says further:

"Progress is the law of God, and under Him, it is going to be the Negro's guiding star in this country." [23]

The context makes plain that by progress is meant the improving of the conditions under which Negroes live and the development of a finer quality of individual living. When one strives to improve his character personally and seeks to raise his status here on the earth, it is the law of God operating in him.

Ideas of God that developed along traditional, compensatory lines in the period before 1914 are to be found in the poetical works of James Madison Bell.

God Vindicates an Injured Race.

"Nor has our birth land been accepted,
Her hundred fields all bathed in blood,
Bear the impress of truth rejected,
And scourging of an angry God.

"The scourging of a God whose justice
And fearful judgment move apace,
And faithful even in the office
To vindicate an injured race.

"Yes, we have sinned and God has scourged us,
And from his chastening we are sore,
Oh! may the deep affliction urge us,
To live in peace and sin no more." [24]

---

[22] Washington, B. T., Black-Belt Diamonds (New York: Fortune and Scott, 1898), p. 34.
[23] Ibid, p. 115.
[24] Bell, James Madison, The Poetical Works of (Lansing: Wynkoop Hullenbeck, Crawford Co., 1904), p. 21.

The idea that God vindicates the Negro is carried further under the caption, "The Black Man's Wrong."

> "For wrongs and outrage shall surcease;
> The millions shall not cry in vain,
> For God the captive will release
> And break the bondsman's galling chain.
>
> "From 'neath the lash they shall extend
> Their bleeding, trembling hands to God,
> And He will to their reserve send
> Stern retribution's chastening rod." [25]

In both of these poems the idea persists that God is just, revengeful, and cruel. Although it is true that God scourges the Negro, the main emphasis is that God will punish those who oppress the Negro and in some way He will vindicate the Negro. The idea does not stimulate the Negro to exert himself very much in his own interest.

The punishment of the Negro's oppressors and the righteous vindication of his cause are to be perfected through God. The Negro's primary desire is to see those who have wronged him punished. Finding no way of achieving his needs and no way of getting even with his oppressors, the author consoles himself with the conviction that in the future God will come to the rescue of his group. The idea says: be patient, have faith, and do not worry about the ills you suffer here—"take your burdens to the Lord and leave them there." Revenge and the wrath of God are the chief desires.

The compensatory character of Bell's ideas of God are further revealed in his poem, "In Commemoration of the Death of Lincoln."

> "We know not why God has permitted
> This tragic scene, this bloody deed;
> An act so seemingly unfitted,
> In this auspicious hour of need,
> Though none perhaps may the intentions,

---

[25] Ibid, p. 30.

> Or the wonderous purpose tell,
> Of this direful life-suspension—
> Yet God, the Lord, doeth all things well." [26]

The idea of God stated here may make life more livable. It may reduce worry and grief to the minimum. It soothes one when perplexity and calamity come upon him. It gives strength and power to stand ill fortune's frowns, but it does not necessarily obligate one to seek to eliminate the source of disasters.

The idea expressed in the next quotation is also a handicap to an interpretation of the idea of God in terms of social rehabilitation:

> "Must we put forth our vain endeavor
> And waste our efforts on the wind
> And learn too late that mortals never
> Can change what heaven has designed?
> We may provoke God's indignation
> And cause the heavens again to frown.
>
> " 'Til his avenging visitations
> Cause us in sorrow to bow down,
> Yet on and on will sweep the current
> Now putting in from freedom's sea,
> Pushing onward like a torrent,
> Floating the land with liberty." [27]

The author seems to believe that what is to come to the Negro is to come by a decree of Heaven and not from effort on the Negro's part.

Equally comforting and satisfying is the idea that God is in charge of the universe. This idea is expressed by William H. Ferris in the following lines:

> "The mind of man is the manifestation of the mind of God. And if God so wills, the conscious, rational life of man will survive the death of the body and the destruction of the brain. God has the whole universe at His command." [28]

---

[26] Ibid, p. 154.
[27] Ibid, p. 158.
[28] Ferris, William H., The African Abroad (New Haven: The Tuttle, Morehouse and Taylor Press, 1913), p. 21.

To believe that the universe is in the hands of God is to believe that there is purpose in the world and that God will guarantee the successful working out of affairs in the universe. In this sense the idea is compensatory. One can rest secure and feel satisfied because he knows that nothing can go wrong in the world since God governs it. On the other hand, the idea that the mind of man reflects the mind of God, is a social interpretation and tends to give man status. It is implied that the mind of any man of whatever race or class is a manifestation of the mind of God. The Negro has equal standing with other groups because he, too, is a reflection of God. Such an idea helps the Negro to develop a more wholesome type of group self-esteem and group self-appreciation. Seen in this light, the author uses the idea to support the view that one man is as good as another in the sight of God.

Charles W. Chestnutt, writing around 1900, presents ideas of God that justify behavior quite different from the types of behavior previously analyzed. The novel, *The House Behind the Cedars*, presents John Warwick and his sister Rena, both fair enough to pass over into the white race, whose ideas of God are used to justify themselves in their pursuit of different courses in life. That is, both of them use God in their argument to justify their course of action. At fifteen Warwick thought:

"His playmates might call him black; the mirror proved that God, the Father of all, had made him white; and God he had been taught made no mistakes,—having made him white, He must have meant him to be white." [29]

As the novel reveals, John Warwick, seeking the larger advantages that come to one who is white, passes over into the white race. His sister does not.

Rena—
"No, she replied firmly, I shall never marry any man,

---

[29] Chestnutt, Charles W., The House Behind the Cedars (New York: Houghton Mifflin Co., 1900), p. 160. Material is used by permission of, and by arrangement with, P. C. Smith, Copyright Department of Houghton Mifflin.

and I'll not leave mother again. God is against it; I'll stay with my own people." [30]

Warwick—

"God has nothing to do with it," retorted Warwick. "God is too often a convenient stacking-horse for human selfishness. If there is anything to be done so unjust, so despicable, so wicked that human reason revolts at it, there is always some smug hypocrite to exclaim, 'It is the will of God.' " [31]

Rena—

"God made us all," continued Rena dreamily, "And for some good purpose though we may not always see it. He made some people white, and strong, and masterful, and heartless. He made others black and homely and poor and weak.....

"He made us too..... and He must have had a reason for it. Perhaps He meant us to bring the others together in His own good time..... God must have meant me to stay here, or He would not have sent me back. I shall accept things as they are." [32]

Both John and Rena are convinced that God made them as they are and that there is purpose or reason for His doing so. According to John, God is infallible and He is the Father of all. John seeks the civic, social, and economic needs of the white race; Rena seeks the satisfaction and emotional security that comes from mingling with her own people. They both develop their ideas of God along the line of racial and social adjustment— to support two opposing views of racial adjustment.

The idea persists with John that since God made him white (though his mother was clearly a Negro), God intends for him to be white and to enjoy the larger opportunities that accrue

---

[30] Ibid, p. 181.
[31] Ibid, p. 181.
[32] Ibid, p. 181.

to those who are white. He passes over and becomes successful in attaining a satisfactory share of civic, social, and economic goods. He urges his sister to do likewise. The idea that God meant for him to be white supported his desire to pass over into the white race in order that he might more nearly secure the things necessary for abundant existence on the earth. There is no remorse, and no sense of sin in doing this. He construes it to be God's will. Though a selfish view with little group significance, it is an idea of God that is used to stimulate an individual to put forth definite steps to improve his status by losing his racial identity.

The idea that God made Rena a Negro, though veiled in a white skin, influences her behavior and interpretation of the God-idea, too. It is true that she makes her final decision to suffer with her people after her white lover, learning that she had Negro blood in her veins, refuses to marry her. It is also true that she revolts against the idea of passing, thinks she is sinning when she does pass, and wants to tell her white lover that she is a Negro. Her brother influences her not to do so. According to Rena's way of thinking, she is a traitor to her race and to deny it is to go against God.

The adjustment that is needed here is wholly social and racial. The idea that God is the Father of all is traditional. But the idea is developed by John to support the view of many people that Negroes who are light enough to pass are justified in doing so, justified on two counts: first, they are in reality white and, second, they have a right to make a more adequate adjustment to the realities of the objective world than they can possibly make if they remain in the Negro race. The idea is developed by Rena to sustain the opposing views.

If the picture presented in Chestnutt's novel is fairly representative of Negroes who are fair enough to pass, it indicates that many Negroes have passed over into the white race believing that God intended it, since He made them white. Either that or they have seized upon and developed the idea to support the adjustment they wanted to make. That a large number do pass over is common knowledge. To what extent they are stimulated by the conviction that God wills it, can hardly be known; and beyond the novel, we do not care to speculate.

The picture also indicates (and it is implied in Rena's statement) that many Negroes remain in the Negro race because they feel that it is God's will that they do so, and that God lays upon them the responsibility of organizing Negroes and working with them in the race's effort to achieve larger privileges. Again, to what extent this idea has encouraged fair Negroes to assume leadership in the interest of their race can hardly be known. It is a fact that many light and able Negroes have assumed leadership in the Negro race with no effort or desire to escape from it.

Most of the writers used in the second period (1865 to 1914) do not survive the third period. Kelly Miller, Benjamin Brawley, and W. E. B. DuBois are notable exceptions. Quotations from these three men prior to 1914 are fewer than they are in the period from 1914 up to the present. One illustration from each of them will suffice for the second period.

God Chooses the Lowly as Spokesmen.

"In olden times, when God communicated with man from burning bush and on mountain top, He selected men of lowly, loving, loyal souls as the chosen channel of revelation. To believe that those who breathe out slaughter and hatred against their fellowmen are now His chosen mouthpiece is to assume that Providence, in these latter days, has grown less particular than aforetime in the choice of spokesmen." [33]

Kelly Miller argues here that Negroes and not their oppressors are chosen by God as His spokesmen. The Negro, therefore, is especially honored because God has singled him out from among the mighty and powerful to make him His special messenger. This idea aims to create in the Negro an appreciation of his race, and it tends to decrease the possibility of the Negro's being ashamed of himself. The belief that he has

---

[33] Miller, Kelly, Race Adjustment (Washington: The Neale Publishing Company, 1909), p. 157.

recognition from God makes the Negro more acceptable to himself, which is more significant than any recognition that man can bestow upon him. The idea that God chooses the weak as His spokesman is developed by Miller to help the Negro to make the proper racial adjustment—to accept himself and be proud of his race. This emphasis blazes forth abundantly in the post-War era.

Mr. Brawley, the second writer whose writings serve both the second and third periods, sees a divine plan at work in the world.

There Is a Plan.

> "Far above the strife and striving,
> And the hate of man for man,
> I can see the great contriving
> Of a more than human plan.
>
> "And day by day more clearly
> Do we see the great design,
> And day by day more nearly
> Do our footsteps fall in line.
>
> "For in spite of the winds repeating
> The rule of the lash and rod,
> The heart of the world is beating
> With the love that was born of God." [34]

The idea that a divine plan permeates the universe saves one from frustration and doubt. It sustains one in hours of deepest need and conflict. It is a belief, many people entertain, that has kept the Negro encouraged through the years—a deep conviction that God has not forsaken His world. How much this idea has saved the Negro from violent, revolutionary tendencies can never be known. But it can hardly be doubted that the idea has helped the race to cling on and endure afflictions rather than die in despair. Though the idea may have enabled the Negro to

---

[34] White and Jackson, Poetry by American Negroes (Durham, N. C., Trinity College Press, 1924), p. 157.

struggle for his needs, it has also helped to make him satisfied and complacent.

God Sends Special Men to Bring Deliverance.

Commenting on John Brown and his fight against slavery, DuBois writes:

> "To the unraveling of human tangles we would gladly believe that God sends especial men—chosen vessels which come to the world's deliverance." [35]

Only this quotation is presented from DuBois' writings prior to 1914, since the ideas prior to 1914 do not differ widely from those we find after 1914.

The idea that God sends special men to deliver the world of certain ills, more than DuBois' ideas generally, adheres to traditional patterns.

And so, though many of the ideas of God in the literature between 1865 and 1914 are traditional and compensatory, the other-worldly ideas are negligible. Furthermore, the ideas of God in this period are developed and interpreted along lines of social rehabilitation probably more than was the case in the "mass" literature. A few ideas are developed along lines of universal, social reconstruction, but for the most part they are developed along social lines that aim at racial adjustment. It is significant, too, that in the two periods from 1760 to 1914, the writers do not doubt God. They raise little protest against the white man's God and never do they doubt God's ability to bring the world out all right. As will be seen later, this cannot be said of the ideas of God that are developed in the literature from 1914 up to the present.

It might be said, too, that Washington's ideas of God are wholly consistent with his policy of social reform. His interpretation of the idea of God to constrain and persuade the white race to assume its task of perfecting social righteousness; his interpretation of the idea to encourage the Negro, and at

---

[35] DuBois, W. E. B., John Brown (Philadelphia: George W. Jacob and Company, 1909), p. 18.

the same time to counsel him to be patient because the long path of upward struggle is God's way for all groups; and his unwavering faith in God—all are thoroughly consistent with his non-hating spirit, and his patience and long-suffering in dealing with the most acute social and racial problems. His social philosophy and his ideas of God go hand in hand.

CHAPTER V

Other-Worldly "Classical" Literature
(*After 1914*)

It should be noted that the other-worldly element in "classical" Negro literature is conspicuous by its small quantity. This is one of the chief distinctions to be drawn between the "mass" Negro literature and "classical" Negro literature. It was set forth in chapter II that much of the recognition and security in the "mass" literature was to be experienced outside the process of history. Only a few writers of "classical" literature of any period are given to other-worldly writing. Note the ideas of God and the desires sought in the writings of Theodore Henry Shackelford and John Wesley Holloway.

Shackelford makes plain that on the other side, God will make everything right. In Heaven there will be no segregation in eating places. Segregation such as forcing Negroes to live on certain streets will be abolished in Glory. There will be no lynching in Heaven and no disfranchisement. On the blissful shore all the wrongs we have suffered here will be made right. There will be freedom from trials, sorrow, prejudice, vice, crime, and injustice. No failures will accompany one in Heaven. In brief, Shackelford wants to be secure from every form of hampering restrictions that the Negro must suffer here. And despairing of this life, he seeks relief in Heaven where God will reward him by giving eternal rest, everlasting security, crowns, robes, and the like.

Examples follow:

Troubles Over

"Some day, my trials here will cease,
Some day, my failures will be o'er;
Some day, I'll close my eyes in peace,
Some day, I'll rest forever more.

"Some day, I'll break these prison bars,
Some day, my soul shall mount up, free;
Some day, my crown bedecked with stars
Some day, I'll dwell, My Lord with Thee." [1]

God Will Make it Right

"For fifty and two hundred years
Did slavery hold its sway;
And now, though fifty more have passed
It still exists today.
You seem to doubt my falt'ring words
But look and you will see
That when a man is bound and gagged
He surely is not free.

"And we are bound for men dictate
Where we must go to eat;
And tell us that we must vacate
Some sections of the street.
And prejudice is sweeping on
With strides both long and fast,
And we are gagged, for in some states
Our vote we may not cast.

"And often in the papers, too
Most dreadful things I see,
Of lynchings and of other things
To hinder you and me.
Unbidden tears flow down my cheeks
As I sit there alone;
'God pity us!' I cry aloud
To Him on heaven's throne.

"Then instant comfort comes to me,
The sun shines out again,
And I a brighter future see,
I have not prayed in vain.
We do not need to fret and grieve
When billows round us roll,
Prayer is the panacea which
Will comfort every soul.

---

[1] Shackelford, Theodore Henry, *My Country and Other Poems* (Philadelphia: Press of I. W. Klapp Company, 1916-18), p. 180.

"For God will help us if our cares
 Upon Him we will cast,
And through the storm will guide the ship
 To harbor safe at last.
No burdens great, like mountains then
 Shall loom upon our sight.
And all the wrongs which we've endured
 The Savior will make right.

"There unjust men shall not dictate
 Nor sit upon the throne.
God rules supreme on that estate,
 It is His very own.
There murmuring brooks forever flow
 Through gardens fair and wide;
There rich and fragrant flowers grow;
 There love and peace abide." [2]

The other-worldly aspect of "classical" Negro literature is further supported by John Wesley Holloway. God operates wholly in the other world. He prepares the way to usher in the final day. He protects people with angels. God even makes one's bed in sickness. Evil and sin and Satan are the fears of this life from which one will be free in Heaven.

Waiting on the Lord.

"I rest me in the Lord,
 And patiently I wait,
Though sin may bud and flower;
Though great be Satan's power;
Though hosts of sin may hedge me round,
And thunders shake the solid ground,
No qualms, no fears, disturb my breast,
For in my Lord I sweetly rest,
 And patiently I wait.

"I rest me in the Lord,
 And patiently I wait,
While He prepares the way
To usher in the day

---

[2] Ibid, pp. 28, 29.

When all His children, bright and fair,
Shall rise to meet Him in the air.
So, till He takes me in His breast,
Forever there in peace to rest,
I patiently will wait." [3]

Insured with God.

"Insured?" 'Gainst everything!
"Company?" Moses' rod.
"Place?" The New Jerusalem.
Yes; I'm insured with God.

"He hedges me round with angels;
Keeps me in all my ways;
Makes my bed in sickness,
With mercy crowns my days.

"I've put my gems and property
Completely in His hands;
With policies maturable,
To every hour's demands.

"He's really more than able
To keep against that day,
Whate'er I put upon Him,
Along life's toiling way.

"From every kind of evil,
He gives you His protection;—
Sometime ten-dollar funerals
But a billion Resurrection!" [4]

The World Is Not My Home.

"I've come from out the darkness,
Direct from God's own hand;
Upon this little island,
My foot first touches land.
I know not whence I came here,

---

[3] Holloway, John Wesley, from The Desert (New York: The Neale Publishing Company, 1919), p. 142.
[4] Ibid, p. 127.

> I know not where I go;
> I know I'm on a journey,
> And this is all I know.
>
> "This world is not the country
> Where I must take my stand;
> I seek another city,
> In some far distant land;
> I'm pausing here a moment
> To catch the air and light;
> Just let me get my bearings
> And I'll resume my flight." [5]

In this brief chapter we are moving within the area of the Spirituals, *God's Trombones*, the other-worldly prayers, and the other-worldly sermons.

There is no clearer indication anywhere of ideas of God that adhere to and support compensatory patterns than those portrayed here. There is little hope or expectation that God will punish the oppressors and provide security on earth, no desire to co-operate with God in building a world where Negroes will come into their own, and no indication that things will be better tomorrow, except that tomorrow which is Heaven after death. Gloom, despair, and hopelessness characterize the poems. But we can, it seems, endure lynching, segregation, prejudice, failures, vice, and crime because in the far-off glory land God will reward us for our long suffering on the earth. The ideas of God set forth here fit perfectly our definition of ideas that adhere to the traditional, compensatory pattern. The idea encourages one to feel and believe that even though things are not right here and will not be made right in this world, they will be made right in Heaven. The ideas just presented do exactly that. They console, they enable one to endure unbearable situations, but they hardly lead one to do anything about them, except to wait on the Lord on the other side of Jordan. Security, recognition, and new experiences are sought in Heaven. The earth is a temporary abode. Such ideas are fertile soil for the

---

[5] Ibid, p. 135.

old time revival, where the chief emphasis is placed upon saving one's soul from the burning wrath of hell. The two authors, Holloway and Shackleford, are sensitive to social maladjustment, but their technique is one of patient waiting until God makes everything right in some far-off glory land. The types of security this idea of God gives may be restated in the following manner:

1. It gives a sense of personal security. Ultimately one's life is safe. It will triumph in God.

2. This idea of God gives certainty. It delivers one from doubts, suspense, and perplexity. If one is absolutely certain that all will be made up in Heaven, there is less need to worry about discomforts, less need to strive, and less need to doubt. It gives serenity and poise.

3. It gives another form of security—deliverance from the grief and worry that come to one who has lost, through death, a person very dear to him. To know that the friend is not destroyed, that he still lives, and that some day the bereaved will meet his beloved dead in Heaven—to know these things helps one to bear grief with comparative ease. There is no effort to develop the idea of God in a way that would relate God to the struggle of perfecting social change here on the earth.

CHAPTER VI

The Impartiality of God and the Unity of Mankind
(After 1914)

The ideas of God in this chapter, for the most part, cluster around the central theme that God is wholly impartial, that from one blood He created all races and nations. In brief the ideas of God revealed in this section are: God made of one blood all nations; God has set no geographical or racial boundaries; there is no divine right of race; the rights of humanity are divine; we are all God's creatures; God created the Negro in His own image; God made no superior races and no inferior man; God loves all mankind; God and humanity are one; He is the source of all life; He unites all mankind; He spins each person from himself and gives him status; He sends the Negro on a special errand.

It is implied and stated throughout that such conceptions as these make all men brothers—black, yellow, brown, and white. The races of the earth are alike in soul and in the possibility of infinite development. God draws no distinction in service and labor. All work is honorable and God makes no distinction between "the black, sweating cotton hands of Georgia and the first families of Virginia." The only distinction that counts with God is that which is based on deeds. It is also inferred that God is interested in having accrued to all peoples proper recognition and status.

These needs run the gamut all the way from mere economic and civic needs to psychological, spiritual values which are also necessary for survival. The Negro group, like all groups, is entitled to space to stretch its arms and its soul. The Negro is entitled to that security and recognition which come to one who

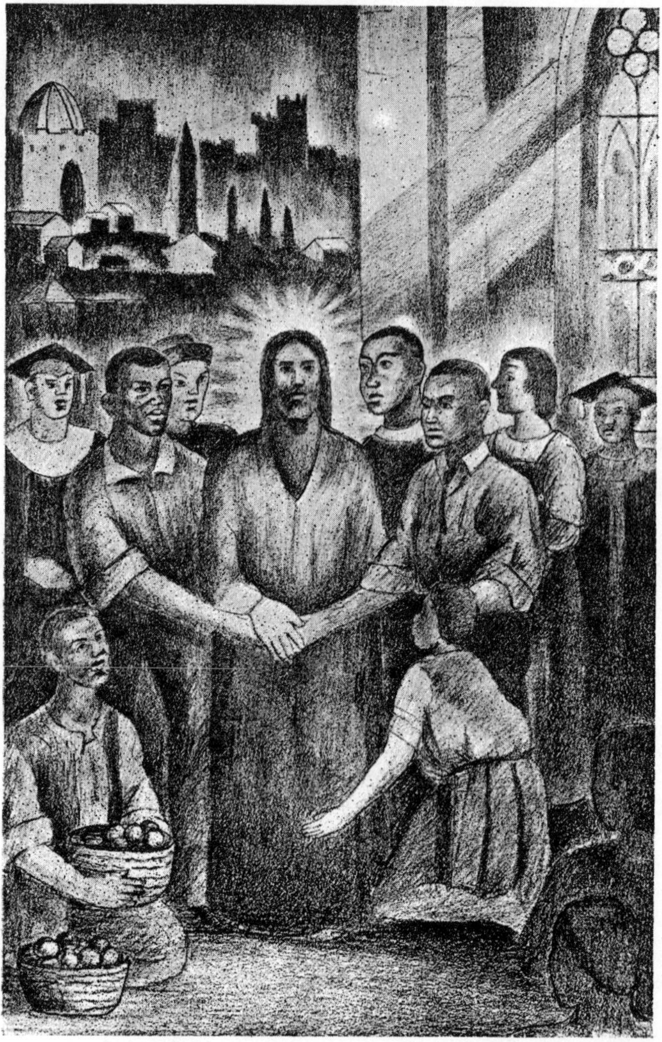

is free to vote, to choose his friends, to enjoy the blessings of nature, and to ride on public conveyances.

It should be noted at the outset that the ideas of God in this chapter are constructively developed to support a growing consciousness of psychological adjustment needed, an adjustment to the conviction that the Negro is not inferior and for that reason he is entitled to the social, economic, and political privileges exercised by other people. It should be noted, too, that, for the most part, the ideas adhere to traditional, but not to compensatory patterns. It is in the interpretation of the ideas of God that the Negro writers in this chapter break with tradition. In a sense they are modernists who take traditional ideas, bring them up-to-date, and fill them with meanings that touch life situations. The quotations embodying these ideas follow in logical succession, beginning with W. E. B. DuBois.

God Made of One Blood All Nations.
"I believe in God, who made of one blood all nations that on earth do dwell. I believe that all men, black and brown and white are brothers, varying through time and opportunity, in form and gift and feature, but differing in no essential particular, and alike in soul and the possibility of infinite development.....

"I believe in service—humble, reverent service, from the blackening of boots to the whitening of souls; for work is heaven, idleness hell, and wage is the "well done," of the Master, who summoned all them that labor and are heavy laden, making no distinction between the black, sweating cotton hands of Georgia and the first families of Virginia, since all distinction not based on deed is devilish and not divine......

"I believe in liberty for all men; the space to stretch their arms and their souls, the right to breathe and the right to vote, the freedom to choose their friends, enjoy the sunshine, and ride on the railroads uncursed by color; thinking, dreaming, working as they will in a kingdom of beauty and love." [1]

---

[1] DuBois, W. E. B., Dark Water (New York: Harcourt, Brace & Howe, 1920), pp. 3, 4.

From a slightly different angle, Kelly Miller sustains DuBois in attributing an impartial character to God. God has not only made all nations of one blood but of one mind and one spirit as well. The impartiality of God is also seen in the fact that God has set no geographical lines; the only limits are those natural boundaries of land and sea which fix the confines of human habitability. God has made the races kin as shown by the fact that in the long run all races will respond to the same stimulus and they will do it in the same way. God has made it impossible for any race to claim any divine right. This idea must be abolished along with that of the divine right of kings. God, according to Miller, is the giver of human rights. He gives them not to one race, but to humanity, and in so doing no human creature can divest these rights from another by virtue of race, color, condition, creed, or climes. God created the Negro in His own image and "nothing created in human guise is a more faithful likeness of that original." It is clear that the author wants for the Negro every right, privilege, and opportunity that other groups enjoy; and he develops his idea of God to support this claim.

The Everlasting Stain, the book from which several of the quotations are taken, is composed of a collection of essays centering about the issues that grew out of the World War and the Negro's relation to them. The productions containing Miller's ideas of God follow:

God Has Set No Geographical Boundaries Nor Racial Limitations.

"The Greek mind reached the loftiest pinnacle of thought and genius as long as the environment favored the development of this peculiar form of culture, but the lapse of two thousand years does not indicate that this race possesses today the slightest trace of that intellectual subtlety which gave rise to "the glory that was Greece." God has made of one blood and of one mind and of one spirit, all nations to dwell on the face of the earth, and has set as the bounds of their habitation no geographical lines nor racial limitations, but the natural boundaries of land and sea which fix the confines of human habitability. Race and color are physical and geographical attributes, and do not permanently determine mind and spirit. All races in the long run will respond to the same stimulus in the same way." [2]

In the following quotation Miller expresses the same idea in another way:

There Is No Divine Right of Race.
"But along with the divine right of kings must go every other semblance of the divine right, including divine right of race. There is no more reason to suppose that God has chosen the white race to exercise lordship over the darker races of men than that He has chosen Germans to lord it over the other European nations. There exists in the minds of many the deep-seated opinion that the white race has some God-ordained mission to which the weaker breeds must bow in humble submission. Rudyard Kipling's 'White Man's Burden' is but the modern refrain of the exploded conceit that God has given His chosen race the heathen for their possession to be broken to pieces with a rod of iron. The divine right of kings is a more acceptable doctrine than the divine right of race." [3]

In chapter XXV of the book under consideration, a chapter entitled "Pessimism of the Negro," Kelly Miller is arguing against the position taken by Fenton Johnson, a Negro poet, who exclaims: "It is better to die then to grow up and find out that you are colored." In this chapter Miller expresses great faith in God and indicates again that the Negro belongs to humanity.

The Rights of Humanity Are Divine and Cannot Be Divested by Reason of Race.
"O! that there might be breathed anew in the nostrils of the Negro that primeval breath of Godhood. The Negro must believe that he is the Son of God and heir and joint heir to the divine patrimony. The rights of humanity are inalienable, of which no human creature can be divested by

---
[2] Miller, Kelly, The Everlasting Stain (Washington, D. C., The Associated Publishers, 1924), pp. 35, 36.
[3] Ibid, pp. 61, 62.

reason of race, color, condition, creed, or clime. Although recognition may be withheld and privileges denied for the while, they can never be effaced or taken away. Only the craven soul can hypothecate his divine birthright.

" 'Though ye have lain among the pots yet shall ye be as doves with wings of silver and feathers of yellow gold.'

"Let the Negro reread Milton's "Paradise Lost" and study closely the character of his imaginary Satan, who is but the embodiment of the tough tenacious Teutonic spirit.

" 'The mind is its own place,
And of itself can make a heaven of hell, a hell of heaven.'

"All is not lost if the mind is not lost. The unconquerable will always find hope in despondency and resolution in despair." [4]

Another work of Kelly Miller's, *Out of the House of Bondage*, carries out the idea of God as set forth in *The Everlasting Stain*. The former was written at the very beginning of the third period stressed in this study and is a collection of essays that originally appeared in a number of the leading magazines of this country. It deals with many of the fundamental principles of the race problem "and with issues that must be involved in any proposed scheme of solution."

We Are All God's Creatures.

"True benevolence is the desire to assist each of God's human creatures to develop his fullest personality." [5]

"The white race, in its arrogant conceit, constituted the personalities and the Negroes the instrumentalities. Man may be defined as a distinction-making animal. He is ever prone to set up barriers between members of his own species and to deny one part of God's human creatures the inalienable birthright vouchsafed to all alike." [6]

---

[4] Ibid., pp. 349, 350.
[5] Miller, Kelly, Out of the House of Bondage (New York: Thomas Y. Crowell Company, 1914), p. 78.
[6] Ibid, p. 84.

God Created the Negro in His Own Image.

"That education of youth, especially the suppressed class, that does not make insistent and incessant appeals to the smothered manhood (I had almost said Godhood) within will prove to be but vanity and vexation of spirit. What boots a few chapters in Chemistry, or pages in History, or paragraphs in Philosophy, unless they result in an enlarged appreciation of one's own manhood? Those who are to stand in the high places of intellectual, moral and spiritual leadership of such a people in such a time must be made to feel deep down in their own souls their own essential manhood. They must believe that they are created in the image of God and that nothing clothed in human guise is a more faithful likeness of that original. This must be the dominant note in the education of the Negro." [7]

The Negro Should Ask God to Help Him Believe in His Inherent Manhood.

"As the white man's faith decreases, our belief in ourselves must increase. Every Negro in America should utter this prayer, with his face turned toward the light: 'Lord, I believe in my own inherent manhood; help Thou my unbelief.'" [8]

Peace and Good Will among Races When They Come to Recognize Their Unity.

"After the red and brown races shall have perished from the face of the earth; after the fragmentary peoples have been exterminated, expelled or absorbed; after the diffusion of knowledge has established a world equilibrium, there will be left the white, the yellow and the black as the residuary races, each practically distinct in its ethnic identity, and occupying its own habitat. We can only prophesy peace, amity and good will among these types, who will more fully appreciate than we do now that God has made of one blood all nations to dwell upon the face of the earth, within assignable bounds of habitation." [9]

---

[7] Ibid, pp. 87, 88.
[8] Ibid, p. 94.
[9] Ibid, pp. 238, 239.

The ideas of God as set forth in the writings of DuBois and Kelly Miller, centering around the belief that God made of one blood all races and that God is wholly impartial in His dealings with the races of men, are further set forth in the writings of Robert Russa Moton, former principal of Tuskegee Institute and successor to Booker T. Washington. The idea that the Negro is God's most perfect handiwork is taken from a speech delivered at a memorial meeting in honor of Booker T. Washington, held in New York City, February 11, 1916. Moton asserts so strongly that Negroes are just as good as other people and that it is disastrous to the fullest development of the race for them to believe that they are inferior and accursed of God, that he virtually accuses God of being partial to the Negro. He not only makes Negroes creatures of God's most perfect handiwork, but he argues that "any lack of appreciation on our part is a reflection on the great Creator." The things sought are self-respect, race pride, and the acceptance of the Negro by himself. The need is for the Negro not to be ashamed of himself and not to try to escape from himself. The idea is developed to support the growing consciousness that the Negro must develop group self-esteem and group appreciation. His exact words follow:

Not to Appreciate the Race Is a Reflection on God.

"If any of us, because of weaknesses and failings within our race, or because of unfairness, injustice, and inconvenience without, or because of the color of our faces and the texture of our hair, have been hitherto lacking in appreciation of our race, or have been afraid to be unmistakably identified with the Negro race, let us, in the name of the God who made us, forever dispel any such foolish, childish, disastrous notions. Let us remember, once and for always, that no race that is ashamed of itself, no race that does not respect, honor, and love itself, can gain the confidence and respect of other races or will ever be truly great and useful.

"Let us remember, also, that we are not an accursed people; that races with whiter faces have, and are still going through difficulties infinitely more trying and embarrassing than much that faces us; that we have in this country vast opportunities for growth and development, as well as for usefulness and service. We are creatures of God's most perfect handiwork, and any lack of appreciation on our part is a reflection on the great Creator. Though we Negroes are black, and though we are living under hampering difficulties and inconveniences, God meant that we should be just as honest, just as industrious, just as skillful, just as pure, just as intelligent, just as Godlike, as any human beings that walk on the face of God's earth." [10]

William Pickens sets the problem in a slightly different area. Speaking on "the kind of democracy the Negro expects," Mr. Pickens gives expression to the conviction that God has made individuals different but God has not made races widely different. A quotation from Pickens follows:

God Made No Widely Different Races.

"Finally, the great colored races will in the future not be kinder to a sham democracy than to a 'scrap-of-paper' autocracy. The private home, private right and private opinion must remain inviolate; but the commonwealth, the public places and public property must not be appropriated to the better use of any group by 'Jim-Crowing' and segregating any other group. By the endowments of God and nature there are individual 'spheres.' Jesus' estimate of the individual soul is the tap root of democracy, and any system which discourages the men of any race from individual achievement, is no democracy. To fix the status of a human soul on earth according to the physical group in which it was born, is the gang spirit of the savage which protects its own members and outlaws all others." [11]

This idea of God is pursued still further by Archibald Grimke, an outstanding lawyer, former Consul in Haiti and champion of Negro rights. Grimke reveals an element of anger bordering on hate. The quotation containing the idea of the

---

[10] Woodson, Carter G., Negro Orators and Their Orations (Washington, D. C., The Associated Publishers, 1925), pp. 605, 606.
[11] Ibid, pp. 657, 658.

impartiality of God or the refutation of the idea that God made some races superior is recorded here:

God Did Not Make the White Man Superior.

"Perceiving the unlimited capacity of mankind for all sorts of folly, no wonder Puck exclaimed, 'What fools these mortals be!' Yes, what fools, but of all the fools who have crawled to dusty death the most stupendous and bedeviled lot are those who strut their fools' feet and toss their fools' head across their little stage of life, thanking their fools' selves that God made them different from other men—superior to other men—to rule over other men." [12]

Reinforcement of this idea of God comes from the Rev. Francis J. Grimke in an address entitled "Victory for the Allies and the United States, a Ground of Rejoicing, of Thanksgiving," delivered at the Fifteenth Street Presbyterian Church, Washington, D. C., December 24, 1918. He claims that the constitutional rights of the Negro are given by God, and the further idea, already stated, that the Negro, or man generally, is made in the image of God. The occasion for his utterance, as in the case of the others, is the social situation in which the Negro finds himself. He is striving for security in America since America claims to have fought to make the world safe for democracy. Grimke says:

Man is Created in God's Image.

"Men of darker hue have no rights which white men are bound to respect. And it is this narrow, contracted, contemptible, undemocratic idea of democracy that we have been fighting to make the world safe for, if we have been fighting to make it safe for democracy at all...... How could we, except in pretense, be fighting to make the world safe for democracy, and at the same time give ourselves no concern about safe-guarding it at home? How can we, with any degree of honesty, of sincerity, claim to be fighting to make the world safe for democracy, when we are trampling upon the sacred, God-given and constitutional

---

[12] Ibid, p. 680.

rights of twelve millions of colored American citizens within our borders?.....That, as a nation, we have little or no interest in true democracy—in the rights of man as man. We have not yet developed sufficiently along moral and spiritual lines to an appreciation of the dignity of man, of the true worth of man as man, created in the image of God; we are still blinded by our narrow racial prejudice; we are still so contemptibly little in our moral ideas that the color of a man's skin is to us of more value, of more importance than anything else in determining the kind of treatment that shall be accorded to him." [13]

In the next statement, Willis J. King not only reinforces the authors quoted above, but also implies that God is impartial by arguing for the solidarity of the human family on the basis of Jesus, the New Testament, and Paul. It is implied that under God all men, of whatever race or nationality, are neighbors; therefore, we are to love them as we do ourselves.

God Made of One Blood All Nations.

"Nothing is more manifest in the teachings and life of Jesus than this note of His interest in others—the conviction that humanity belongs together. He Himself was sociable and craved friendship. Most of the time He was to be found where needy people were. Nor did He confine Himself to the members of His own race. Now it is a woman of Syro-Phoenicia whose daughter is healed. Again, He is seated on a well beside a despised Samaritan woman of questionable character, expounding the truths of the Kingdom. In one of the most beautiful parables recorded of Him His hero was a member of this same Samaritan race. The manifest implication of that story is that our world is a little neighborhood, and that all men, of whatever race or nationality, are our neighbors, whom we are to love as we do ourselves.....If there is any doubt as to the mind of Jesus on that matter, His ablest interpreter—Paul, the great Apostle to the Gentiles—is very explicit on that point. God has made of one blood all the nations of men and desires that all men seek and find Him. This note of the

---

[13] Ibid, pp. 695, 696.

solidarity of the human race runs through the New Testament." [14]

The poem in the foreword of Kelly Miller's *Out of the House of Bondage* bears upon the idea of human solidarity. Miller argues there that God is to love mankind of whatever clime or hue. The idea of the impartiality of God still persists in virtually all of the authors quoted. Miller also claims here that all those who love God must love mankind, too. The words of the poem are:

God Loveth All Mankind.

"I hate a cat. The very sight
Of the feline form evokes my wrath
Whene'er one goes across my path,
I shiver with instinctive fright.

"And yet there is one little kit
I treat with tender kindliness,
The fondled pet of my darling, Bess;
For I love her and she loves it.

"In earth beneath, as Heaven above,
It satisfies the reasoning,
That those who love the self-same thing
Must also one another love.

"Then if our Father loveth all
Mankind of every clime and hue,
Who loveth Him must love them, too;
It cannot otherwise befall." [15]

In another quotation from DuBois, another idea of God is revealed and it is developed along universal, social lines. God possesses all things. He owns the gold. He suffers when man suffers because it is clear that God and humanity are completely fused. God agonizes and pleads with men to come to his rescue as He struggles to make a decent world. Whatever wrong man does to man, he does to God, too. To lynch man is to

---

[14] From The Negro in American Life by W. J. King, Copyright 1926, p. 135. By permission The Methodist Book Concern.
[15] Miller, Kelly, Out of the House of Bondage (New York: Thomas Y. Crowell Company, 1914), p. 11.

lynch God. To draw blood in war from human beings is to draw blood from God. The cruelties and injustices of men constitute God's crucifixion. To steal gold from the helpless is to steal it from God—the gold is God's. Definitely, God is against all forms of injustices and has allied Himself against them but He needs help. This point of view is best expressed by quoting from the "Prayers of God" in DuBois' *Dark Water*. It follows;

God and Humanity Are One.

"This gold?
I took it.
Is it Thine?
Forgive; I did not know.

"Blood? Is it wet with blood?
'Tis from my brother's hands.
(I know; his hands are mine).
It flowed for Thee, O Lord.

"War? Not so; not war—
Dominion, Lord, and over black, not white;
Black, brown, and fawn,
And not Thy Chosen Brood, O God,
We murdered.
To build Thy Kingdom,
To drape our wives and little ones,
And set their souls a-glitter—
For this we killed these lesser breeds
And civilized their dead,
Raping red rubber, diamonds, cocoa, gold;

"For this, too, once, and in Thy name,
I lynched a Nigger—
(He raved and writhed,
I heard him cry,
I felt the life-light leap and lie,
I saw him crackle there, on high,
I watched him wither):

"Thou?
Thee?
I lynched Thee?

"Awake me; God; I sleep!
What was that awful word Thou saidst?
That black and riven thing—was it Thee?
That gasp—was it Thine?
This pain—is it Thine?
Are, then, these bullets piercing Thee?
Have all the wars of the world,
Down all dim time, drawn blood from Thee?

"Have all the lies and thefts and hates—
Is this Thy Crucifixion, God,
And not that funny, little cross,
With vinegar and thorns?
Is this Thy Kingdom here, not there,
This stone and stucco drift of dreams?

"Help!
I sense that low and awful cry.
Who cries?
Who weeps?
With silent sob that rends and tears—
Can God sob?

"Who prays?
I hear strong prayers throng by,
Like mighty winds on dusky moors—
Can God pray?

"Prayest Thou, Lord, and to me?
Thou needest me?
Thou needest me?
Thou needest me?
Poor, wounded soul!
Of this I never dreamed. I thought—
Courage God,
I come!" [16]

God Is the Source of All Life.

The fact that man's life is tied up with God's is expressed in another connection by Howard Thurman. To him, God is the source of all life and from this fact three things follow which will be stated presently. Since out from God emanates all

---

[16] DuBois, W. E. B., *Dark Water* (New York: Harcourt, Brace & Howe, 1920), pp. 250–252.

creation, there is an underlying unity for all of them. There is not only a unity of all things that emanate from God, but there is essential kinship; one man can never be the kind of man he ought to be until everybody else is the kind of person "that everybody else ought to be." "Even God," Thurman argues, "cannot be what he ought to be until man is what he ought to be." Beginning with a traditional idea of God, he goes far beyond traditional ideas in his interpretation.

It is God-ideas that drive men on in quest of fulfilment. The quest for fulfilment is the quest for God. This quest which drives men on is exemplified in men like Horace, when he said that he was unable to sleep at night because of the pressure of unwritten poetry; Bunyan, when he declared that he had to set aside the writing of sermons and other serious tracts in order to write *Pilgrim's Progress,* and Jesus, when he said that the Spirit of the Lord was upon Him. The drive is always in the direction of some need, often the need of others as specifically illustrated in the life of Jesus. Thurman's own words are illuminating at this point:

"We have heard it affirmed that it was His faith" (speaking of Jesus) "and the faith of the speakers, that at the heart of this universe there is personality which is at once the source of life and the goal of life. If that affirmation is valid, then a series of things must follow therefrom, and it is along the line of these that I think the quest for fulfilment, the quest of God, drives one.

"First of all, if God is the source of all life, if from Him emanates all creation, then there must be an underlying unity for all of them, and wherever one digs in honestly, living up to the limit of the light that one has at the particular time, one does make contact with that unity.....

"If there is the unity of which we are thinking, the next thing which comes out of that is an essential kinship of all the creations of all the people in the world and if that kinship is true, is genuine, then I can never be the kind of person that I ought to be until everybody else is the kind of person that everybody else ought to be. When Jesus of

Nazareth says, 'I came to seek and to save the lost,' He is not only thinking about the need that a certain group of people will have for the kind of life which is His, but He is also reminded of the fact that not only do the lost need Him but He needs the lost, and He will never be what He ought to be until they are what they ought to be.....God needs them, and God will never be what He hungers to be in His world until these people are what they ought to be.

"If I need every one else, then by the same process I must be sensitive to the needs of other people. Human need is infinite but when I respond to it to the limit of my power and become thereby painfully conscious of my own inadequacy, I seem to send my soul through the air and the sky and the sea in quest of an infinite energy that I may release for an infinite task." [17]

This idea of God finds expression not only among Negro ministers and social scientists, but also among Negro poets. These poets sing of a God who does not discriminate and who unites all human kind. Writing during and at the close of the World War, Walter Everette Hawkins gives us an idea of God which united the human race.

God Unites All Human Kind.
 "Islam and Buddha and Christ, all but tend
  Toward the same goal,—these but means toward an end.
  In full depths or winged flights of my mind,
  That which unites me to all human kind,
  Links the All-Good to the goodness in me,
  Makes life sublime today, not life to be,
  Lifts my soul off the harsh rack and the rod,
  Gives me soul-consciousness,—this is my God." [18]

Not only is this idea that God is no respecter of person implicit in the writings of Negro social scientists and Negro poets, but it blazes forth in the writings of Negro novelists as well. The idea that God has made no difference in the quality

---

[17] Miller, Francis P., Religion on the Campus (New York: Association Press, 1927, pp. 49 ff.
[18] Hawkins, W. E., Chords and Discords (Boston: The Gorham Press, 1920), p. 45.

of soul of different races and that every life comes from a source of love and purity is brought out in *Redder Blood* by William M. Ashby. Ashby also makes it clear that each life comes from God. *Redder Blood* is a novel showing that where two persons love each other deeply neither custom, nor convention, nor law is a great enough barrier to keep them apart, else we should never have had an Othello and a Desdemona. The implication is that we are all one, united in God through love. Stanton Birch, a wealthy white man, falls in love with and marries a Negro woman, Zelda Marston, not knowing she has Negro blood in her veins. When he finds out that she is colored, he raves, leaves her, but finally returns. Adrian is the son of Zelda Marston and Stanton Birch. In trying to reconcile his father who raves when he discovers that there is Negro blood in his wife, the author makes Adrian say that love is divine since it is a smile from God's own lips which imprints itself on man's heart. The implication is that love irrespective of race comes from God.

The Soul Comes into the World with Love for Man and God.
Adrian speaking to his father says:
"I tell you, dear father, the only thing in all the world worth while is love. It is the only smile from God's own lips that imprints itself ineradicably on man's heart and returns again to God; it is the only human thing that is unchangeable, unchanging, and unchanged.".........

"See, father, she loves you. Take her and forget. In her love for you she is no different now from what she was before you knew."

In reply the father says:
"Take her, you say! Do you suppose I'm going to be made the laughing-stock of society—She is not my kind—She's different."

Adrian continues:
"Yes, she is different because society says so, not because her soul is different. I tell you that every life that is ushered into this world comes from one pure undefiled source of love and purity. We are not conceived in iniquity; anger,

envy, hate, jealousy, are the qualities that men give to themselves. The soul itself comes into the world with one predominating attitude,—love for man and love for God.

"See, father, those two little children in the driveway. Look how they play; the black one is the son of the cook; the white one, the son of a man of millions. In their actions toward each other, there is no discord......All the bliss of heaven is in their little hearts now. Let them go on this way; let society not meddle with them and they will live endlessly in that same happiness in which you now see them." [19]

The father again:

"The very thing over which the church should rejoice, Adrian, the only God-created thing which has been defiled, polluted, desecrated,—love." [20]

Wanda is a Caucasian girl who is in love with Adrian. When he refuses to marry her because he has Negro blood in his veins, the author makes Wanda say:

"When God spins each out from Himself He gives each a selfhood into which no other self can ever get perfectly, into which He cannot even get Himself and be Himself." [21]

God Made No Inferior Man.

In another novel, *The Chosen People*, written by W. Forest Cozart, this idea of God is set forth:

"Man was created free and God never intended that man should be held in human slavery, as all men were made of one blood, free and equal, God did not make an inferior man, therefore, there are no inferior races, only in places where surrounding conditions, circumstances and the lack of opportunity for mental and physical development is denied them, or is unobtainable, under such conditions any race in course of time on account of ennui would deteriorate." [22]

---

[19] Ashby, William M., Redder Blood, (New York: The Cosmopolitan Press, 1915), pp. 165, 166.
[20] Ibid, p. 180.
[21] Ibid, p. 180.
[22] Cozart, W. Forest, The Chosen People (Boston: The Christopher Publishing Company, 1924), p. 16.

Let us note the idea of God in a poem written by Leslie Pinckney Hill. Not only does he believe that God created all races and nations but also that He sends the Negro out to perform a special mission on the earth. A brief summary of this mission is most illuminating.

Hill maintains that God has chosen the weak, the foolish, the base, and the despised to work his will. Negroes are not the dupes of Providence, he declares; they have been selected by God and specially honored by Him. Although God is omnipotent and has the stars for His citadels, "with time and space their pylons," He builds "His favored home upon the docile trust of lowly hearts." He goes on to argue that he sees no hope for future man in the people who stand upon the pinnacle and heights of fame and power. These people will decline and fall primarily because they deny brotherhood and look with contempt upon the humble.

The things which the Negro is commissioned by God to accomplish are significant. They are: cheerful confidence in men, calm endurance, infinite capacity for pain and suffering, unfeigned humility, a feeling for all forms of life, hope in trouble, and an abiding faith in God. The Negro, he believes, is also chartered to be the minister of the truth, to search for the things of the spirit, to win poise and control, to breed and rear children in prayer, and he is to shun the examples set by the powerful and the strong who build kingdoms but to fall. The author, Leslie Pinckney Hill, feels that Negroes, developing such powers, will become counsellors of peace and the embodiment of the idea of brotherhood.
The poem follows:

God Sends the Negro on a Special Errand.

"But have I

A certain warrant? Does the cannon roar
Above the mangled myriads washed in blood
Upon a hundred fields embolden me
To vent the doctrine of a private heart!

Nay, ask it not, for God hath chosen still
The weak thing, and the foolish, and the base,
And that which is despised to work His will;
And humble men are chartered yet to run
Upon His errands round the groaning sphere.
Not many of the mighty shall be called,
Not many that dispute, Not many wise,
That so the prophecy may be fulfilled.
....

"I have been bred and born beneath the stern
Duress and cold inhospitality
Of that environment which prejudice
Fills consciously with bane; and I have sought—
Blessed be the God of mercy—at the shrine
Of thought inviolate the wells of peace.
There, fortified and unmolested, long
Have I in contemplation rued the plight
Of all my kind, and reverently aspired
To ponder out our mission, unconvinced
That we are born the dupes of Providence,
To be a nation's burden and her taunt
Or Ishmaels of an unchosen land.

"My quest has been to know the good of life,
And why a race should be, and what endures
Of that which man has called society,
And—last and highest aim of these pursuits—
To learn what perfect service, born of throes
Dreadful but purgative, we yet might dare
To offer thee, O country of our hope.

"And from these musings—thanks to Him
Whose citadels are stars, with time and space
Their pylons, but who builds His favored home
Upon the docile trust of lowly hearts—

Proceeded comfort, patience to endure,
And strength increasing of a faith sublime
Which neither infidelity in arms,
Nor all the bitter usage of the world
Can e'er the avail to tarnish or impair—
For looking out upon the world I saw
No hope for future man in those who stand

Upon the heights of power, Save in the tales
Transmitted of their slow decline and fall.
Because they spurn the truth of brotherhood,
And trade in life, and mock the living God
By high contempt of all His humbler sons,
The strong battalions of eternal right
And nature's law make their discomfort sure.
. . . .

"And they have dreamed
Of a peculiar mission under heaven,
And felt the force of unexampled gifts
That make for them a rare inheritance
The gift of cheerful confidence in men,
The gift of calm endurance, Solacing
An infinite capacity for pain
The gift of an unfeigned humility
That blinds the eyes of strident arrogance
And bigot pride to that philosophy
And that far-glancing wisdom which it veils,
The gift of feeling for all forms of life,
Of deathless hope in trouble, and of wide
Adaptive power without a parallel
In chronicles of men, and over all,
And more than all besides, the gift of God
Expressed in rhythmic miracles of song. . . . .

"So viewing all my brothers in distress,
Hindered and cursed and aliens, I have wept
And prayed for them in solitude apart,
That they might know themselves a chosen folk,
Unrecognized but potent, chastened still,
But chartered to be ministers of truth,
To search the depths of spirit, to go forth
To woo and win a perfect self-control,
To breed strong children exercised in prayer,
Shunning as they would death the patterns set
By those who hold the Kingdoms and the sway.
So might they with the pregnant years become
New Arbiters of social destiny,
New health veins in the body politic,
A high-commissioned people, mingled through
With all the bloods of men, and, counselling
Peace, and the healing grace of brotherhood,

'Have power in this dark world to lighten it,
And power in this dead world to make it live.' "[23]

We know that the idea of a God-chosen race is not new. It is traditional in Hebrew religion and the idea exists among other races. But the interpretation which the author places upon the idea is adapted to suit the modern scene. It has great racial and social implications. The idea is developed to help the Negro to make a saner psychological adjustment to his world, and to maintain a belief in his intrinsic worth. The race under God is to lead the world into a new social structure. The idea is developed to support the growing consciousness of the kind of social adjustment needed. It is developed wholly along racial lines. One cannot despise his race or look with contempt upon it, if he believes that God has chosen it to perform a certain mission on the earth. The idea presented by Hill tends to lead the Negro to believe that he has a higher status in God's eye than those who oppress him. The Negro can feel proud of his race and can accept it without apology.

Claude McKay, in his poem, "To the White Fiends," comes to the rescue of Leslie Pinckney Hill in the contention that God sends the Negro on a special errand. McKay expresses bitterness in the first half of the poem, but in the latter part he contends that God has set the Negro here to be a light to burn on a benighted earth. He expresses the view that the world will be swallowed up in darkness; nevertheless, God has put the Negro here to prove himself of greatest value before this darkness comes. The poem is:

"Think you I am not fiend and savage too?
Think you I could not arm me with a gun
And shoot down ten of you for every one
Of my black brothers murdered, burnt by you?
Be not deceived, for every deed you do
I could match—out match: am I not Africa's son,
Black of that black land where black deeds are done?

---

[23] Hill, Leslie P., The Wings of Oppression (Boston: The Stratford Company, 1911), p. 5 ff.

> "But the Almighty from the darkness drew
> My soul and said: Even thou shall be a light
> Awhile to burn on the benighted earth,
> The dusky face I set among the white
> For thee to prove thyself of highest worth;
> Before the world is swallowed up in night,
> To show thy little lamp: go forth, go forth!" [24]

This idea, like the idea in Hill's poem, helps the Negro to believe in himself as a person of intrinsic value. Denied proper recognition and status by men, the Negro receives a higher status with God.

James Weldon Johnson, sometimes called the dean of Negro poets, in his poem, "Fifty Years," written in 1913, expresses the belief that God has some great plan for the Negro. It is clear that God will not let the good come to naught. It is implied in the poem that God sent out Garrison, Phillips, John Brown, and Lincoln to do what they did in behalf of freeing the Negro. God, then, continues to protect the work of these men. He cannot allow the work to come to naught. Being thus convicted, Johnson admonishes the Negro to have faith in his God-known destiny.

Negro Is a Part of Some Great Plan.

> "Courage! Look out, beyond, and see
> The far horizon's beckoning span!
> Faith in your God-known destiny!
> We are a part of some great plan.
>
> "Because the tongues of Garrison
> And Phillips now are cold in death,
> Think you their work can be undone?
> Or quenched the fires lit by their breath?
>
> "Think you that John Brown's spirit stops?
> That Lovejoy was but idly slain?
> Or do you think those precious drops
> From Lincoln's heart were shed in vain?

---

[24] Johnson, James Weldon, The Book of American Negro Poetry (New York: Harcourt, Brace and Company, 1922), p. 135.

> "That for which millions prayed and sighed,
> That for which tens of thousands fought
> For which so many freely died,
> God cannot let it come to naught." [25]

Georgia Douglas Johnson implies the belief that God is leading the Negro on. She says in her note attached to *Bronze* that she knows that God's sun will shine upon the Negro as an unhampered group.

> "This book is the child of a bitter earth-wound. I sit on the earth and sing—sing out, and of, my sorrow. Yet fully conscious of the potent agencies that silently work in their healing ministries, I know that God's sun shall one day shine upon a perfected and unhampered people." [26]

In both of these poems there is a quest for group recognition and there is a quest for security—a kind of security that comes to one who is convinced that despite the troubles and disappointments of life all is well. God is the Master of the ship. As Georgia Douglas Johnson sings in her sorrow, she rests satisfied that silently God is at work and that some day God's sun will shine upon a perfected people. It is a comforting, soothing idea and it adheres somewhat to the compensatory pattern. In James Weldon Johnson's poem, the plan is unknown and the idea savors slightly of complacency. It nevertheless helps the Negro to make a finer psychological adjustment to his world— to accept himself, if he believes he is a part of some great plan.

Though not an American Negro, Marcus Garvey did spectacular work in America. His work was significant too. He called the colored man's attention to his numerical strength in the world. He helped to develop race pride in the American Negro. He had much to say about God. He joined other Negro leaders in their efforts to convince the members of his race that they were not an accursed people. He insisted that the Negro was created in the image of God and that in every

---

[25] Johnson, James Weldon, Saint Peter Relates an Incident (New York; The Viking Press, 1935), p. 96 ff.
[26] Johnson, Georgia Douglas, Bronze (Boston: B. J. Brimmer Company 1922), p. 3.

particular the Negro race is the equal of other races. To accept the idea that the Negro is inferior is to insult God. Garvey moves on from this point to prove that since the Negro is made in God's image, he is entitled to enjoy the rights and privileges exercised by members of the dominant race. Garvey argues that the highest tribute the Negro can pay to God is to recognize and appreciate the fact that he is God's masterpiece. It was Garvey who placed emphasis on the conception that the Negro must see God not through the spectacles of white men nor yellow men, but through the eyes of Ethiopians. He dramatised the idea of a black God and black angels. It is clear that there is nothing compensatory in the way Garvey used the idea of God. He utilized it definitely to arouse the Negro to a sense of deep appreciation for his race. He used it, too, to stimulate the Negro to work to improve his social and economic conditions.

Chapter Summation.

It must not be forgotten that these ideas of God, involving for the most part a growing consciousness of the psychological needs of the Negro, developed in the post-War period. While this development is not due wholly to the post-War period, as was proved in chapter III, this particular use of the idea of God to support a growing conviction that Negroes should accept themselves, that they should not despise themselves, that they are as good as any other group, and the development of these theories to support the Negro's claim for complete social, economic, and political justice, flower forth to full fruition only in the post-War period. They developed simultaneously with one of the major emphases in Negro life, the one advocated by the Association for the Study of Negro Life and History, that Negroes should be proud of themselves. The Association was organized by Carter G. Woodson in 1915 for the express purpose of developing in Negroes a sane degree of group self-esteem and racial self-appreciation.

Furthermore, the development of the idea that God made

---

[27] Garvey, Amy Jacques, *Philosophy and Opinions of Marcus Garvey* (New York: The Universal Publishing House, 1923), pp. 89 ff.

the Negro equal to other groups and the use of the idea to support the conviction that the Negro should share equally in the privileges and opportunities of American life, burst forth also simultaneously with other major social emphases in Negro life—those of the National Association for the Advancement of Colored People and of the National Urban League. Both of these organizations have done their major work in the post-War period.

The ideas of God developed in this chapter move away from compensatory patterns more completely than those developed in previous chapters. The ideas developed in this chapter, more than in previous ones, are used in the three areas of social reconstruction. There are ideas that support the need of social change along universal lines as seen in the development of the ideas of God by DuBois and Thurman. There are ideas that support the need of social adjustment which is confined solely to the Negro as is the case in many of the quotations from Kelly Miller and Robert Moton. Most of the ideas are developed to support the conviction that God has made the Negro potentially equal to other races.

Although the idea that God created of one blood all races and nations is traditional in the Christian religion, it is nevertheless significant that it is a dominant note in the "classical" writings of Negroes in the post-War period. Obviously, it grows out of the social situation in which Negroes in America find themselves. As already intimated, this idea finds expression during the period in which Negroes are most race conscious—a time when they feel their importance, for it is during the period of our study (1914–1937) that they have been delving into the archives of the past in quest of their racial history. The development of this idea began at a time when the experiences of the World War had caused the Negro to feel that he was a part of the total scheme of things. And it is not without significance that it was throughout this period that certain sociologists and psychologists were attempting to prove that the Negro is inferior.

Denied the recognition he craves, the Negro has consciously

or unconsciously seized upon and developed an idea of God that gives him a higher status than he can expect to receive from his contemporaries—a cosmic status which is found in God. The vast majority of Negro "classical" writers have refused to believe in an unjust, partial God. Their constant insistence upon the idea that the human family is one and that God has made all races from the same pattern has been an effective weapon whereby Negroes have been inspired to feel that the race is not an inferior one. Kelly Miller's statement that "the Negro must believe that he is the Son of God," Moton's belief that the Negro is "God's most perfect handiwork," and that "God is the Creator of all" are dynamic utterances. These ideas go a long way toward eliminating from the minds of the Negro the belief that he is destined to an inferior status. Being convinced of this, the "classical" Negro writers, for the most part, have not sought salvation in Heaven but have encouraged Negroes to seek a foothold in this world as a God-given privilege, which no man has the right to deny. It is the most militant Negro writers of the older group who insist on the idea that God has made of one blood all races and, as a result, all races are entitled to "space to breathe and to stretch their arms."

This idea of God may not be peculiar to suppressed groups. Its significance in the case of the Negro lies in the fact that he uses the argument in a unique way to prove that he is not different from other groups, as many writers of the dominant group have endeavored to show, and to give weight to his claim that he is entitled to a fair chance. As part of the Christian tradition, man has generally insisted that he is made in the image of God, and that he is so important that God breathed into him the breath of life. As Dr. Aubrey of the University of Chicago has pointed out, the conservatives fought evolution not merely because it undermined the authority of the Bible and upset the scheme of salvation, but because they felt that if God did not create man in His own image and breathe into his nostrils the breath of life, man does not have the status he desires, and the line of demarcation between man and the lower animals is not sufficiently drawn.

The Negro has not only emphasized a God-idea which creates man in God's own image, but he has insisted that God cut him from the same cloth that He used in fashioning other races. He gets status because God created him as He did other groups and made him just as good as other groups. Believing this, he is stimulated not only to plead for social changes in civic and economic areas, but he is probably stimulated to use more militant tactics in his effort to achieve needs.

Since, as Whitehead says, ideas work slowly in transforming behavior and in perfecting social change, it is not possible to measure the degree in which this idea of God has served the Negro in accepting himself as "somebody." It is common knowledge that the idea has been and is constantly used by Negro parents, teachers, and preachers in their effort to teach Negro boys and girls that they are as good as members of other races. The phrase "you are as good as he is, God made you all alike" is commonly heard in Negro circles, especially where the color line is tightly drawn and where Negro children are called derogatory names by members of the dominant group.

It is the belief of many Negroes that the Negro preacher of long ago made his greatest contribution at this point. The Negro, crushed and humiliated everyday in the week and made to feel that he was "nobody," was greatly helped by "ignorant" Negro preachers who said to their bewildered and discouraged congregations on Sundays, "you are God's children." This idea was more than an opiate; it did more than help the Negro to bear the burdens of the day. It gave him more faith in himself and a firmer belief in his intrinsic worth. It was perhaps this slowly developing but transforming idea that has enabled the Negro to accept himself as much as he does.

CHAPTER VII

Miscellaneous Ideas of God in "Classical" Negro Literature (1914–1937)

In the two preceding chapters and in the chapter that follows, the ideas of God are so closely related that they are easily grouped around a central theme. In this chapter they are rather varied and do not lend themselves to that sort of treatment. The effort is made here to draw together those ideas of God in the literature of the third period that cannot be grouped around a central idea though many of them are similar to those in the "mass" literature and those in the "classical" literature of the pre-War era. The variety of the ideas may be seen in a brief summary. When storms are raging, God takes care of us; if we trust God, He will bless us; God supplies every need; God is on the throne, all is right with the world; all happens in the providence of God; God is just; He is on the side of right; He will bring things out victoriously; God has a plan for the Negro; God is leading the Negro on; He has the Negro on a special errand; and God is love. In the first poem presented in this chapter emotional security is the watchword. Peace of mind is the thing most desired. The author, John Wesley Holloway, wants God's comfort when things are in turmoil.

Life is pictured as a raging sea. Storms, deluge, doubts, and fears of all kinds beset us. But we would never fear if we only had faith to know that God takes care of us. God is only testing our faith when things seem to go wrong.

Security in God.
> "If we just but knew who's with us
> On this raging sea of life,
> When the gale blows like a tempest,
> And the wind cuts like a knife,
> No doubts nor fears would daunt us,
> Our hearts would still be true,

No demon's self could flaunt us,
If—we just but knew.
"If we just but knew who's with us
When the deluge is at hand,
When high the seething waters
Pile upon the shifting sand,
Our minds would still be resting
On him who seems asleep;
Who but our faith is testing,
And safe our souls will keep.

"If we just but knew who's with us
When the wind and wave are strong,
And when total wreck seems certain,—
E'en then a joyful song
Our faithful lips would utter,
And we, with no ado,
Might walk upon the waters,
If—we just but knew!" [1]

The belief that God is testing us out when troubles fall upon us thick and fast is one that makes it possible for us to bear the load without complaint. It is equally soothing and comforting if one can believe that God is with him in the midst of his trouble. The person is less lonesome if he believes this. The idea seems to strengthen one to endure and to hold on rather than to work to eliminate the source of irritation. It gives one confidence but the idea adheres closely to traditional, compensatory patterns. It is a call to complacency and there is no effort at constructive rehabilitation of the idea of God in terms of social and economic adjustment.

In another connection, Theodore Henry Shackelford represents God as a God who tries the patience of men. He tests them by sending afflictions upon them. The thing to do in a crisis of this kind is to be patient and trust God. If you trust God, he will multiply your riches and give peace and rest. This was the situation in Job's case and it is implied that what God did for Job, He will do now.

---

[1] Holloway, John Wesley, The Desert (New York: The Neale Publishing Company, 1919), p. 142.

Trust God and He Will Bless You.
"No mark of His displeasure
Doth trials always show,
Those whom God blessed most largely
Did oft' most troubles know,
For Job lost all his cattle
And all his earthly store
And then with boils was covered
Till he grew sick and sore.

"But God, when Job still trusted,
His every effort blest.
He multiplied his riches
And gave him peace and rest.
So be thou not discouraged,
Though burdened down with care,
Thou still has friends around thee
Who will thy trials share." [2]

Trusting God means to have faith and to believe that God will bring one out all right—victorious in every struggle. It is the belief that God gives abundant trouble to those He blesses most. The implication is that the way for one to get riches and prosperity is to trust God and never doubt or question His ways. If troubles are prerequisites for great blessings from God, they should be welcomed and they should be easy to bear. If troubles are sent by God incident to showers of blessings, one has no right to try to avoid them, and he should be able to carry them with a smile and with comparative ease. The idea serves as an opiate for the people and it supports and tends to perpetuate the traditional, compensatory views so prevalent among the Negro masses.

In the next quotation, Shackelford expects God to operate in the capacity of supplying all one's needs. Then, too, God is close to man and through prayer one may depend on God to protect him from all danger. God shields one from the power of the tempter; during the darkest hour, God gives cheer and

---

[2] Shackelford, Theodore Henry, My Country and Other Poems (Philadelphia: Press of I. W. Klapp Company, 1916–1918), p. 180.

comfort. The quotation, in addition to reflecting a quest for emotional and physical security, shows a desire for response.

God Supplies Every Need.

> "O, God, to Thee I come today,
> And with true repentance kneeling.
> The while I bend my knee to pray,
> The tears from mine eyes are stealing.
> But for Thy grace lost would I be,
> Or ship-wrecked on life's hidden shoals,
> Or left to drift upon the sea
>   Where dwelleth all earth's derelict souls.
> But Thou didst free from all alarms
>   And shield me from the tempter's power;
> Thou broke the shackles from my arms
>   And thou didst cheer my darkest hour.
> Thou hast supplied my every need,
> And made me free, and free indeed." [3]

The ideas of God expressed here are also compensatory. God cheers in the darkest hour, but it is cheer or consolation in complacency and not consolation in an effort to improve life or to reduce the number of dark hours. The idea exalts one, but it makes no constructive contribution toward the effort to adjust one to the realities of the objective world. The adjustments are left to God and there is no challenge to man to work to gain the necessities of life for himself. It is not a co-operative effort whereby man and God are co-partners in the enterprise. It is God's task and the idea tends to justify the laissez-faire attitude. The fact that God is near and ever present is a most comforting idea. It satisfies the feeling and makes life more endurable.

Expressing the desire for security, the poet, Raymond G. Dandridge, confirms the belief that God takes care of the Negro group. This is seen in a supplication dedicated to the Cincinnati Branch of the N.A.A.C.P. He expects God to give the Negro liberty. He prays that God will protect the group from foes that oppress and from repression by vain thoughts.

---

[3] Ibid, p. 175.

He asks God to send world democracy that will include equality for all—justice, truth, and right. God is seen here as cruel and revengeful. The prayer is a quest for security and recognition both of which come from God.

> "Dear Lord we come to Thee,
> In quest of Liberty
> Thy mercy lend.
> We know no better way
> Than serve, obey and pray,
> Almighty Friend.
>
> "Unsheathe Thy vengeful sword
> Cleave us a way, O Lord,
> As naught else can.
> Let no base foe oppress,
> Let no vain thought repress
> Our future usefulness
> To God and man.
>
> "We have no ancient creed,
> We have no glutton's greed
> To satisfy.
> We seek the lofty height,
> Where Justice, Truth and Right,
> Condemn oppressor's might,
> Like God on high.
>
> "May World Democracy
> Include equality
> For every one.
> Father, all-wise and just,
> Do as Thou wilt with us,
> In Thee, alone, we trust
> Thy will be done." [4]

The impression is given here that the author trusts God to bring in a democracy that will include the Negro. A God who answers prayers, who is just and all-wise can be depended upon to bring the Negro out all right. There is resignation to this end. One can hardly glean from the poem the idea that resigna-

---
[4] Dandridge, Raymond Garfield, The Poet and Other Poems (Cincinnati: Copyright by author, 1920), p. 31.

tion comes after one has done all he can do to achieve justice, truth, and right. It seems to come prior to the struggle. The idea expressed here lends itself to the interpretation that in times of sore distress one is justified to wring his hands, weep, pray, and wait for God to relieve the situation. God with His vengeful sword is to cleave us a way. He is to keep back the oppressor. It is not even implied that God will help us as we struggle nor that He will stimulate us to work toward the realization of our needs. The idea adheres to complacency and to a vocalization of needs through prayer and it seems to end there.

Despite Conditions, God Is on the Throne—All Will Be Well.
This idea is vividly expressed in an address delivered by Rev. Francis J. Grimke, December 14, 1918.

> "Out of this awful baptism of blood that has deluged the earth, I can't help feeling that God is getting ready for some great spiritual awakening—that He is getting ready to shake Himself loose from this miserable semblance of Christianity that exists, and to set up in the earth a type of religion that will be as the inspired penman conceived it:
>
> > 'Fair as the moon,
> > Clear as the sun,
> > Terrible as an army with banners.'....
>
> "Whether we realize it or not, God is on the throne; and, sooner or later, He will make even the wrath of man to praise Him." [5]

It is not clear how God is to bring into being the kind of religion the author is talking about. It seems clear though that it is to be ushered in through some spectacular, cataclysmic, catastrophic means. There is nothing to indicate clearly that God will use men as instruments to this end. The idea is not otherworldly, but it may justify those people who sit on the anxious seat waiting for God in some miraculous way to bring into being a new age. But it must be said here that Grimke

---

[5] Woodson, Carter G., Negro Orators and Their Orations (Washington, D. C., The Associated Publishers, 1925), p. 705.

himself did not sit complacently by expecting God to perform without his aid. His idea of God gave him a militant religion and he was in the forefront with those who sought social righteousness for this world.

The idea that right must win is supported by the views of Theodore H. Shackelford. God guarantees victory and ushers in the kingdom of right. God will see to it that the good conquers evil. He will right the evil of the rich having enough and to spare, while the righteous beg for food. He will right the wrong of the strong oppressing the weak. God will also right the wrongs of war where might makes right. These are the chief ideas of God presented in this poem of Shackelford. Justice, the abolition of evil, economic security, abolition of war—these are the things most desired in the poem.

The World Is in the Hands of God.

"Oh, tell me not that 'right' is dead
That 'justice' is asleep,
That 'Providence' doth not exist,
Nor God His vigil keep.

"Too firm indeed is my belief
In 'God's eternal plan'
To e'er believe He could forget
His promises to man.

"Though 'justice' seems perverted oft',
And 'evil' conquers 'good,'
And while the rich their substance waste,
The 'righteous' beg for food.

"Though carnal 'lust' despoils the 'pure,'
And leaves a crimson trail,
And helpless souls stretch out their hands,
And cry to no avail.

"Though nations, strong, oppress the weak,
And wars are won by might,
Yet all of this, somewhere, somehow,
Must be dethroned by right." [6]

---

[6] Shackelford, Theodore H., My Country and Other Poems (Philadelphia: Press of I. W. Klapp Co., 1916–18), p. 133.

Nothing can be more emotionally satisfying or soothing than to believe that whatever happens and however disastrous the events of life may be, the world is in the hands of God. The idea helps one to keep emotional sanity and it gives peace and calm. Otherwise, one might be bewildered and emotionally upset. This poem was written during the World War and it probably indicates the only way many people were able to keep themselves together. Seeing no way out, they would probably have sunk in despair if they had been compelled to believe that the task was theirs to set the world right. They could suffer in apparent ease since God was guaranteeing the dethroning of wrong by the right.

The same idea that God has charge of the world is expressed in the next quotation and it is equally compensatory in character. It supports the traditional view that "God will bring things out all right, so why worry?"

Secure Because God Liveth.

"What have I fathomed of life,
What of its medley of strife,
Sorrow and solace profound?
What can we creatures of dust
Stand upon, swear by, and trust,
What my unshakable ground?

"This that though evil be strong,
Goodness prevaileth ere long,
However betrayed or beset;
That he his own spirit doth smother
Who willeth the hurt of another
And this: that God liveth yet." [7]

God Permeates His World.

"In the still night there comes to me
The blessed boon of liberty.
From all the cares that chafed and choked,
The spirit is at last unyoked
To seek her heaven, as she ought

---

[7] Ibid., p. 118.

On sturdy wings of fearless thought.
Then come the dreams which through the day
The moil of living shuts away.
Then can one soul her fountains fill,
While all the universe is still,
From streams of quietness that rise
Out of the hills of Paradise.
And I can tell the day was meant
For some design beneficent,
For sweet-imagined sounds I hear,
And forms of beauty hover near
To win me to perfect trust
That life is good, and God is just,
And permeates His world whereof
The essence and the end is love." [8]

The ideas that God permeates His world, that life is good, and God is just may help people in a marked way. The idea may give tone and sweetness to one's life. It may give optimism, hope, and buoyancy. Seeing life as good and God as penetrating His world, one may be encouraged to treat lightly the unpleasant tragic things of life. As corrupting as the social and economic problems may be, one may see that life is good and all is well because God is in control of His world. The idea lends support to those who wish to take flight from the stern realities of this life.

After the cares and toils of the day have vexed and annoyed one, he can let his spirit soar at night and content himself with the belief that after all life is good, God is just, and He rules His world. In a way, the idea drugs a person so that he may endure the toils of the next day. The idea creates an optimism that may blind one to the realities of life and make it impossible to view the world with objective impartiality.

According to Kelly Miller, God gives rights to men, and there are certain God-given rights which no man is mighty enough to take away. It is implied that God guarantees the victory of right. As the context from which the quotation is taken seems to indicate, the rights which Miller claims are God-given are the right to vote, the right to be protected from mob rule and

---

[8] Ibid, p. 119.

lynching, and the right to earn a living unhampered—in fact, the right to enjoy all the opportunities and privileges that the most fortunate American enjoys. It is a quest for physical and emotional security and the security that comes to one who enjoys complete citizenship rights.

Miller is speaking of the Negro in the New World order, and he sets forth a conviction of triumph for the Negro based on the belief that God is just and right must win.

The Negro Will Win Because His Cause Is Right.

> "The Negro represents a minority in the midst of a more powerful and populous people; but, unlike minority races in the Balkan states, he does not hope to win his cause by primary conflict. He must rely upon the essential righteousness of his claim and the aroused moral sense of the nation. He is a coward who will not exert his resistive power to its utmost for the unlimited enjoyment of every right which God or man has conferred upon him. There are certain God-given rights which man may be mean enough to deny but never can be mighty enough to take away. The contest which the Negro must wage incessantly and unceasingly is not a conflict that would result in the destruction of the social fabric of which he forms a part, but would rather lead to the fulfilment of its declared aims and ideals. The Negro's cause is right, and right must finally win. The devils believe this, and tremble." [9]

The idea that God is on the Negro's side as he wages a battle to exercise the rights and privileges enjoyed by the dominant group in American life and the idea that he will win because of God's assistance are wholly traditional ideas. But they are so developed that they lend support to the Negro's desire to reconstruct the social order.

Without the use of violent means the Negro is to stage a battle that will ultimately lead to the complete fulfilment of the aims and ideals of America—the unlimited enjoyment of the

---

[9] Miller, Kelly, The Everlasting Stain (Washington, D. C., The Associated Publishers, 1924), pp. 70–80.

rights that God and man have given. As the Negro struggles to achieve these, he is consoled and urged on by the conviction that God guarantees the triumph of the right. It is not claimed that God will do the job for the Negro. It is clearly revealed that the achievement of complete citizenship rights is a long struggle. They are to be fought for on the ground that these rights are given by God and no man can take them away though he may deny them. These privileges must eventually be won by the Negro. God is on the side of right, guaranteeing the victory.

Here is an idea of God that is developed to support the conviction that one should struggle to perfect social change. In the use of the idea the author has interwoven it into the very fabric of the kind of social justice that the Negro desires. The idea gives the Negro hope and encourages him not to sit and wait but to travel in the direction of desired goals. Miller continues in a similar vein in the next quotations:

God Is on the Side of Right.

Believing in the essential rightness of the Allies' cause, Miller again reveals his conception of God. Evidently God moves in His own good time and in His own way. It matters not how dark things may look, right cannot be ultimately defeated because God operates on the side of right. It is inferred that the heaviest battalion if on the wrong side cannot win. The quotation follows:

"Power may seem to triumph for a while; might may be enthroned while right is enchained; but final defeat is never accepted until the verdict is reversed, and right is crowned victor. If it appears that God is on the side of the heaviest battalion, a deeper insight and closer scrutiny reveal the fact that ultimately the heaviest battalion gets itself arrayed on the side of right..... The victorious outcome of this titanic struggle has given to the cause of right a sanction that can never again be shaken." [10]

---

[10] Ibid, pp. 46–47.

"The arbitrament of triumph does not consist in the mightiness of might, but in the righteousness of right. This is the one divine event to which the whole creation moves. Herein lies the Negro's protective device and defensive philosophy." [11]

God Is Just.

In an open letter to President Wilson, entitled "Disgrace of Democracy," written August 4, 1917, Kelly Miller insinuates that God is just; that if America is to thrive, it must seek to apply the principles of democracy at home. Here, as in previous quotations, the author is contending for security of life and property, freedom from mob rule, and other domestic evils that were being experienced by the Negro at the entrance of America into the World War. The letter was stimulated by the indifferent attitude of the Government toward the race riots in East St. Louis and Memphis. In this letter to the President, Miller writes:

"The East St. Louis outbreak convinces the nation, as it has never been before, that the time for action has come. The press is not content with a single editorial ebullition, but by repeated utterances insists that the nation shall deal with its most malignant domestic evils. Reproach is cast upon your contention for the democratization of the world, in face of its lamentable failure at home. Ex-President Roosevelt, who is the greatest living voice now crying aloud for individual and national righteousness, has openly proclaimed in dramatic declaration, that these outbreaks make our moral propaganda for the liberation of mankind but a delusion and a snare. Mr. President, can this nation hope to live and to grow in favor with God and man on the basis of a lie?.....

"The Declaration of Independence, which declared for the equality of all men, was written by a slaveholder... But Thomas Jefferson was keenly sensitive of the moral inconsistency of this attitude that God is just, and that His justice would not slumber forever." [12]

---

[11] Ibid, pp. 351–352.
[12] Ibid, pp. 150–1.

Justice for the Negro and justice for America means, according to Miller, the protection of the Negro from physical violence and the application of the principles of democracy to his situation. Unless this is done, America cannot continue to prosper. Though based on the traditional views that God is just and that He prospers a righteous nation, the ideas are interpreted to give force to the argument and claim of the Negro that the Federal Government should use its influence to bring civic protection to colored Americans and practice the principles of democracy in all of its phases here at home.

Robert Russa Moton, successor to Booker Washington, in his autobiography, states most emphatically that what the Negro has suffered in this country is a part of the plan of God. The Negroes' experiences in slavery, and the oppression and difficulties experienced since emancipation were, and are, designed by God. It is to be understood that it was God's way of lifting the Negro. Moton contends further that God gave the white man the superior position which he occupies in the world and it is thereby understood that God expects the white race to use its superior position to help safe-guard the rights of the Negro—to see to it that he has an equal opportunity along all lines. Moton argues further that the Negro and the white man here in America were put here to demonstrate to the world that groups of varying backgrounds can live together in peace, each enjoying all necessary rights and privileges. Moton writes:

In the Providence of God.
"Thinking of the experiences through which my ancestors passed, along with thousands of other slaves, in their contact with the white people of America, I have often felt that somehow in spite of the hardships and oppression which they suffered—that in the providence of God, the Negro, when all is summed up dispassionately, has come through the ordeal with much to his credit, and with a great many advantages over his condition when he entered the relationship." [14]

---
[13] *From Finding a Way Out* by Robert Russa Moton, Copyright, 1920 by Doubleday, Doran and Company, Inc., p. 15.

God Gave the White Man His Position.

Speaking to white American soldiers in France just after the Armistice, Principal Moton carries forth the idea expressed above. What the white man has, was given to him by God.

"You are heirs of all the ages. God has never given any race more than He has given to you. The men of my race who return will have many unnecessary hardships and limitations along many lines. What a wonderful opportunity you have, therefore, and what a great responsibility for you, to go back to America resolved that so far as in your power lies you are going to see that these black men and the twelve millions of people whom they represent in our great country.....shall have a fair and absolutely equal chance with every other American citizen, along every line. This is your sacred obligation and duty." [14]

That Mr. Moton believes that the Negro's presence in America is a part of the great plan of God is further attested to in a speech he delivered at the dedication of the Lincoln Monument in Washington, D. C., on May 30, 1922.

America Is God's Experimental Station in Human Relations.

"And how shall we account for it, except it be that in the providence of God the black race in America was thrust across the path of the onward-marching white race to demonstrate, not only for America, but for the World, whether the principles of freedom are of universal application, and ultimately to extend its blessings to all mankind." [15]

In the same address Mr. Moton continues:

"And now the whole world turns with anxious hearts and eager eyes toward America. In the providence of God there has been started on these shores the great experiment of the ages—an experiment in human relationships where men and women of every nation, of every race and creed, are thrown together in daily contact. Here we are engaged, consciously or unconsciously, in the great problem of determining how different races can not only live together in

---
[14] Ibid, p. 264.
[15] Woodson, Carter G., Negro Orators and Their Orations (Washington, D. C., The Associated Publishers, 1925), p. 574.

peace, but co-operate in working out a higher and better civilization than has yet been achieved. At the extremes the white and black races face each other. Here in America these two races are charged under God with the responsibility of showing the world how individuals, as well as races, may differ most widely in color and inheritance and at the same time make themselves helpful and even indispensable to each other's progress and prosperity." [16]

The ideas of God in Moton's quotations counsel patience. If God placed the Negro in America for a purpose, and this divine plan is being worked out, the Negro can afford to be patient in the midst of under-privileges. He can suffer and endure a great deal because the eternal God is working out His objectives. But the ideas of God set forth here are not wholly compensatory. God lays upon the white man the responsibility of seeing to it that the Negro is given an equal chance in every particular to work out his destiny unhampered. Furthermore, God holds both Negroes and white people responsible to prove to the world that two races differing in attainment and inheritance can live together in peace, each contributing to the progress and enrichment of the other. These two races, according to Mr. Moton, are commissioned under God to co-operate in working out a higher and better civilization. Clearly the ideas presented here are not unrelated to social and economic problems. Each idea is developed by him to show that social change should be perfected in the area of improved opportunities and privileges for the Negro and in the area of improved race relations generally.

In *Dark Water*, W. E. B. DuBois, in his plea for the emancipation of women, identifies God with love. In setting forth the kind of world love demands, he sets forth the kind of world God demands. By implication, love or God works to open the doors of opportunity to men irrespective of position or circumstances. Whatever contributes or helps to make the greater world possible is God. God is identified with love and with the forces in

---

[16] Ibid, p. 577.

our world that seek to build a kingdom of love and beauty. Mr. DuBois argues for security and recognition for all groups—the gates of opportunity must be opened to women, peasants, laborers, and the socially damned. It is strongly implied in the next quotation that God is interested in working to realize for all people the necessities required for the most complete living. The following words make vivid the point advanced here:

God Is Love.

In the section on "The Damnation of Women" in which the author pleads for the liberation of all women, he identifies God with love. He writes: "Civilization must show two things: the glory and beauty of creating life and the need and duty of power and intelligence. This and this only will make the perfect marriage of love and work."

> "God is Love
> Love is God;
> There is no God but Love
> And work is His prophet!"

This verse is set in his argument for economic independence for women and his insistence that women should have a life work. Love demands that women be emancipated. The kind of world love demands, which is the kind of world God demands, is set forth.

"The vast and wonderful knowledge of this marvelous universe is locked in the bosoms of its individual souls. To tap this mighty reservoir of experience, knowledge, beauty, love, and deed we must appeal not to the few, not to some souls, but to all. The narrower the appeal, the poorer the culture; and the wider the appeal the more magnificent are the possibilities. Infinite is human nature. We make it finite by choking back the mass of men, by attempting to speak for others, to interpret and act for them, and we end by acting for ourselves and using the world as our private property. If this were all, it were crime enough—but it is not all; by our ignorance we make the creation of the greater world impossible; we beat back a world built of the playing of dogs and laughter of children, the song of Black

Folk and worship of Yellow, the love of women and strength of men, and try to express by a group of doddering ancients the will of the world." [17]

Following further what is inferred in this concept 'love," this statement is significant:

"However desperate the temptation, no modern nation can shut the gates of opportunity in the face of its women, its peasants, its laborers, or its socially damned." [18]

The God-ideas expressed and inferred in the quotations above challenge one to work to create a life of love and beauty for all peoples—women, peasants, laborers, and the socially damned. God opposes restrictions and barriers that impede the infinite development of human nature. The author takes the traditional idea that God is love and develops it to show the kind of world we ought to have. In the interpretation of the idea, he gives it universal application and packs into it a meaning that is dynamic enough to revolutionize the social order— to create a new world.

James Weldon Johnson implies in the "Young Warrior" that God gives one strength and courage to battle against the wrong. He makes the young warrior urge his mother to pray not that God would keep harm and danger from him; but that God would give him the ability to fight "the battle well," to keep his "purpose strong," and to go against the wrong with his sword unsheathed.[19]

Though slightly less definite in her social implication, Esther Popel also prays to God for strength. Admiring the potency of the hills, she asks God to give her strength "like that of the hills." It seems not too much to infer that as the strength of the hills enables them to "lift their heads

"Above the petty, lowland, valley things,
And shake their shoulders free
Of bonds that hold
Them close to earth,".....

---

[17] DuBois, W. E. B., Dark Water (New York: Harcourt, Brace & Howe, 1920), pp. 140–1.
[18] Ibid, p. 154.
[19] Johnson, James Weldon, Saint Peter Relates an Incident (New York: The Viking Press, 1935), p. 33.

a similar strength is desired by her, a strength which will enable her to rise above the petty things of life. The words of the poem are:

> "Give me the strength
> Of verdant hills
> Washed clean by summer rain;
> Of purple hills
> At peace when weary Day
> Sinks quietly to rest
> In Night's cool arms;
> Of rugged, wind-whipped hills
> That lift their heads
> Above the petty, lowland, valley things,
> And shake their shoulders free
> Of bonds that hold
> Them close to earth;
> Of snow-capped hills
> Sun-kissed by day, by night
> Companioned by the stars;
> Of grim volcanoes
> Pregnant with the fires
> Of molten fury!
>
> Grant me strength,
> Great God,
> Like that of hills!" [20]

From this point on, two kinds of revolt or protest are to be noted: the one is a protest against the Negro's traditional ideas of religion and God; the other is that, too, but it is more a protest against the kind of religion and God which the Negro has accepted from the white man; or a revolt against the white man's God.

Walter E. Hawkins, poet, has been quoted in another connection. His ideas of God are implied. Obviously, a God of fear, one who damns one's soul to hell, would be rejected in the following poem. It is a protest against other-worldliness:

---

[20] Popel, Esther, A Forest Pool (privately printed, Washington, D. C., 1934), p. 11.

> "I can see no cause for worry
> 'Bout a future heaven or hell,
> For the thing has long been settled
> And it's plain as tongue can tell;
> And it's mighty poor religion
> That won't keep a man from fear,
> For the next place must be heaven
> Since 'tis hell we are having here." [21]

In the next poem a God of love is implied, a God who demands right conduct and not adherence to creeds and doctrines—a God who cares. Mr. Hawkin's words are impressive:

> "There is too much talk of doctrine,
> Too much talk of church and creeds;
> Far too little loving kindness,
> To console the heart that bleeds;
> Too much Sunday Church religion,
> Too many stale and bookish prayers;
> Too many souls are getting ragged,
> Aping what their neighbor wears.
> Too much stress upon the washing,
> Whether in a creek or bowl,
> Does it matter since devotion
> Reigns supreme within the soul?
> All the unction and the washing
> That the church on earth applies,
> Won't suffice to clean a sinner,
> If his heart is choked with lies.
>
> "There is too much talk of heaven,
> Too much talk of golden streets,
> When you can't be sympathetic
> When a needy neighbor meets,
> Too much talk about the riches
> You expect to get "up there,"
> When one will not do his duty
> As a decent being here." [22]

---

[21] Hawkins, W. E., Chords and Discords (Boston: Richard G. Badger, The Gorham Press, 1920), p. 28.
[22] Ibid, p. 49.

The next poem suggests the same idea of God—a God who is concerned primarily with what people are and with what they do. Like the other two, it is a revolt against the emphases in current traditional religion—it is an effort to set forth the true conception of religion.

> "I hold no dogmas and no creeds,
> It recks me not what be thy faith;
> How stands thy life, how shine thy deeds,
> Dost thou e'er bless the heart that bleeds?
>   The hungry heart in sorrow sayeth:
> Thy dogmas, doctrines, scarce prevail
> To save a soul or form a tale.
> 'Tis of thyself and not thy creeds, I have a care.
>
> "I have no care for preachers' moans,
> Nor for the prelates' studied prayer;
> What need has heaven for grunts and groans,
> These offerings of the churches' drones,
> What benediction do they bear?
> What boon to bless humanity
> Is treasured up for good to thee?
> What contribution hast thou made
> To give men life and liberty?
> Not of thy creeds, but of thy deeds, I have a care.
>
> "I have no care how men proclaim
> Their piety or gifts of grace;
> How fares thy absent neighbor's name
> Upon thy tongue for good or blame?
>   Thy fellow-friend before thy face
> Is lost in sin and sore distressed,
> While heaven which needs thee not is blest.
> What dost thou give the cause to win,
> To save man from himself and sin?
> 'Tis of thy deeds and not thy creeds, I have a care." [23]

The author yearns and craves for a religion that consoles bleeding hearts; he desires a religion that makes for purity of heart; he wants a religion that responds helpfully and sympathetically to human needs; he insists on a religion that gives men

---

[23] Ibid, pp. 72–3.

abundant life and liberty; and he argues for a religion that will save men from their worst selves and from sin. It is clearly and strongly inferred that God is a God of social justice. He is concerned with developing and improving life. He is more interested in the quality of life one lives than He is in the quantity of liturgical services or doctrinal formulae to which one subscribes.

According to the God-idea suggested in the quotations from Hawkins, it is not conceivable that God could exist without having intense interest in the ethical and social welfare of man. The idea is interpreted wholly in terms of ethics and improved human relations. Though the idea of God is not explicitly stated, the author's interpretation of religion is one of the finest and most constructive efforts to rehabilitate the idea of God along social lines thus far presented. The ethical and social views of God as set forth by prophets like Amos and Micah are used to sustain the theory that society needs reconstruction along the lines of the highest and best that an ethical religion affords.

Walter White, novelist and Secretary of the National Association for the Advancement of Colored People, makes a protest against present forms of religion and ideas of God in his novel, *Fire in the Flint*. He describes in this book the racial situation in the South, aiming primarily to show the cruelty and savagery of the institution of lynching and mob rule. Speaking of Kenneth Harper, the central figure in the novel, Mr. White revolts against an other-worldly religion and the malignity of God as pictured by most ministers. If any kind of God is deduced, it is a God who is interested in improving life here and now. The quotation follows:

"He was not essentially religious in the accepted meaning of the word. He believed, though he had not thought much on the subject of religion, so immersed had he been in his beloved profession, in some sort of a God. Of what form or shape this being was, he did not know. He had more or less accepted the beliefs his environment had forced upon him. He doubted the malignity of the God described by most of the ministers he had heard. As a matter of fact, he was rather repelled and nauseated by the religion of the modern church. Narrow, intolerant of contrary opinions, prying into the lives and affairs of its communicants with which it had no concern, its energies concentrated on raising money and not on saving souls, of little real help to intelligent people to enable them to live more useful lives here on earth, and centering instead on a mysterious and problematic life after death, he felt the church of Jesus Christ had so little of the spirit of the Christ that he had little patience with it." [24]

In another section the author makes Kenneth Harper protest against the established other-worldly phase of religion. It was occasioned by a conversation which Kenneth Harper, the Negro physician, had had with Mr. Ewing, a leading white man in the small Georgia town where the scene of the novel is laid. The physician told Mr. Ewing that fifty men of his type could stop lynching. Ewing advised Harper to stay away from such talk and assured him that it would be dangerous for his own life if the boys of the Ku Klux Klan knew that he had even discussed such matters with a Negro. Speaking of Harper's reaction, the author says:

"The whole situation seemed so vast, so sinister, so monstrous, that he shuddered involuntarily, as he had done as a child when left alone in a dark room at night. Religion, which had been the guide and stay of his father in like circumstances, offered him no solace. He thought with a faint smile of the institution known as the church. What was it? A vast money machine, interested in rallies and pastors' days and schemes to milk more money from its communicants, in preparing people to die. He wasn't interested in what was going to happen to him after death. What he wanted was some guide and comfort in present problems." [25]

White is revolting against other-worldliness and against religion that serves a narcotic for the people. The things sought

---

[24] White, Walter, Fire in the Flint (New York: Alfred A. Knopf), pp. 168–9.
[25] Ibid, p. 72 ff.

are physical security and a religion that seeks to improve life and make it more livable on the earth. It is implied that God is not malignant and cruel, but loving, and that He is greatly desirous of having life improved here. One is expected to work for the realization of the good life in this world rather than to look forward to it on the other side of Jordan. Whatever the implications of God may be, the author is primarily concerned with a humanitarian religion that brings justice on the earth. The traditional, compensatory ideas are discarded as useless in the present racial situation.

Carter G. Woodson is the director and founder of the Association for the Study of Negro Life and History. He is one of the most prolific writers the Negro race in America has produced. In the examples given below, his ideas of God are also implied. His references to God and religion are protests against what is. Often the protests are sarcastic and ironical. The following quotation is a protest against the other-worldly elements in the Negro's religion. He writes:

"Under almost any sort of protest a Negro lawyer, physician, or dentist may be driven out of a rural community, if a few whites decide that he should go; but the Negro preacher is seldom disturbed, if he "sticks to the Bible." He is regarded as a factor in making the church a moral police force to compel obedience to what is known as moral obligations. He is also an asset in that he keeps Negroes thinking about the glorious time which they will have beyond this troublesome sphere and that enables them to forget their oppression here. White people, therefore, give more readily to religious work among Negroes than to any other of their needs, although what they do give is inadequate." [26]

In the next quotation Woodson sets forth his revolt (by implication) against the rural Negro's conception of God which gives God credit for the helpful things but refuses to accredit God with the evils that befall the race. Woodson seems to

---

[26] Woodson, Carter G., The Rural Negro (Washington, D. C., The Association for the Study of Negro Life and History, 1930), p. 149.

infer a slight disbelief in an all-seeing Providence and a disbelief in the divinity of Christ. Speaking of the rural Negro, he says:

> "They laugh at those who doubt the existence of an all-seeing Providence and question the divinity of His Son. The Lord has delivered these Negroes from too many trials and tribulations for them to doubt His power or His interest in mankind. God is not held responsible for the Negroes' being carried away captive to be the slaves of white men; but He is given credit for delivering them from bondage. God has nothing to do with their long persecution and the intolerable conditions under which they have to live, but great praise should be given Him for permitting them to exist under the circumstances. The evils from which these Negroes suffer, they believe, resulted from the sins of their forefathers and their own short comings, but as soon as they can be purified in the fire of persecution necessary to burn away the dross, they will come into the enjoyment of the privileges now monopolized by the highly privileged race." [27]

The following quotation is a protest against a revengeful God with the inference that God is a loving Father:

> "The appeal of the Negro rural church, then, very much like that of the whites, is based upon fear. God is not so much the loving Father who has provided many good things for His obedient children; He is rather Jehovah, Lord of Hosts, working the destruction of those who do not heed His commands." [28]

A Protest Against Other-worldliness.

> "The large majority of Negro preachers of today, then, are doing nothing more than to keep up the mediaeval hell-fire scare which the whites have long since abandoned to emphasize the humanitarian trend in religion through systematic education." [29]

The last reference on this protest against the Negro's religion and God shows that the author is opposed to a religion

---
[27] Ibid, p. 152.
[28] Ibid, p. 166.
[29] Woodson, Carter G., The Mis-Education of the Negro (Washington, D. C., The Associated Publishers, 1933), p. 70.

which drives Negroes to their knees rather than a religion which makes them fight for what they need. From the context, it is clear that the author's sympathy is with the riffraff Negro who fights his battle in the open rather than with the cultured Negro who works indirectly. The quotation follows:

> "Sometimes one inquires as to what the enlightened Negroes are doing to direct attention to these things. The inevitable answer is that they are doing absolutely nothing in the open. What bearing their service has on the situation is indirect. The intelligent Negroes in the South are more timid than the riffraff. The Southern whites stand less in fear of the schooled Negroes than they do of the rabble. When cornered, the Negro rough element will sometimes fight it out down to death, but under such circumstances, the Christianized Negroes hold indignation meetings or take their troubles to God in prayer." [30]

In most of his writings where conceptions of religion and God are given, Woodson is an enemy to views of God that lead the Negro to look for salvation in Heaven and to ideas of God that blind the Negro so that he cannot see the seriousness of the plight in which he finds himself. Woodson in his revolt merely dramatizes the facts already presented that many ideas of God held by Negroes, however valuable they may be psychologically in helping Negroes to endure and hang on, are ideas that are compensatory in result. According to Woodson, if God is a reality, He is primarily concerned with life here. It is strongly inferred that the Negro must rely on his own strength and resources to improve his conditions and not expect God's assistance. The idea of God implied is inseparable from the social demands of justice and fair play.

A Protest Against the Negro's Acceptance of the White Man's Religion and God.

Having dealt with the classical Negro writers' revolt against the impractical and other-worldly aspects of the religion cur-

---

[30] Woodson, Carter G., The Rural Negro (Washington, D. C., The Association for the Study of Negro Life and History, 1930), p. 238.

rently practised by most Negroes, we now turn to another phase of this protest—a protest against the Negro's acceptance of the white man's religion and a revolt against his idea of God. The call is to abandon the white man's religion as inadequate for the Negro.

A Disbelief in the White Man's Religion.

The first expression in this series setting forth the Negro's repudiation of the white man's religion is taken from an address delivered by Mordecai Wyatt Johnson, now President of Howard University, Washington, D. C. This address was one of the three Commencement parts delivered at Harvard University Commencement, June 22, 1922.

"Another and larger group among us believes in religion and believes in the principles of democracy, but not in the white man's religion and not in the white man's democracy. It believes that the creed of the former slave states is the tacit creed of the whole nation, and that the Negro may never expect to acquire economic, political, and spiritual liberty in America. This group has held congresses with representatives from the entire Negro world, to lay the foundations of a black empire, a black religion, and a black culture; it has organized the provisional Republic of Africa, set going a multitude of economic enterprises, instituted branches of its organization wherever Negroes are to be found, and binds them together with a newspaper ably edited in two languages." [31]

Carter Woodson's protest is similar.

A Slaveholder's Religion Inadequate for the Negro.

"It is very clear, then that if Negroes got their conception of religion from slaveholders, libertines, and murderers, there may be something wrong about it, and it would not hurt to investigate it. It has been said that the Negroes do not connect morals with religion. The historian would like to know what race or nation does such a thing? Certainly, the whites with whom the Negroes have come in contact have not done so." [32]

---

[31] Woodson, Carter G., Negro Orators and Their Orations (Washington: The Associated Publishers, 1925), p.
[32] Woodson, Carter G., The Mis-Education of the Negro (Washington, D.C., The Associated Publishers, 1933), p. 73.

"Following the religious teachings of their traducers, the Negroes do not show any more common sense than a people would in permitting criminals to enact the laws and establish the procedure of the courts by which they are to be tried." [33]

Speaking of the kind of education the Negro needs, Woodson revolts again against what he calls the religion of the enslaver.

God Is the Lover of All Mankind.
"Such subjects of certitude as mathematics, of course, would continue and so would most of the work in practical languages and science. In theology, literature, social science, and education, however, radical reconstruction is necessary. The old worn-out theories as to man's relation to God and his fellowman, the system of thought which has permitted one man to exploit, oppress, and exterminate another and still be regarded as righteous must be discarded for the new thought of men as brethren and the idea of God as the lover of all mankind." [34]

Continuing his criticism as to the mis-education of the Negro, Woodson speaks of the sermon of a college graduate as follows:

"Recently an observer saw a result of this in the sermon of a Negro college graduate, trying to preach to a church of the masses. He referred to all the great men in the history of a certain country to show how religious they were, whether they were or not. When he undertook to establish the Christian character of Napoleon, however, several felt like leaving the place in disgust. The climax of the service was a prayer by another 'miseducated' Negro who devoted most of the time thanking God for Cicero and Demosthenes. Here, then was a case of the religion of the pagan handed down by the enslaver and segregationist to the Negro." [35]

In this connection, the ideas expressed in Johnson's quotation and those set forth in Woodson's revolt against the white

---

[33] Ibid, p. 147.
[34] Ibid, pp. 149–150.
[35] Ibid, pp. 64–6.

man's religion, and his idea of God, implied and expressed, grow out of the social situation in which the Negro finds himself. That is, the Negro in almost every instance is concerned with a God who serves him and who helps him to secure the necessities of life. Woodson revolts against the white man's religion because it is a religion that has been used to justify slavery; the group for whom Johnson speaks revolts against it because economic, political, and spiritual liberties are denied. It is a religion held by a people who still oppress and exploit the weak. Their idea of God is that of a God who opposes exploitation and who loves all mankind. Woodson takes the loftiest conception of God as set forth in the Christian tradition and brings it to bear upon the Negro's crucial problems. It is strongly inferred in the writings of both that those who believe in the God of Jesus, a God who loves all mankind, would not exterminate and exploit. Both authors are primarily concerned with social reconstruction that will serve more adequately the social and economic needs of the Negro.

James M. Harrison, a poet, also protests against current religious practices, particularly those preached and practiced by the powerful; he, too, supports Woodson and Johnson. The implied idea is that God is just and loving and that in the end God will use his chastening rod.

>"Preach not to me of heathen far away,
>Whose souls have ne'er tasted God's sweet love,
>And to whose images they bow and pray,
>Made from richest jewels, gold and clay—
>Wandering aimlessly, no light above.

>"Preach not to me of justice and of right,
>Nor dare lie to me that your Christ is God
>While rule is based on cruel power and might
>Yet we the under dogs you urge to fight,
>Forgetting the coming of the chastening rod." [36]

Walter White in one of his novels, hurls a criticism at those who pray to a God of their own making, implying an idea of

---

[36] Harrison, James M., Southern Sunbeam (Richmond: The Saint Luke Press, 1926), p. 89.

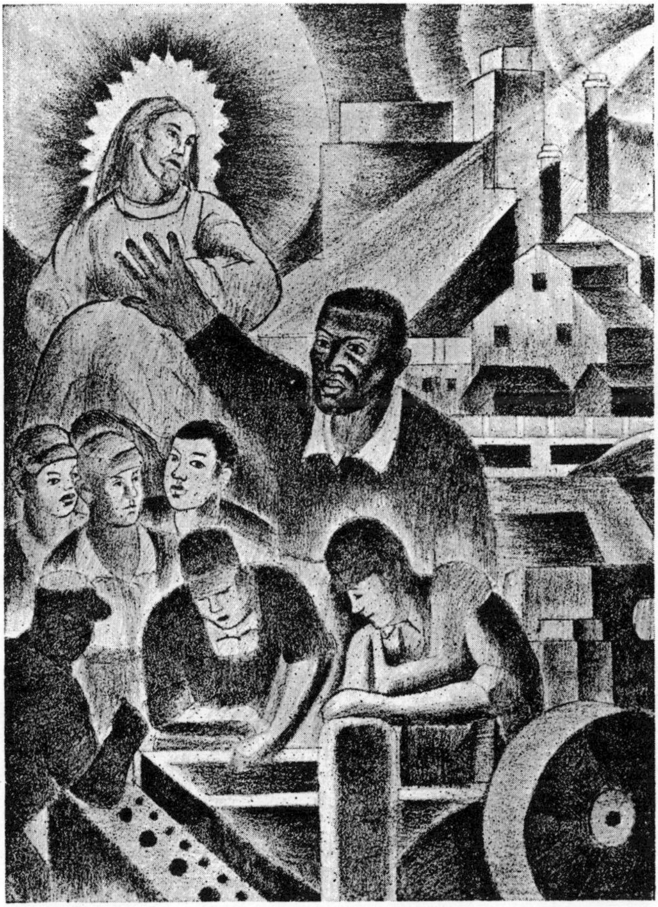

God which does not cater to the whims and caprices of men—an impartial God; or he is implying the idea that the man-created God is the only kind of God that there is. The protest follows:

"Men, as always, prayed to a God of their own creation, a Divinity which only mirrored the petty minds of its worshippers. This man, and of wealth and power, prayed devoutly and absentmindedly to his conception of God, a being of unlimited wealth, plastered with diamonds, fat, vulgar, and, through his wealth, able to dictate the lives of countless millions of creatures, scattered throughout a boundless universe.

"Another man prayed to a God of vengeance, a God who had wisely taken counsel of man and decreed that this race or that one should be crowned as the chosen people. Blindly by obsessions of superiority, unbelievable cruelties were prayed over and asked of God by these molelike creatures who fancied their own infinitesimal wisdom superior to that of any other beings, human or divine.

"Above all, they demonstrated through their prayers that they believed only in themselves, and they were unable to accomplish the miracles they sought." [37]

In the quotations from Harrison and those from White, the things opposed are: cruel power and might, wealth that dictates the lives of millions, chosen races and superior races. It is implied that if God exists, these things are against Him. He is not cruel. He has chosen no one race. He has made no one race superior.

The views of God in this wave of protest against current religious practices of Negroes and that against the God of the white man, protesting on the ground that this religion is far removed from social problems, are consistent with and in harmony with the post-War social trend of the Negroes as expressed in the N.A.A.C.P., and the program of the National Urban League, both of which have fought courageously for social adjustment that would accrue to the Negro adequate civic and economic protection.

---

[37] White, Walter, Flight (New York: Alfred A. Knopf, 1926), pp. 287-288.

CHAPTER VIII

Ideas of God Involving Frustration, Doubt, God's Impotence and His Non-Existence

We move now into new territory. For the first time, the third main emphasis of the study is reached. The Negro writers treated up to this point have put new wine into old bottles. They have, on the whole, taken the idea of God, traditional or otherwise, and made it a useful instrument in supporting the growing consciousness of the kind of social adjustment needed. The ideas have been interpreted in social terms and there has been no attempt to abandon God. In this section that is not true. The chapter is designed to show that in the development of the idea of God in Negro literature there is a tendency or threat to abandon the idea of God "as a useful instrument" in social adjustment, as evidenced by the following facts:

1. There is a strong tendency to doubt God's value to the Negro in his struggle to gain a stable economic, social, and political foothold in America.

2. God is described as having outlived His usefulness. Historically, when gods have outlived their usefulness, either they have been abandoned or a new conception of God has been developed to meet the new experiences. The younger Negro writers seem to be inclined to abandon the idea rather than develop new conceptions.

3. There is a denial of the existence of God.

It is clear that this third development does not mean that the idea of God is unrelated to the growing demand for social change—not that at all. But rather it seems to mean that these heretical ideas of God develop because in the social situation the "breaks" seem to be against the Negro, and the authors are unable to harmonize this fact with the God pictured by Christianity.

The first of these suggestions that God is probably useless in the Negro's struggle for decent existence comes from Countee Cullen, born in New York in 1903. Unlike the mere protest against the white man's practice of religion and against his conception of God as discussed in the previous chapter, one finds here a protest against a God who is accepted as white. The idea that God is helpful to the Negro is abandoned or it is highly doubted. Cullen, along with Langston Hughes, is possibly the best known of the younger post-War poets. In his poem, "Heritage," Cullen expresses the view that possibly a black God would understand and sympathize with him more than a God who is white. The quotation follows under the captions:

Wishing He I Served Were Black.

"Quaint, outlandish heathen gods
Black men fashion out of rods,
Clay, and brittle, bits of stone,
In a likeness like their own,
My conversion came high-priced;
I belong to Jesus Christ,
Preacher of humility;
Heathen gods are naught to me.

"Father, Son, and Holy Ghost,
So I make an idle boast;
Jesus of the twice-turned cheek,
Lamb of God, although I speak
With my mouth thus, in my heart
Do I play a double part.
Ever at Thy glowing altar
Must my heart grow sick and falter,

"Wishing He I served were black,
Thinking then it would not lack
Precedent of pain to guide it,
Let who would or might deride it,
Surely then this flesh would know
Yours had borne a kindred woe.
Lord, I fashion dark gods, too,
Daring even to give you

> "Dark despairing features where,
> Crowned with dark rebellious hair,
> Patience wavers just so much as
> Mortal grief compels, while touches
> Quick and hot, of anger, rise
> To smitten cheek and weary eyes.
> Lord, forgive me if my need
> Sometimes shapes a human creed." [1]

It seems clear that Cullen's wish "that God were black" is simply a poetic way of expressing his belief in the futility of expecting any significant help from God, be He black or white. Of course, it is a tirade against the view that God is white. But underneath, it is a tirade against God, against the idea that He guides, understands, and sympathizes with black people in their toil. Abandoning altogether the traditional, compensatory idea of God, the author threatens to abandon the idea that God is a useful instrument in racial uplift. Certainly it is futile to pray to the Father, Son, and Holy Ghost. They do not understand. A black God might.

DuBois in *Dark Water* expresses similar doubt and frustration when he exclaims:

> "Keep not Thou Silent, O God!
> Sit not longer blind, Lord God, deaf to our prayer
> And dumb to our dumb suffering. Surely Thou,
> Too, are not white, O Lord, a pale, bloodless,
> Heartless thing." [2]

Perhaps the most expressive of these doubts, ending in denial of the existence of God, is to be found in *Quicksand*. The novel is built around Helga Crane, a Chicago girl, whose father was a Negro and whose mother was a white immigrant. Quite early her father deserted her mother, and when she was six years old, her mother married again—this time a white man. Helga's mother died when she was fifteen. Her uncle, Peter Nilssen, took care of her for awhile and educated her.

---

[1] Cullen, Countee, Color (New York: Harper & Brothers, 1925), pp. 39, 40.
[2] DuBois, W. E. B., Dark Water (New York: Harcourt, Brace & Howe, 1920), pp. 275, 276.

While Helga was teaching in a Negro school in the South, her Uncle Peter married. On resigning her work in the Negro school, Helga returned to her uncle's house in Chicago. His wife made Helga understand that because of her Negro blood, she was not wanted; and that she was not a legitimate niece of her husband, since it was claimed that Helga's mother and father were never married. This hurt Helga very much because Uncle Peter had at least patronized her and helped her, even if she did feel that he did it out of pity rather than out of pure affection. Since she was a Negro, her step-father, her step-brothers and sisters, her numerous cousins, aunts and uncles—all repudiated her and shunned her.

Through the employment office of the Negro Y. W. C. A. in Chicago, Helga got an opportunity to go with an outstanding race woman, Mrs. Hayes-Rore, to New York, and through Mrs. Hayes-Rore she obtained a job with a Negro insurance company. She enjoyed Harlem life for a while but finally it became disgusting to her. After being in New York for more than a year, Helga received a letter from Uncle Peter who expressed regret for the cold treatment she received from his wife on her return to Chicago from her teaching position in the South—more than a year ago. Speaking of the incident her uncle writes:

"Dear Helga:

"It is now over a year since you made your unfortunate call here. It was unfortunate for us all, you, Mrs. Nilssen, and myself. But, of course, you couldn't know. I blame myself. I should have written you of my marriage.

"I have looked for a letter, or some word from you; evidently, with your usual penetration, you understood thoroughly that I must terminate my outward relation with you. You were always a keen one.

"Of course, I am sorry, but it can't be helped. My wife must be considered, and she feels very strongly about this." [3]

---

[3] Larsen, Nella, Quicksand (New York: Alfred A. Knopf, 1928), pp. 118, 119.

In his letter her uncle sent her five thousand dollars and suggested that she visit her Aunt Katrina in Copenhagen. Finally, she accepted the suggestion and went to Denmark. No prejudice greeted her in Denmark and she had the opportunity to marry in high circles but refused. In refusing to accept the hand of a prominent gentleman in Denmark the author makes Helga say:

"You, I couldn't marry a white man. I simply couldn't. It isn't just you, not just personal, you understand. It's deeper, broader than that. It's racial. Someday may be you'll be glad. We can't tell, you know; if we were married, you might come to be ashamed of me, to hate me, to hate all dark people. My mother did that." [4]

Finally, she began to hunger for America, not so much for America, but for association and companionship with Negroes. She says: "I'm homesick not for America, but for Negroes. That's the trouble." [5]

The author says that this experience of yearning to be with Negroes caused Helga Crane, for the first time, to feel sympathy for her father rather than feel contempt and hatred, which she had often felt, because he deserted her mother. Helga returned to America, partially determined never to marry because she felt that it was a sin to bring black children into the world. In reply to the question asked her about marriage by one who was proposing to her, she replies:

"Some day, perhaps. I don't know. Marriage—that means children to me. And why add more suffering to the world, why add any more unwanted tortured Negroes to America? Why do Negroes have children? Surely it must be sinful. Think of the awfulness of being responsible for the giving of life to creatures doomed to endure such wounds to the flesh, such wounds to the spirit, as Negroes have to endure." [6]

---

[4] Ibid, p. 196.
[5] Ibid, p. 207.
[6] Ibid, p. 231.

But in spite of this attitude toward marriage, she finally married the Reverend Mr. Pleasant Green and became the mother of five children. It was at the Reverend Mr. Green's revival that she became converted. Later on, she repudiated this simple religious faith—during a period of convalescence when she had time to think through the racial situation. It is here that she revolts against the white man's God and denies the existence of God.

God Does Not Exist.

"In that period of racking pain and calamitous fright Helga had learned what passion and credulity could do to one. In her was born angry bitterness and an enormous disgust. The cruel, unrelieved suffering had beaten down her protective wall of artificial faith in the infinite wisdom, in the mercy, of God. For had she not called in her agony on Him? And He had not heard. Why? Because she knew now, He wasn't there. Didn't exist. Into that yawning gap of unspeakable brutality had gone, too, her belief in the miracle and wonder of life. Only scorn, resentment, and hate remained—and ridicule. Life wasn't a miracle, a wonder. It was, for Negroes at least, only a great disappointment. Something to be got through with as best one could. No one was interested in them or helped them. God! Bah! And they were only a nuisance to other people......

"Within her emaciated body raged disillusion. Chaotic turmoil. With the obscuring curtain of religion rent, she was able to look about her and see with shocked eyes this thing that she had done to herself. She couldn't she thought ironically, even blame God for it, now that she knew that He didn't exist. No. No more than she could pray to Him for the death of her husband, the Reverend Mr. Pleasant Green. The white man's God.—And His great love for all people regardless of race! What idiotic nonsense she had allowed herself to believe. How could she, how could any one, have been so deluded? How could ten million black folk credit it when daily before their eyes was enacted its contradiction?" [7]

---

[7] Ibid, pp. 291, 292.

God Does Not Exist for the Negro; The White Man's God Deceives Him.

"Her mind, swaying back to the protection that religion had offered her, almost she wished that it had not failed her. An illusion. Yes. But better, far better, than this terrible reality. Religion had, after all, its uses. It blunted the perceptions. Robbed life of its crudest truths. Especially it had its uses for the poor—and the blacks.

For the blacks. The Negroes.

"And this, Helga decided, was what ailed the whole Negro race in America, this fatuous belief in the white man's God, this childlike trust in full compensation for all woes and privations in 'Kingdom Come.' Sary Jones' absolute conviction, 'In de nex' worl' we's all recompense,' came back to her. And ten million souls were as sure of it as was Sary. How the white man's God must laugh at the great joke He had played on them! Bound them to slavery, then to poverty and insult, and made them bear it unresistingly, uncomplainingly almost, by sweet promises of mansions in the sky by and by." [8]

In the quotation just presented, Helga Crane gives us ideas of God that not only involve doubt, frustration, and bewilderment; but primarily, she repudiates the validity of the idea of God and denies His existence. The personal, physical suffering through which she had passed, the mental agony and torture which she had suffered, owing to race, had not only caused her to cast aside the white man's God, but these experiences had led her to the conclusion that God did not even exist. In Helga Crane, there is complete abandonment of the idea that God is helpful in personal, social, and racial adjustment. Even before she expressed flat denial, she doubted God as shown by her belief that Negroes should not bring children into the world. Her denial of the existence of God is due not only to her personal rebuffs, suffering, and disappointment but also to the social situation of her people. The idea that God loves all people, regardless of race, is nonsense because there are ten million Negroes who see nothing in daily practice to sustain the belief.

---
[8] Ibid, pp. 296, 297.

In Walter White's *Fire in the Flint* Kenneth Harper in his soliloquy, brooding over the intense racial situation in the South, calls out to God in despair.

"Here I am, 'he soliloquized,' with the best education money can buy. And yet Roy Ewing, who hasn't been any further than high school, tells me I'd better submit to all this without protest. Yet he stands for the best there is here in Central City and I suppose he represents the most liberal thought of the South. How's it all going to end? Even a rat will fight when he's cornered, and these coloured people aren't going to stand for these things all the time. What can I do? God, there isn't anything—anything I can do?.....Oh, God I'm helpless! I'm helpless." [9]

One could hardly find in this quotation any deep abiding faith that God was going to come to the rescue of Kenneth Harper. He is, at least, suspicious as to God's help. His incredulity is too strong for him to find comfort and consolation in his hour of trial.

In Jessie Redmond Fauset's *Plum Bum*, there is bewilderment with the implication of a strain of agnosticism with respect to God.

Puzzled About God.

" 'Granted,' said something within her rooted either in extreme hard common sense or else in a vast sophistry, 'granted, but does that carry with it as penalty the shattering of a whole life, or even the suffering of years? Certainly the punishment is far in excess of the crime.' And it was then that she would lie back exhausted, hopeless, bewildered, unable to cope further with the mysterious and apparent ferocity of life. For if this were a just penalty for one serious misdemeanor what compensation should there not be for the years in which she had been a dutiful daughter, a loving sister? And suddenly she found herself envying people possessed of a blind religious faith, of the people who could bow the head submissively and whisper: 'Thy will be done.' For herself she could see how beaten and harried, one might subside into a sort of blind passivity, an acceptance of things as they are, but she would never be able to understand a force which gave one the imagination to paint

---

[9] White, Walter, The Fire in the Flint (New York: Alfred A. Knopf, 1924), p. 73.

a great desire, the tenacity to cling to it, the emotionalism to spend on its possible realization but which would then with a careless sweep of the hand wipe out the picture which the creature of its own endowment had created." [10]

Georgia Douglas Johnson, though expressing a great faith in God, questions God so as to imply bewilderment and distrust. In the poem entitled "Moods" she expresses it thus:

Faith and Doubt.

> "My heart is pregnant with a great despair
> With much beholding of my people's care,
> 'Mid blinded prejudice and nurtured wrong,
> Exhaling wantonly the days along:
> I mark Faith's fragile craft of cheering light
> Tossing imperiled on the sea of night,
> And then, enanguished, comes my heart's low
> cry, 'God, God! I crave to learn the reason
> why!' Again in spirit loftily I soar
> With winged vision through earth's outer door,
> In such an hour, it is mine to see,
> In frowning fortune smiling destiny." [11]

In the next poem by the same author, though God is not mentioned, there is concealed a great doubt, a lack of faith in God to the extent that the author fears to bring children into the world. She speaks for the black woman.

A Lack of Faith in God.

> "Don't knock at my door, little child,
> I cannot let you in,
> You know not what a world this is
> Of cruelty and sin.
> Wait in the still eternity
>   Until I come to you,
>   The world is cruel, child,
>   I cannot let you in!

---

[10] Fauset, Jessie Redmond, Plum Bum (New York: Frederick A. Stokes Company, 1928), pp. 308, 309.
[11] Johnson, Georgia Douglas, Bronze (Boston: B. J. Brimmer Company, 1922), p. 32.

> "Don't knock at my heart, little one,
> I cannot bear the pain
> Of turning deaf-ear to your call
>
> Time and time again!
> You do not know the monster men
> Inhabiting the earth,
> Be still, be still, my precious child,
> I must not give you birth." [12]

These quotations involving ideas of God filled with agnosticism and a lack of faith in God reveal at least the fact that positive conviction as to the usefulness of the idea of God in perplexed racial situations is lacking. There is the inability to rely upon God with calm assurance that somehow He will give positive aid. To the orthodox mind, it is the will of God that children be brought into the world; not to do so is sin. Georgia Douglas Johnson's argument with the Negro child that the world is too cruel for it to enter, may show a lack of faith in God; certainly, it seems to be an abandoning of the orthodox view of God, or any other for that matter, so far as His help goes in making the world a fit place for black babies to be born in.

The next quotations taken from the *Black Christ* contrast the simple faith of a mother with that of her children.

Questioning the Usefulness of God.

> "We had no scales upon our eyes;
> God, if He was, kept to His skies,
> And left us to our enemies.
> Often at night fresh from our knees
> And sorely doubted litanies
> We grappled for the mysteries:
> 'We never seem to reach nowhere,'
> Jim with a puzzled, questioning air,
> Would kick the covers back and stare
> For me the elder to explain.
> As like as not, my sole refrain
> Would be, 'A man was lynched last night.'
> 'Why?' Jim would ask, his eyes star-bright.

---

[12] Ibid, p. 43.

'A white man struck him; he showed fight.
Maybe God thinks such things are right.'
'Maybe God never thinks at all—
Of us,' and Jim would clench his small,
Hard fingers tight into a ball.
'Likely there ain't no God at all,'
Jim was the first to clothe a doubt
With words, that long had tried to sprout
Against our wills and love of one
Whose faith was like a blazing sun
Set in a dark, rebellious sky.
Now then the roots were fast, and I
Must nurture them in her despite.
God could not be, if He deemed right
The grief that ever met our sight.
. . . .
"Nay, I have done with deities
Who keep me ever on my knees,
My mouth forever in a tune
Of praise, yet never grant the boon
Of what I pray for night and day.
God is a toy; put Him away.
Or make you one of wood or stone
That you can call your very own,
A thing to feel and touch and stroke,
Who does not break you with a yoke
Of iron that he whispers soft;
Nor promise you fine things aloft
While back and belly here go bare,
While His own image walks so spare
And finds this life so hard to live
You doubt that He has aught to give.
Better an idol shaped of clay
Near you, than one so far away......
Better my God should be
This moving, breathing frame of me,
Strong hands and feet, live hearts and eyes;
And when these close, say then God dies.
Your God is somewhere worlds away
Hunting a star He shot astray;
Oh, He has weightier things to do
Than lavish time on me and you." [13]

---

[13] Cullen, Countee, The Black Christ (New York: Harper & Brothers, 1929), p. 77 ff.

Ancient Gods Were Beneficial

"When Rome was a suckling, when Greece was young,
Then there were Gods fit to be sung,
Who paid the loyal devotee
For service rendered zealously,
In coin a man might feel and spend,
Not marked 'Deferred to Journey's End.'
The servant then was worth his hire;
He went unscathed through flood and fire;
Gods were a thing then to admire.
'Bow down and worship us,' they said.
'You shall be clothed, be housed and fed,
While yet you live, not when you're dead.' " [14]

Substantiating the view of Nella Larsen in *Quicksand*, Countee Cullen abandons the idea "that God is a useful element in the social conflict." There is doubt as to whether God has anything to give, and He is too far away to help. But the main emphasis seems to be that He does not exist. The reason for abandoning the idea of God as helpful is clearly stated:

"A man was lynched last night;"
"God, if He was, kept to His skies,
And left us to our enemies;"

the things prayed for are never given; "life is hard to live"; and, God is accused of promising "fine things aloft while back and belly go bare." Therefore, the idea of God is abandoned and He is branded as useless in the area of social and racial justice. "God is a toy" and a God of wood and stone might do as much good.

In another poem, Cullen expresses his faith in God—faith that God can solve the mysteries and paradoxes of life. But into the final couplet he pours "an infinity of irony and bitterness, and pathos and tragedy." In a real sense, it implies the kind of doubt and cynicism characteristic of other expressions. In addition to the pathos and tragedy expressed, it is a sonnet of rare beauty. Though not so radical as the previous expression,

---

[14] Ibid, p. 85.

the idea persists in the next two quotations that God may not be too heavily relied upon; He is deaf to our plaints.

Mingling of Convictions and Doubt.

> "I doubt not God is good, well-meaning, kind,
> And did He stoop to quibble could tell why
> The little buried mole continues blind,
> Why flesh that mirrors Him must some day die,
> Make plain the reason tortured Tantalus
> Is baited by the fickle fruit, declare
> If merely brute caprice dooms Sisyphus
> To struggle up a never-ending stair.
> Inscrutable His ways are, and immune
> To catechism by a mind too strewn
> With petty cares to slightly understand
> What awful brain compels His awful hand.
> Yet do I marvel at this curious thing:
> To make a poet black, and bid him sing!" [15]

In the following poem, "Pagan Prayer," one sees that the author wants to have faith, that he wants to believe in God and the teachings of Christianity, but apparently he cannot. He accuses God of being deaf to "our plaints" and implies that God has lost the Negro race and begs God to "retrieve my race again."

God Is Deaf to Our Plaints.

> "Not for myself I make this prayer,
> But for this race of mine
> That stretches forth from shadowed places
> Dark hands for bread and wine.
>
> "For me, my heart is pagan mad,
> My feet are never still,
> But give them hearths to keep them warm
> In homes high on a hill.
>
> "For me, my faith lies fallowing,
> I bow not till I see,
> But these are humble and believe;
> Bless their credulity.

---

[15] Cullen, Countee, Color (New York: Harper and Brothers, 1925), p. 3.

> "For me, I pay my debts in kind,
>   And see no better way,
>   Bless these who turn the other cheek
>   For love of you, and pray.
>
> "Our Father, God; our Brother, Christ—
>   So are we taught to pray;
>   Their kinship seems a little thing
>   Who sorrow all the day.
>
> "Our Father, God; our Brother Christ,
>   Or are we bastard kin,
>   That to our plaints your ears are closed,
>   Your doors barred from within?
>
> "Our Father, God; our Brother, Christ,
>   Retrieve my race again;
>   So shall you compass this black sheep,
>   This pagan heart.   Amen." [16]

In the "A Litany at Atlanta," there are confusion, doubt, and frustration. Mr. DuBois has there no clear cut conviction as to what or who God is. He is disturbed that God should allow men, especially his own people, to suffer. Here the impression is given that God can be consciously reached and appealed to—He can be moved to act in the name of justice. The author seems to attribute to God in his frustration and confusion a plan, a purpose. The inference is that God could do something about the situation *if He would*. God is almost accused of being insensitive to wrong and of being a cause of injustice. A few excerpts from "A Litany at Atlanta" are illustrative:

Doubts God's Help.

> "O silent God, Thou whose voice afar in mist and mystery hath left our ears an-hungered in these fearful days—Hear us, good Lord!
>
> "Listen to us, Thy children: our faces dark with doubt are made a mockery in Thy Sanctuary. With uplifted hands we front Thy heaven, O God, crying:

---

[16] Ibid, pp. 20, 21.

"We beseech Thee to hear us, good Lord! We are not better than our fellows, Lord; we are but weak and human men. When our devils do deviltry, curse Thou the doer and the deed, curse them as we curse them, do to them all and more than ever they have done to innocence and weakness, to womanhood and home.

"Have mercy upon us, miserable sinners! And yet, whose is the deeper guilt? Who made these devils! Who nursed them in crime and fed them on injustice? Who ravished and debauched their mothers and their grandmothers? Who bought and sold their crime and waxed fat and rich on public iniquity? Thou knowest, good God!....

"Wherefore do we pray? Is not the God of the Fathers dead? Have not seers seen in heaven's halls Thine hearsed and lifeless form stark amidst the black and rolling smoke of Sin, where all along bow bitter forms of endless dead? Awake, Thou that sleepest!

"Thou art not dead, but flown afar, uphills of endless light, through blazing corridors of suns, where worlds do swing of good and gentle men, of women strong and free—far from the cozenage, black hypocrisy, and chaste prostitution of this shameful speck of dust!.....Hear us, O Heavenly Father!

"Doth not this justice of hell stink in thy nostrils, O God? How long shall the mounting flood of innocent blood roar in Thine ears and pound in our hearts for vengeance? .....Forgive us, good Lord; we know not what we say! Bewildered we are and passion-tossed, mad with madness of a mobbed and mocked and murdered people; straining at the armposts of Thy throne, we raise our shackled hands and charge Thee, God, by the bones of our stolen fathers, by the tears of our dead mothers, by the very blood of Thy crucified Christ: What meaneth this? Tell us the plan; give us the sign!" [17]

The author seems to want to believe that God can do things. But he certainly is in doubt as to whether aid from God can be expected. That God is a helpful agency in the Negro's desire for social reconstruction is to be doubted.

---

[17] DuBois, W. E. B., Dark Water (New York: Harcourt, Brace & Howe, 1920), pp. 25 ff.

It cannot be strongly argued, but there seems to be in some respects, an echo of eighteenth century Deism in DuBois' conception of God as stated here and in chapter VI. For example, a first cause is implied in the first paragraph of the Credo which was quoted in a previous connection. God seems to be far away in the moral realm—remote "from the particular cases exhibiting the working of His laws." God seems to be the ultimate source of things. All these are elements common to Deism. Although the Deists held to a belief in the possibility of occasional interference on the part of the Deity, they also held that it was highly improbable that he would interfere. Though pleading for God to interfere with the working of moral law, Mr. DuBois doubts that God will do anything about existing wrongs and evils. According to Deism, God's relationship to the world is that of a builder to the building. Just as a builder determines the character of the building, so God determined the character of the world—but He could not be expected to make the world better.

I may do violence to the author here. He would hardly accept God as a real person as I believe Deism did. I also doubt that he would agree with eighteenth century Deism in saying that in the moral world as in the physical world, there is no need for the special interposition of the Supreme Deity. Being so keenly sensitive to the evils of the world, I feel he would admit the need of such intervention but would certainly deny the probability of its happening. I believe the context makes clear that Mr. DuBois would probably follow the Deist in his claim that human personality is to be preserved, that man is to retain his freedom, and that he is to accept responsibility for what he does. "As he sows so shall he reap, according to laws that admit of no exception."[18]

In another section, "A Hymn to the Peoples," the idea of frustration is further demonstrated and God seems to be a human God. Even here one gets the impression that the author does not expect any aid from external superhuman forces.

---

[18] Joyce, G. C., "Deism," Encyclopedia Religion and Ethics, Vol. IV, p. 541 (Edited by James Hastings).

"We are but weak and wayward men,
  Distraught alike with hatred and vain glory;
  Prone to despise the Soul that breathes within—
  High visioned hordes that lie and steal and kill,
  Sinning the sin each separate heart disclaims,
  Clambering upon our riven, writhing selves,
  Besieging Heaven by trampling men to Hell!

"We be blood-guilty! Lo, our hands be red!
Not one may blame the other in this sin!
But here—here in the White Silence of the Dawn
Before the womb of Time,
We face the birth-pangs of a world.
We hear the stifled cry of Nations all but born—
The wail of women ravished of their stunted brood!
We see the nakedness of Toil, the poverty of Wealth,
We know the Anarchy of Empire, and doleful Death of life!
And hearing, seeing, knowing all, we cry:
Save us, World-spirit, from our lesser selves!
Grant us that war and hatred cease,
Reveal our souls in every race and hue!
Help us, O Human God, in this Thy truce,
To make Humanity divine." [19]

The next quotation is taken from one of James Weldon Johnson's most recent and widely read books, *Along This Way*. The idea of God presented here differs greatly from the idea presented in Mr. Johnson's poem, "Fifty Years," in which the view is expressed that the Negro is a part of some great plan. In that poem, Mr. Johnson does not doubt God. He believes that there is purpose in the universe. In this quotation, Mr. Johnson presents his views of religion and future life, in addition to his idea of God.

Doubting Purpose and a Personal God.
"My glance forward reaches no farther than this world. I admit that through my adult life I have lacked religiosity. But I make no boast of it; understanding, as I do, how essential religion is to many, many people. For that reason, I have little patience with the zealot who is forever trying

---

[19] DuBois, W. E. B., Dark Water (New York: Harcourt, Brace & Howe, 1920), pp. 275-276.

to prove to others that they do not need religion; that they would be better off without it. Such a one is no less a zealot than the religionist who contends that all who "do not believe" will be consigned to eternal hell fires. It is simply that I have not felt the need of religion in the commonplace sense of the term. I have derived spiritual values in life from other sources than worship and prayer. I think that the teachings of Jesus Christ embody the loftiest ethical and spiritual concepts the human mind has yet borne. I do not know if there is a personal God; I do not see how I can know; and I do not see how my knowing can matter. What does matter, I believe, is how I deal with myself and how I deal with my fellows. I feel that I can practice a conduct toward myself and toward my fellows that will constitute a basis for an adequate religion, a religion that may comprehend spiritually and beauty and serene happiness.

"As far as I am able to peer into the inscrutable, I do not see that there is any evidence to refute those scientists and philosophers who hold that the universe is purposeless; that man, instead of being the special care of a Divine Providence, is a dependent upon fortuity and his own wits for survival in the midst of blind and insensate forces. But to stop there is to stop short of the vital truth. For mankind and for the individual this state, what though it be accidental and ephemeral, is charged with meaning. Man's sufferings, his joys, his aspirations, his defeats, are just as real and of as great moment to him as they would be if they were part of a mighty and definite cosmic plan.

"The human mind racks itself over the never-to-be-known answer to the great riddle, and all that is clearly revealed is the fate that man must continue to hope and struggle on; that each day, if he would not be lost, he must with renewed courage take a fresh hold on life and face with fortitude the turns of circumstances. To do this, he needs to be able to touch God; let the idea of God mean to him whatever it may." [20]

---

[20] Johnson, James Weldon, Along This Way (New York: The Viking Press, 1933), pp. 431, 414.

Whatever the nature of the God Mr. Johnson believes in, it is clear that this God does not operate in some future place called Heaven, and his God does not consign one to Hell. With respect to the idea that God is personal, Mr. Johnson is an agnostic, admitting that there may be a God of some sort. Johnson's inclination to accept the idea of a purposeless universe, his idea that man is not under the special care of a Divine Providence, and his inclination to accept the view that man is dependent upon chance and his own ability for survival, imply that God does not exist. The author's conviction that "man's sufferings, his joys, his aspirations, his defeats" are not parts of any definite cosmic plan, and his strong implication that man's state here is accidental and ephemeral also infer the non-existence of God. The last paragraph of the excerpt, however, insists that man needs a God if he is to possess sufficient faith to enable him to face life with fortitude. The logic of this paragraph might easily lead one to conclude that there is a plurality of gods and that whatever it is that enables one "to continue to hope and struggle on" is God. If this is true, there would be as many gods as there are things that stimulate man to live courageously in a world of blind chance. On the other hand, Mr. Johnson may intend to say that for the brave and strong of heart, there is no need of a belief in God; but for the weak and frail, the "so-called" masses, the belief in God is a necessity; otherwise, life for them would have no meaning. Here is a clear case where the idea of God as a useful instrument in the area of social reconstruction is clearly abandoned. This is certainly true for Mr. Johnson, although the idea may have value for the masses. The next writer makes a definite confession of atheism.

George S. Schuyler, who for twenty years has been in the public eye as a writer, lecturer, and critic of American social life, also presents an interesting view substantiating the third main contention of this study. In an unpublished statement, he writes:

"It is well known, of course, that I am an atheist. I have said so time and again, and long before any of my literary contemporaries in Senegambia began to be assailed with doubts and said so in public.

"However, I am realist enough to agree with Voltaire that 'if there were no God, it would be necessary to create Him.' There is much that is noble and beautiful in religion and I would not take one iota of faith away from any human being who is comforted and can escape from harsh reality thereby. Much of the ranting against religion and the church is utterly devoid of sense. True, as religion comes to be highly institutionalized it develops into a racket and eventually suffers the fate of all rackets; that is, makes place for another racket. But what is here true of religion is likewise true of all the rest of man's activities."

In some respect Schuyler's statement coincides with that of James Weldon Johnson previously quoted. Both agree that belief in God is necessary for many people and that if they find comfort and solace in the belief, they should not be ridiculed or criticised. Both find something noble and beautiful in religion. There is no effort on Schuyler's part nor in Johnson's recent statement to molest or deride the simple faith of the masses. Though critical of institutionalized religion, there is a profound appreciation for the church. The attitude expressed by Schuyler is in striking contrast to that revealed by the editors of the *Messenger* and Langston Hughes. In one sentence Schuyler implies that religion is compensatory; but he also implies that compensatory religion has value for those who believe in God and religion.

When the Messenger Magazine was in operation, it served as an outstanding critic of the Negro Church and religion. The editors believed that the Negro ministry should center its attention on economics, history, sociology, and physical science—less on Bible. In a Thanksgiving editorial in 1919, the *Messenger* denied allegiance to the traditional God. It said: "We do not thank God for anything nor do our thanks include gratitude for which most persons usually give thanks at this period. With us we are thankful for different things and to a different

Deity. Our Deity is the toiling masses of the world and the things for which we thank are their achievement."[21]

In the next poem, Langston Hughes turns Communist and repudiates Christ. This selection is also a repudiation of God and religion, which is a radical departure from the faith implicit in his earlier writings.

Good-bye Christ.

"Listen Christ,
You did all right in your day I reckon
But that day's gone now.
They ghosted you up a swell story, too,
Called it Bible—
But its dead now.
The popes and the preachers've
Made too much money from it
They've sold you to too many
Kings, generals, robbers, and killers—
Even to the Tzar and the Cossacks
Even to Rockefeller's church,
Even to the Saturday Evening Post.
You ain't no good no more.
They've pawned you
Till you've done wore out
Goodbye.

"Christ Jesus Lord God Jehovah,
Beat it on away from here now.
Make way for a new guy with no religion at all.
A real guy named
Marx Communist Lenin Peasant Stalin,
Worker ME—
I said, ME
Go ahead on now.
You're getting in the way of things Lord
And please take Saint Becton
Of the Consecrated Dime
And step on the gas, Christ
Don't be so slow about moving;
Move.

---

[21] *Messenger*, Dec., 1919, p. 4.

The world is mine from now on—
And nobody's gonna sell me
To a king or a general
Or a Millionaire
Go ahead on now." [22]

Langston Hughes is easily the most Communistic of the writers used in this study. According to his view point Christ and perhaps God have all outlived their usefulness. The world must be left for reconstruction in the hands of Communists. Christ is not only of no use in perfecting social change, but He is a decided handicap. He gets in the way of things. Here again we have total abandonment of the idea of God as being a constructive force in building a better world.

Chapter Summation.

It is not surprising to find frustration, doubt, cynicism, and denial of God's existence in the writings of Negroes during this post-War period. In the case of the Negro, this temper of doubt is peculiar to the group in many respects; but it has its setting in the larger area of disillusionment which followed after the War, and which was and is characteristic of the world at large. Walter Horton has well described the latter situation—before and after the War. He says:

"In a sense, it was not the War itself which did most to shake the foundations of our ways of thinking; it was its aftermath of disillusionment.

"The decade which led up to and included the War was a period of intense social idealism and social optimism. In public life, it was the period of the rapid rise of Progressivism in both of the major political parties; when Theodore Roosevelt took his stand at Armageddon to do battle for the Lord, and Woodrow Wilson stirred the blood of youth with his attacks upon 'dollar diplomacy' and his enlightened plea for 'the new freedom.' In religious circles, it was the period of the immense popularity of the Social Gospel;

---

[22] This Poem appeared in the November-December issue of the *Negro Worker*, 1932, a thirty-six page bi-monthly magazine published by Reds in Hamburg, Germany.

when 'Service' and 'Self-Sacrifice' were the watchwords of the day, and the liberal coming of the Kingdom of God on earth seemed only a matter of a perfectly measurable and practicable amount of time and co-operative effort.

"Now the amazing thing is, not that some people lost their optimism when the War began, but that the great mass of people held on to it tenaciously, with certain inevitable modifications, to the very end of the War—only to abandon it in disgust not long after the Armistice. The tide of social idealism and social millennialism did not abate during the War; it rose to heroic and almost incredible heights. The War was to 'make the world safe for democracy;' it was to 'end war' forever; in the 'new age' after the War, all human institutions were to be reconstructed on a basis of ideal justice; through the awful travail and sacrifice of the great conflict, the coming of the Kingdom of God was to be hastened, even as by the sacrifice of the Son of Man on Calvary......

"We trusted our political leaders, when they told us of the villainy of our enemies, and the unimpeachable purity of the aims by which we and our allies were inspired; and, rightly or not, the impression is now abroad that they betrayed us. We trusted our religious leaders, when they proclaimed their apocalyptic visions of a new heaven and a new earth, whose coming was contingent upon the military victory of the Allied Powers; and, at any rate since the collapse of the Inter-Church World Movement, we are pretty well convinced that they betrayed us. We trusted that God would, somehow, balance the stupendous evils of the War by an equal weight of good, that would immediately accrue to us in the post-war period; and if faith in God is declining today, it is because many feel that faith, too, has betrayed them." [23]

This extended quotation from Horton is included because it describes adequately the larger background that has given rise to this protest and cynicism of Negro writers since the War, particularly the younger Negro writers. It is necessary now to sharpen the issue still further by special reference to the disillusionment of the Negro group.

---

[23] Horton, Walter Marshall, Theism and the Modern Mood (New York: Harper & Brothers, 1930), pp. 1 ff.

God's Impotence and His Non-Existence 241

Whatever one may think to the contrary, there can be no denying the fact that the Negro, in the World War, made a two-fold fight for freedom—"to make the world safe for democracy" and to make America safe for the Negro. The Negro was told by Negro and white leaders that after the War, things were going to be better for him. He was made to believe that lynching would cease, that gross injustices in the distribution of public funds would be eliminated, that crippling social and economic proscriptions would be rapidly abolished, and that brotherhood would soon become a reality. The Negro soon discovered, however, that these were preachments of the imagination and had no basis in fact. Almost before the Armistice was signed, movements were on foot to work out plans whereby the Negro might be kept in "his place." He was advised to return to America and settle down as before—not to expect anything different from what he had experienced before the War. Lynching did not cease; in some instances, it increased; race riots multiplied; conflicts in labor continued; social proscriptions remained as before; and discriminations in the distributionof public funds actually increased. The church of God took no courageous stand to right these wrongs.

The disillusionment experienced by the Negro as a result of the World War is ably expressed by Mordecai W. Johnson, in a Commencement address at Harvard University in 1922.

> "At the close of the War, however, the Negro's hopes were suddenly dashed to the ground. Southern newspapers began at once to tell the Negro soldiers that the War was over and the sooner they forgot it the better. 'Pull off your uniform,' they said, 'find the place you had before the War and stay in it.' 'Act like a Negro should act,' said one newspaper, 'work like a Negro should work, talk like a Negro should talk, study like a Negro should study. Dismiss all ideas of independency or of being lifted up to the plane of the white man. Understand the necessity of keeping a Negro's place.' In connection with such admonitions there came the great collective attacks on Negro life and property in Washington, Chicago, Omaha,

Elaine, and Tulsa. There came also the increasing boldness of lynchers who advertised their purpose in advance and had their photographs taken around the bodies of their victims. There came vain appeals by the colored people to the President of the United States and to the Houses of Congress. And finally there came the reorganization and rapid growth of the Ku Klux Klan." [24]

It is not surprising then, as the previous chapter shows, that we get protest against other-worldly religion in Negro churches, protest against the "white man's God," and repudiation of the simple faith of former days; and, in this chapter expressions of doubt, cynicism, and a flat denial of God's existence. The marvel is that despite these facts we find the majority of the Negro writers maintaining some kind of faith in God.

Revolt against the other-worldly religion is really a protest against those who seek to achieve the complete needs of the group in a far off, future heaven rather than put forth an active effort to get them here. The revolt against the white man's religion is due to the conviction shared by some Negroes that it serves as an opiate for the Negro, makes him satisfied with occupying an inferior social status and with occupying an economic position that is unstable. This was clearly brought out in our reference to Helga Crane in the novel *Quicksand*. Helga Crane's protest is based wholly on the fact that her mother, after marrying a Negro man, developed hatred for all Negroes, thinking she was superior to them; and the fact that her white relatives and the white group refused to recognize her, refused to give her the warm response that human beings crave and must have. She found this recognition and response, in America, in the Negro group with whom she cast her lot.

Doubt, frustration, and denial of God's existence arise also from social crises. God must not be interested in helping the group to achieve the needs necessary for existence. God does not exist; if He does, He is indifferent to the needs of the group.

---

[24] Woodson, Carter G., Negro Orators and Their Orations (Washington: Associated Publishers, 1925), p. 660.

They arise at the point where physical security is denied; economic privilege cut off; the free exercise of the ballot prohibited; segregation in every area sustained by custom and law; and, the free development of spiritual powers almost completely stifled.

The repudiation or negation of God may influence the behavior of Negroes in many ways. It may lead many of them into the humanistic camp of the Haydon-Otto variety. Negroes would then seek to perfect social change by combining religious idealism and the technique of modern science without relying on God or supernatural aid. The negation of the idea of God may also drive Negroes into the communistic camp, whereby more militant or violent means would be used to achieve political and economic status. The negation of the idea of God may lead weaker souls into the realm of despair encouraging suicide; or it may induce them to a happy-go-lucky state in which case the motto may well be: "enjoy life and get what pleasure you can out of it." The same holds true with those ideas of God involving frustration and doubt.

The last quotation from James Weldon Johnson in which he states the inability of man ever to know that there is a personal God, and the uselessness of it if he did know; his statement that what does matter is the kind of conduct one exercises toward himself and his fellows; and, his further declaration that he agrees with scientists and philosophers who say that the universe is purposeless and man is dependent upon his "own wits for survival in the midst of blind and insensate forces"—these trends are definitely humanistic.

The case of Langston Hughes is clear. The absolute repudiation of Christ, God, and religion, and the reliance upon Marx, Lenin, and Stalin is the extreme left to which the negation of God in the life of the Negro may lead. The negation stimulates the Negro to become Communistic and to resort to more violent means of attaining social, economic, and political justice.

It can hardly be denied that an appreciable number of Negroes, learned and untutored, are Communists not so much by choice but because Communism offers, they think, the only ray of hope for the Negro, though the way of achievement is anti-God and anti-religious.

Though it is beside the point in this study, it is the belief of the writer that the Negro's firm faith in God has saved him, up to this point, from violent revolutionary methods of achieving his rights. His faith in God has not only served as an opiate for the Negro, but it has suggested and indicated that pacific and legal methods are to be used in achieving them. It is not too much to say that unless liberal prophetic religion moves more progressively to the left in the effort to achieve complete citizenship rights for the Negro, he will become more irreligious and he will become more militant and communistic in his efforts to attain to full manhood in American life. It is significant to note that prior to 1914, one finds no ideas of God that imply doubt and repudiation. Since the War, and particularly since 1920, there is a wave of cynicism, defeat, and frustration in the writings of young Negroes where God is discussed.

CHAPTER IX

Summation

The ideas of God in Negro literature are developed along three principal lines: (1). Ideas of God that are used to support or give adherence to traditional, compensatory patterns; (2). Ideas, whether traditional or otherwise, that are developed and interpreted to support a growing consciousness of social and psychological adjustment needed; (3). Ideas of God that show a tendency or threat to abandon the idea of God as "a useful instrument" in perfecting social change.

The compensatory ideas are those that are commonly taught and exposed to the mass of Negroes; they are reflected in sermons, particularly the other-worldly type; such ideas are found in practically all of the stenographically reported prayers; the compensatory ideas are also set forth in the Spirituals; and they are revealed in the Church School Literature of three major Negro denominations. These ideas support the first trend and they adhere strictly to traditional, compensatory patterns. Though recognizing notable exceptions, they are compensatory and traditional in character because they are neither developed nor interpreted in terms of social rehabilitation. They are conducive to developing in the Negro a complacent, laissez-faire attitude toward life. They support the view that God in His good time and in His own way will bring about the conditions that will lead to the fulfilment of social needs. They encourage Negroes to feel that God will see to it that things work out all right; if not in this world, certainly in the world to come. They make God influential chiefly in the beyond, in preparing a home for the faithful—a home where His suffering servants will be free of the trials and tribulations which beset them on the earth. A brief summary of such ideas follows:

God fights the battles of His chosen people, and He will bring them out victors in every crisis. Not only is God to fight our battles, but He is to prepare a place for us in Heaven. For example, "Fight our battle for us and lead us to the rock of Salvation." "Oh, Lord, here we are down here in a world of trouble; down here in a world of sorrow—Oh, Lord, have mercy right now this day our Heavenly Father and in the end, give us a lasting resting place in that city where we can praise Thy name forever." Whatever happens is "permitted by God" and there is nothing we can do about it. God will protect us from physical danger, sickness, and disease if our ways are pleasing to Him. If they are pleasing to Him, He will solve our problems. For example, "If a man's ways please God, He can awake at the hour of midnight with a smile on his face and solve the problems and he will defeat those who try to retard his progress. He simply kneels down and tells God about his problems and God will solve them." A mother prayed to God and asked Him to save her four sons from death in France. God answered her prayers. Notwithstanding the fact that millions were killed in the War, her four sons were saved. God is in His Heaven; all is right with the world. God is a rock in a weary land and a shelter in a mighty storm. God knows all our needs and He will provide for them. All things work together for good for those who love the Lord. God takes care of His own during the depression.

This brief summary of ideas is fairly representative of those that are commonly taught to the mass of Negroes in sermons of the other-worldly type, in the Spirituals, in prayers, and in Church School Literature for pupils between the ages of six and sixteen. They adhere to traditional, compensatory patterns.

These ideas are dominant in some of the writings of Hammon, Wheatley, and the Reverend Mr. Cannon; in some of Dunbar's writings; in the writings of Shackelford and Holloway; in the fifty-four other-worldly sermons revealed in an analysis of one hundred stenographically recorded sermons; and in fully twenty-one of the other forty-six which are not so characteristically other-worldly. That this is true of most of the spirituals, is too obvious to need further proof. Of the fifty-one stenographically reported prayers, thirty-five were dominantly other-worldly. It is clear from the prayers that many Negroes consider this world a land of sorrow and trouble and not of joy. Life is looked upon as a temporary affair—their real home is beyond Jordan. There are frequent references to the fact that they are packing up to leave. As indicated previously, journeying through this world is wearisome, and they need God to guide them through. This world is also a world of trouble and it is friendless. Other ideas of God (scattered throughout the literature under discussion), though not other-worldly, are traditional and compensatory. Particularly is this true of the Church School Literature which covers the literature of all grades, including a time span of fifteen months for one denomination, nine months for another, and a period of three months for the third.

Although the literature under discussion contains ideas of God as described above, it must be pointed out that there are ideas in this literature that are not compensatory, though in essence traditional. They represent the second trend and they are developed and interpreted along social lines. In the "mass" literature numerous ideas show that God is against slavery; that of one blood God created all races; that it is against God to take life; that the Negro is not an inferior person; that God is just; and that, in due time, He will bring slaveholders to His judgment seat.

There is found an idea of God which makes one's relationship to God inseparable from his relationship to his fellows, which challenges one to become reconciled with his fellowmen—to live a life that is in harmony with God and man—to develop an attitude of appreciation and sympathy for all human beings. There is also expressed an idea of God which makes Him a transforming agency. God's spirit works wonders upon the individual. "Family life makes the man a loving father, it makes him a man the people will trust, a man the bank will trust—a man who will not be dishonest and work the life out of people and steal their blood and bread. This is what God's Holy Spirit will do." The idea is implicit in the quotation that when God gets into a man he will want economic security for others, not for himself alone, and that he will work to that end. Another idea is, that we are indebted to God for everything and the way to pay God is to use our talents to benefit and improve humanity. Again there is given an idea which shows that God liberates human personality for the sole purpose of transforming the social order so that the abundant life might accrue to all. It is expressed that God requires us to become worthy factors in bringing about world peace. Finally, the idea is clearly set forth that man belongs to God, and, organically, one is a part of God and man. "There is a divine value in human life, and every recipient is under obligation to God to respect that value, for all human life is precious unto Him." The ideas that are developed in terms of social reconstruction are found primarily in the writings of ministers prior to the Civil War, in writers of the reconstruction era, in the twenty-five this-worldly sermons, in a few of the spirituals and in the quarterlies for young people and adults. This, in brief, concludes the summary of the ideas of God as found in the literature of the Negro masses.

"Classical" Negro literature is composed of the writings of poets, novelists, biographers, orators, and social scientists— productions that have come out since the time of Jupiter Hammon.

It is significant to note that there is virtually no difference between the ideas of God found in the "classical" literature between 1760 and 1860, and those found in the "mass" Literature of the same period. In fact compensatory, other-worldly views in this period are comparatively rare. Negro writers of this period were primarily concerned with emancipation and they developed their conceptions of God to that end. The same is true of the period between the Civil War and 1914. The writers of "mass" Literature are just as much concerned with social reform as the writers of "classical" literature. But there is a striking difference between the ideas of God found and developed in "classical" Negro literature since 1914 and those ideas of God of the Negro masses since 1914. Four distinctions might be mentioned:

1. The ideas of God in this literature, more than is the case with the "mass" literature, are ideas of God that are developed to substantiate the growing conviction of Negro writers that radical changes are needed in social and economic areas.

2. The "classical" Negro literature is more definitely this-worldly in its emphases. The literature which reflects the ideas of God of the masses was found to be more other-worldly in its emphases.

3. Although there is found the same desire for security and recognition in both types of literature, in the "classical" literature it is a desire for security based on a firm economic foundation which has group significance; whereas the "mass" literature reveals more a desire to be protected from danger, sickness, disease, death, hell, and enemies. It is the desire for personal security based primarily on the fear of men or on the fear that comes to one who is afraid of life generally because of experiences that make life a precarious and hazardous undertaking. Similarly, the desire for recognition in the "classical" literature is not so much a personal thing as it is an effort to have the group recognized. In the other literature, this desire is highly personal.

4. In the "mass" literature there is found without exception a deep, abiding faith in God; while in the "classical" literature there are found strains of doubt, revolt, frustration, cynicism, agnosticism, and atheism. These points of difference will become clearer in the analysis which follows.

A brief summary of the most significant ideas of God in "classical Negro literature that are used to support the second development, the need of psychological and social readjustment, is given below:

God is agsinst slavery, war, and injustices of any description. God created all races from one blood. God is love. God is beauty. God and humanity are one. God has set no geographical boundaries nor racial limitations. There is no divine right of race. The rights of humanity are divine and they cannot be divested by reason of race. We are all God's creatures. God created the Negro in His own image. He has made no superior races and no inferior races. The Negro is God's most perfect handiwork. The human family is united in God. The Negro is on a special errand for God. Every soul comes into the world with love for man and love for God. He spins every person from Himself. He is on the side of right, actively engaged in the struggle, but in co-operation with man. God has put the Negro and the white man here in America to prove to the world that two races varying in culture and color can live together, each contributing to the welfare of the other. God, if one lets Him, erases from one's heart race hatred and prejudice. God gives a person strength and courage to battle and contend for the right. Peace and good-will will come among races whenever they recognize their unity in God. Finally, God desires that every individual be given the right to grow to perfection without the imposition of artificial barriers from without. These ideas of God clearly support the growing consciousness that social change should be perfected along the lines of racial and social justice. It was pointed out in the analysis of data that the ideas supported the need of social rehabilitation along three fronts that slightly vary:

a. Some of the ideas of God are developed to show the need of social reconstruction on a universal scale, rising beyond the narrow confines of race.

b. There are ideas developed and interpreted along social lines that are confined wholly to the social and economic needs of the Negro.

c. Then too, there are ideas that aim primarily to help the Negro to make a more wholesome psychological adjustment—to support the view that the Negro is the potential equal of other races and for that reason is entitled to a fair chance in the struggle for existence.

It should be repeated here that all ideas of God in "classical" Negro literature are not developed in terms of the need of social change. Many of them are highly other-worldly and lead to complacency as much as any of the ideas in the "mass" literature. The ideas that the Negro should accept slavery until God sees fit to abolish it; that it is more important for the slave to prepare for Heaven than to struggle to be free; that God will make every thing right in Heaven where there are no segregation, lynching, prejudice, crime nor vice; and waiting on the Lord, are illustrative of ideas in "classical" literature that are compensatory.

The third and final trend in the development of the ideas of God in this study shows that there is a tendency on the part of recent Negro writers to consider the idea of God as useless in any effort to reconstruct the world socially. Many of these ideas are not flat denials of the existence of God, but they show incredulity, frustration, and pessimism which make the idea of God of little value in social crises. In every case, in this third emphasis, the traditional views of God as exemplified in the Negro masses and in the white man's conceptions of God are abandoned as useless in the social struggle. They run the entire gamut from mere protest against traditional ideas and abandonment of the same to a complete denial of the existence of God.

In addition to the summary of the way the ideas of God have developed in Negro literature, it is necessary to record the following outstanding revelations:

1. It is interesting to note that there is probably more other-worldliness in Negro literature during the World War and immediately following the War than there is in the Literature of the early periods. This does not mean, however, that the ideas in the third period (1914–1937) are more compensatory. The reverse is probably true.

2. It is most significant to note that we strike all the trends in the development of the idea of God in the post-World War period; whereas, only two are found in the

pre-World War period. Prior to 1914, God is neither doubted nor is His existence denied. Doubt, lack of faith, and denial are definitely post-War developments. In other words, from 1760 to 1914 God's existence is not denied.

3. We get, therefore, three widely opposing views in the post-War era—all three, however, developing logically out of the social crisis. As has been stated, there is a wave of other-worldliness during and immediately following the War. After 1920, one finds no other-worldliness in "classical" literature, but there is a heavy strain of denial, frustration, cynicism, doubt, and bewilderment. As strange as this may seem it is not surprising. The development of apocalyptic literature in times of disappointment and distress, and the desire to escape the hardships of this life by taking a flight into the other world are facts well-known to students of history. Other-worldliness arose in Jewish history at a time when Israel had been subject for generations to domination by one or another of the imperial powers. It is natural that the Negro who has suffered much in American life would be further baffled by the World War, would read into it supernatural meaning, and would be more inclined than ever before to seek peace and solace in Heaven. Nor is it contradictory to see that in the same period, from 1914 to the present, literature would be produced revealing atheism, doubt, cynicism, and bewilderment. This would naturally come after the War when the Negro had become fully aware of his disillusionment. He had been led to believe that conditions would be better for him after the War; but it was not so. Democracy did not follow the War. Lynching did not cease. The Negro fared no better in the courts. Race riots broke out in various sections. Segregation increased and conditions generally grew worse. Out of this situation came floods of Negro literature expressing a lack of faith in God never before witnessed in the history of the Negro in this country. The Negro who had been considered to be the most religious of all groups, and whose faith in God was irresistible began to develop literature after 1920 fraught with agnosticism and atheism. "The faith of the fathers" was shaken

for the first time. The other widely opposite view is not denial and it is not other-worldly. It is the development of the idea of God by that type of Negro modernists who took God out of the compensatory setting and used the idea in areas of social reconstruction.
It was an effort to bring the conception of God up to date—to make God equal to the task required in social rehabilitation stimulated by the War.

4. With respect to the idea of God, there are three strains that are rather constant and tend to persist in certain types of literature.

   a. There is continuous insistence upon the view that God is no respecter of person; that from one blood, He created all mankind. The Negro will not accept the idea of a partial God.

   b. The idea seems to persist that somehow things will work out to the advantage of the Negro—our cause is just; God is just; God is on the side of the right. This being true, the Negro cannot lose. The Negro insists upon having a God of justice and a God who is going to see to it that he wins through.

   c. There is a constant note of doubt, frustration, protest, and cynicism; especially among the younger writers and particularly among the post-War writers. There are also expressions of atheism.

5. It is tremendously revealing to note that Negro "classical" writers have, for the most part, adhered rather closely to the orthodox, traditional views of God. In fact, there are to be found only a few astonishing ideas of God in the whole survey. Where there has been a radical departure from orthodoxy, it has been a departure toward atheism as expressed in Humanism or Communism. There are two other notable exceptions: In *Redder Blood* the idea is advanced that God gives each person a selfhood into which He Himself cannot enter. Howard Thurman advances the view that God cannot be what he ought to be until every other person is what he ought to be. Orthodoxy proclaims the omnipotence of God, asserting that with Him nothing is impossible. Though adhering to orthodoxy, Negro "classi-

cal" writers are very discriminating in their selection and use of the traditional ideas of God. They have used, in most instances, only those ideas that are compatible with the needs and hopes of a suppressed group—God made of one blood all races, God is just, God is on the side of right, God is love, God is beauty, and God and humanity are one. The Negro is on an errand for God—they employ the ideas of God that embody the values the Negro seeks.

6. There are contradictions in the views of God expressed by the same writers. Both Dunbar and Washington held views of God that are compensatory; they also held views of God that are developed along social lines. At one time James Weldon Johnson states that God has a plan for the Negro; at a very recent date he denies purpose in the universe, except what man gives to it. DuBois is firm in the affirmation of the existence of God and in the implication that He is a God of social righteousness, while he seems to doubt God as being of any help in the social struggle. He never seems to rely upon God to right the ills of society. DuBois' non-reliance upon God in the area of social reconstruction and Washington's firm faith in God at all times may account for their opposing social philosophies. There are authors who assert that God is wholly impartial; yet they indicate that God has chosen the Negro for a unique mission on the earth.

7. The most outstanding revelation of this study is the fact that the Negro's idea of God grows out of his social situation. The cosmological and teleological conceptions of God are conspicuous by their absence in Negro literature. Modern views such as Mathew's "God is the personality producing activity;" the identifying of God with some evolutionary process as in Bergson's "Elan Vital;" the implication that "God is the ultimate, synthetic, ordering, organizing, and regulative activity in the universe which accounts for all the structural groupings in it" as seen in Smuts' "Holism;" that "God is progressive integration or the growing good" as maintained by Wieman; the idea that "God is the struggle toward the next higher level" as represented by

Alexander; the mystical approaches to God in which one is completely absorbed in the Deity; and the view of Barth that "God is wholly-other" have not permeated Negro literature. The moral, traditional approach is the one the "classical" Negro writers have used. They have apparently been indifferent to modern expressions of God, except the variations mentioned under point four.

The data show that however the ideas are used, they develop at the point of social crisis; at the point where justice is denied, hopes thwarted, and plans shattered, owing in part to the hampering proscriptions imposed upon the Negro by the dominant group. His ideas of God, so to speak, are chiseled out of the very fabric of the social struggle. Virtually all of them express the unfilled yearnings of the Negro group, whether they be worldly or other-worldly. They developed, as can be validated historically, along the line of the Negro's most urgent needs and desires. Prior to 1860, the Negro's ideas of God were developed around slavery. After the Civil War, they grew out of the wrongs of Reconstruction. Since 1914, they are inseparable from the social and economic restrictions which the Negro meets in the modern world.

Unlike that of many people, the Negro's incredulity, frustrations, agnosticism, and atheism do not develop as the results of the findings of modern science nor from the observation that nature is cruel and indifferent; but primarily because in the social situation, he finds himself hampered and restricted. It is not surprising, therefore, that the Negro group has produced great preachers but few theologians. The Negro is not interested in any fine theological or philosophical discussions about God. He is interested in a God who is able to help him bridge ths chasm that exists between the actual and the ideal. The Negro's life has been too unstable, too precarious, too uncertain, and his needs have been too great for him to become sufficiently objective to theologize or philosophize about God.

BIBLIOGRAPHY

ALLEN, RICHARD — THE LIFE, EXPERIENCE AND GOSPEL LABORS; Philadelphia: A.M.E. Book Concern.

A.M.E. REVIEW, VOL. VI

ASHBY, WILLIAM M. — REDDER BLOOD; New York: The Cosmopolitan Press, 1915.

BANNEKER, BENJAMIN — Copy of a Letter to Secretary of State; Philadelphia: Printed and Sold by Daniel Lawrence, No. 33, 1792.

BELL, JAMES MADISON — POETICAL WORKS OF JAMES MADISON BELL; Lansing: Wynkoop Hullenbeck, Crawford Company, 1904.

BRAWLEY, BENJAMIN G. — SOCIAL HISTORY OF THE AMERICAN NEGRO; New York: The Macmillan Company, 1921.

CANNON, N. C. — THE ROCK OF WISDOM, 1833: Moorland Room, Howard University.

CHESTNUTT, CHARLES W. — THE HOUSE BEHIND THE CEDARS; New York: Houghton Mifflin Company, 1900.

COKER, DANIEL — JOURNAL OF DANIEL COKER; Baltimore: Edward J. Coole, Publisher, 1820.

COZART, W. FOREST — THE CHOSEN PEOPLE; Boston: The Christopher Publishing Company, 1924.

CULLEN, COUNTEE — THE BLACK CHRIST; New York: Harper and Brothers, 1929.

CULLEN, COUNTEE — COLOR; New York: Harper and Brothers, 1925.

CRUMMELL, ALEXANDER	Sermons Preached in Trinity Church, Monrovia, W. Africa; Boston: Press of T. R. Marion and Son, 1865.
DANDRIDGE, RAYMOND GARFIELD	THE POET AND OTHER POEMS; Cincinnati: Copyright by author, 1920.
DAVIS, FRANK MARSHALL	I AM THE AMERICAN NEGRO; Chicago: Black Cat Press, 1937.
DOUGLASS, FREDERICK	MY BONDANDE AND MY FREEDOM; New York: Miller, Orton, and Milligan, 1855.
DuBOIS, W. E. B.	DARK WATER; New York: Harcourt, Brace and Howe, 1920.
DuBOIS, W. E. B.	ON BEING ASHAMED OF ONESELF; Article—Crisis, 1935, September Issue.
DuBOIS, W. E. B.	JOHN BROWN; Philadelphia: George W. Jacob Company, 1909.
DuBOIS, W. E. B.	BLACK RECONSTRUCTION; New York: Harcourt Brace and Company, 1935.
FAUSET, JESSIE REDMOND	PLUM BUM; New York: Frederick A. Stokes Company, 1928.
FERRIS, WILLIAM H.	THE AFRICAN ABROAD; New Haven: The Tuttle, Morehouse and Taylor Press, 1913.
FLOYD, S. X.	LIFE OF CHARLES T. WALKER; Nashville: National Baptist Publishing Board, 1902.
FRAZIER, E. FRANKLIN	THE NEGRO FAMILY IN CHICAGO; Chicago: The University of Chicago Press, 1932.
GARVEY, AMY JACQUES	PHILOSOPHY AND OPINIONS OF MARCUS GARVEY; New York: The universal Publishing House, 1923.

BIBLIOGRAPHY

HAMMON, JUPITER	An Address to Negroes in State of New York: Carroll and Patterson, 1787.
HARRISON, JAMES M.	SOUTHERN SUNBEAM; Richmond: The Saint Luke Press, 1926.
HAWKINS, W. E.	CHORDS AND DISCORDS; Boston: The Gorham Press, 1920.
HILL, LESLIE P.	THE WINGS OF OPPRESSION; Boston: The Stratford Company, 1912.
HOLLOWAY, JOHN WESLEY	THE DESERT; New York: The Neale Publishing Company, 1919.
HORTON, WALTER MARSHALL	THEISM AND THE MODERN MOOD; New York: Harper and Brothers, 1930.
JOHNSON, GEORGIA DOUGLAS	BRONZE; Boston: B. J. Brimmer Company, 1922.
JOHNSON, JAMES WELDON	THE BOOK OF AMERICAN NEGRO POETRY; New York: Harcourt, Brace and Company, 1922.
JOHNSON, JAMES WELDON	GOD'S TROMBONES; New York: The Viking Press, 1927.
JOHNSON, JAMES WELDON	THE BOOK OF AMERICAN NEGRO SPIRITUALS; Binghampton, New York: The Vail-Bollan Press, 1925.
JOHNSON, JAMES WELDON	THD BOOK OF NEGRO SPIRITUALS AND THE SECOND BOOK OF NEGRO SPIRITUALS; New York: The Viking Press, 1925, 1926.
JOHNSON, JAMES WELDON	ALONG THIS WAY; New York: The Viking Press, 1933.
JOHNSON, JAMES WELDON	SAINT PETER RELATES AN INCIDENT; New York: The Viking Press, 1933.

JOYCE, C. C.	DEISM; Encyclopedia Religion and Ethics, Vol. IV, Edited by James Hastings.
KING, W. J.	THE NEGRO IN AMERICAN LIFE; New York: The Methodist Book Concern, 1926.
LARSEN, NELLA	QUICKSAND; New York: Alfred A. Knopf, 1928.
LYND, ROBERT S., AND HELEN MORRELL	MIDDLETOWN; New York: Harcourt, Brace and Company, 1929.
MATNEY, W. C.	EXPLOITATION OR CO-OPERATION; Crisis, Vol. 37–38, February, 1930, 69 Fifth Avenue, New York.
MAYS AND NICHOLSON	THE NEGRO'S CHURCH; New York: Institute of Social and Religious Reserach, 1933.
MILLER, KELLY	THE EVERLASTING STAIN; Washington, D. C.: The Associated Publishers, 1924.
MILLER, KELLY	OUT OF THE HOUSE OF BONDAGE; New York: Thomas Y. Crowell Company, 1914.
MILLER, KELLY	RACE ADJUSTMENT; Washington, D. C.: The Neale Publishing Company, 1909.
MILLER, FRANCIS P.	RELIGION ON THE CAMPUS; New York: Association Press, 1927.
MILLER, H. A.	RACES, NATIONS AND CLASSES; Philadelphia: J. B. Lippincott Company, 1924.
MOTON, ROBERT RUSSA	FINDING A WAY OUT; New York: Doubleday, Page and Company, 1920.

Bibliography

PAUL, NATHANIEL — An Address on the Celebration of the Abolition of Slavery in New York: Library of Congress.

PENNINGTON, J. W. C. — Address Delivered before the Glasgow Y.M.C.A. Moorland Room, Howard University. Philadelphia Gazette, December 31, 1799.

PHILLIPS, PHILIP LEE — The Negro, Benjamin Banneker, Astronomer and Mathematician, Plea for Universal Peace; Reprint from Records of the Columbia Historical Society, Vol. 20, 1917.

POPEL, ESTHER — FOREST POOL; Washington: Privately printed, 1934.

RENFRO, HERBERT G. — LIFE AND WORKS OF PHILLIS WHEATLEY: Washington: Published by Robert L. Pendleton, 1916.

SCOTT, EMMETT J. — NEGRO MIGRATION DURING WORLD WAR; New York: Oxford University Press, American Branch.

SHACKELFORD, THEODORE HENRY — MY COUNTRY AND OTHER POEMS; Philadelphia: Press of I. W. Klapp Company, 1916–18.

STILL, WILLIAM — THE UNDERGROUND RAILROAD; Philadelphia: Peoples Publishing Company, 1879.

VASSA, GUSTAVUS — LIFE OF GUSTAVUS VASSA, THE AFRICAN; Boston: Isaac Knapp, Published 1837—Library of Congress.

WASHINGTON, BOOKER T. — BLACK-BELT DIAMONDS; New York: Fortune and Scott, 1898.

WASHINGTON, BOOKER T. — UP FROM SLAVERY; New York: Association Press, 1900, 1904.

WASHINGTON, BOOKER T.	STORY OF HIS LIFE AND WORK; Booker T. Washington Copyright 1901; J. L. Nichols and Company, 1915.
WASHINGTON, BOOKER T.	A NEW NEGRO FOR A NEW CENTURY; Chicago: American Publishing House, date about 1900.
WASHINGTON, BOOKER T.	THE FUTURE OF THE AMERICAN NEGRO; Boston: Small, Maynard and Company, 1899.
WASHINGTON, E. DAVIDSON	SELECTED SPEECHES OF BOOKER T. WASHINGTON; New York: Doubleday, Doran and Company, 1932.
WEGELIN, OSCAR	JUPITER HAMMON, AMERICAN NEGRO POET; New York: Printed for Charles Fred Heartman, 1915.
WESLEY, CHARLES	RICHARD ALLEN, APOSTLE OF FREEDOM; Washington: Associated Publishers Inc., 1935.
WHEATLEY, PHILLIS	MEMOIRS AND POEMS; Boston: Published by Isaac Knopf, 1838.
WHITE AND JACKSON	POETRY BY AMERICAN NEGROES; Durham, N. C.: Trinity College Press, 1924.
WHITE, WALTER	FLIGHT; New York: Alfred A. Knopf, 1926.
WHITE, WALTER	FIRE IN THE FLINT; New York: Alfred A. Knopf, 1924.
WIGGINS, LIDA KECK	THE LIFE AND WORKS OF PAUL LAURENCE DUNBAR; Washington, D. C.: Mulliken-Jenkins Company.
WOODSON, CARTER G.	THE RURAL NEGRO; Washington, D. C.: The Association for the Study of Negro Life and History, 1930.

Bibliography

WOODSON, CARTER G. — THE MIS-EDUCATION OF THE NEGRO; Washington, D. C.: The Associated Publishers, 1933.

WOODSON, CARTER G. — NEGRO ORATORS AND THEIR ORATIONS; Washington, D. C.: The Associated Publishers, 1925.

WOODSON, CARTER G. — THE NEGRO IN OUR HISTORY; Washington, D. C.: The Associated Publishers, 1922, 1924, 1927 and 1928.

WOOFTER, T. J., JR. — STUDY OF THE ECONOMIC STATUS OF THE NEGRO; Mimeographed: June, 1930.

WORK, MONROE N. — BIBLIOGRAPHY OF THE NEGRO; New York: H. W. Wilson Company, 1928.

WORK, MONROE N. — THE NEGRO YEAR BOOK; Tuskegee Institute, Alabama: Negro Year Book Publishing Company, 1931, 1937–8.

The Negro in Chicago, University of Chicago, 1922.
The N.A.A.C.P., Its History, Achievement, Purposes; New York, The National Association for the Advancement of Colored People, 1933.
Sunday School Quarterlies.
Messenger Magazine—Editorial, December, 1919.

INDEX

Allen, Richard, 30 ff.
  birth of, 30
  bishop and founder of A. M. E. church, 30
  forced from knees during prayer, 30
  ideas of God, development of, 38–39
Alexander, S. S., 18
  God, definition of, 18
Ashby, William M., 177 ff.; 253
  Redder Blood, 177–178, 253
Association for the Study of Negro Life and History, 13, 185–186, 211

Bannecker, Benjamin, 107, 109
  astronomer and mathematician, 107
  ideas of God, development of, 109
Bell, James Madison, 146 ff.
  Black Man's Wrong, The, 147
  Ideas of God, development of, 146–148
  Lincoln, In Commemoration of the Death of, 147–148
Bergson, H. L., 18
  God, definition of, 18
Brawley, Benjamin, 8 ff.; 152 ff.
  Far Above the Strife and Striving, 153
  ideas of God, development of, 153–154
Brown, John, 154

Cain, Richard H., 63
  ideas of God, development of, 63
Cannon, W. C., 57 ff.
  ideas of God, development of, 57–58
Chestnutt, Charles W., 149 ff.
  House Behind the Cedars, 149–151
  ideas of God, development of, 149–151
Coker, Daniel, 39 ff.
  birth, 39
  idea an instrument in colonizing Africa, 41
  ideas of God, development of, 39–41
  missionary to Liberia, 39
  pioneer and martyr of A. M. E. church, 40
Communism, 13
Compensatory, definition of, 14–15
Constructive development, definition of, 15
Corr, Joseph M., 44 ff.
  ideas of God, development of, 44–45
Cozart, W. Forest, 178
Crisis, The, 4, 7, 8, 10
Crummell, Alexander, 60 ff.
  ideas of God, development of, 60–61
Cullen, Countee, 219 ff.; 227 ff.
  Black Christ, 227–231
  Heritage, 219–220

Dandridge, Raymond G., 192 ff.
Deism, 233
Douglass, Frederick, 121 ff.
  early life, 121
  ideas of God, development of, 121–126, 128
Douglass, Williams, 55 ff.
  ideas of God, 55–56
Du Bois, W. E. B., 10, 12, 152; ideas of God, development of 154, 163 ff.; 168, 173 ff.; 186, 203 ff.; 220, 231 ff.
  Litany at Atlanta, 231–232
  Prayers of God, The, 173–174
Dunbar, Paul Laurence, 2 ff.; 130 ff.; 246, 253
  By Rugged Ways, 137–138
  ideas of God, development of, 130
  interpreter of Negro life, 2–3

Lead Gently, Lord, and Slow, 131–132
Long Had I Grieved, 133
O Lord, the Hard-won Miles, 133
Religion, 134
Warrior's Prayer, The, 135–136
When Storms Arise, 132

Fauset, Jessie Redmond, 225 ff.
Ferris, William H., 148 ff.
   ideas of God, development of, 149
Forten, James, 112

Garnet, Highland, 45 ff.
   birth and early life, 45
   ideas of God, development of, 45–48
Garvey, Marcus, 184 ff.
God, approaches to, 18
God, ideas of
   vide: Ideas of God
Greener, Wichard T., 129 ff.
Grimke, Archibald, 169 ff.
Grimke, Francis J., 170 ff.; 194
Groups, suppressed, 16
   needs of, 16
   reaction of, 16

Hammon, Jupiter, 1, 97 ff.; 100, 102, 109, 246, 248
   An Evening Thought: Salvation by Christ, 102
   Dialogue Between the Master and Slave, 100
   ideas of God, development of, 97–103, 109, 246, 248
Harper, Mrs. Frances Watkins, 118 ff.
Hawkins, Walter E., 176, 206 ff.
Haynes, Lemuel, 58 ff.
   ideas of God, 58–59
Hegel, G. W. M., 18
   God, definition of
Hill, Leslie Pinckney, 179 ff.

But Have I a Certain Warrant?, 179–182
Holloway, John W., 156, 158 ff.; 189, 246
   I Rest Me in the Lord, 158–159
Horton, Walter M., 239 ff.
Hughes, Langston, 219, 237 ff.; 243
   Listen Christ, 238–239

Ideas of God
   anodyne for the people, 86
   brotherhood, 179
   chosen people, 179
   compensatory, 14, 23 ff.; 28, 30, 56, 69, 71 ff.; 77, 90, 92, 99 ff.; 105, 132 ff.; 139 ff.; 142 ff.; 146 ff.; 152 ff.; 156, 160 ff.; 184 ff.; 189 ff.; 195 ff.; 245
   constructive development of, 15, 77 ff.; 82, 108, 110 ff.; 119 ff.; 125, 128, 130, 139
   denial and doubt, 15, 212, 218, 223 ff.; 230, 237, 243
   developed at point of social crisis, 27, 255
   ethical development of, 77
   faith, 191
   God as unity, 175 ff.
   how developed, 14 ff.
   ideas of protest, 206 ff
   impartiality of God, 162, 164, 168 ff.; 172
   in prayers summarized, 83
   militant idea of God, 195, 199, 200
   omnipotence, 179
   opiate for the people, 55, 75, 130, 149, 153 ff.; 188, 244
   other-worldly, 24 ff.; 27 ff.; 56, 69 ff.; 87 ff.; 105 ff.; 154 ff.; 206, 210, 251, 255
   personal security, 161, 170, 172, 184, 193 ff.; 198

INDEX

psychological adjustment, 163, 184 ff.; 188
quest for fulfillment, 176
resignation, 193
social adjustment, 154, 172 ff.; 182
social change, 199, 250, 255
social development of, 77, 95, 209
social reconstruction, 108, 110, 186, 198
social righteousness, 78 ff.; 84, 95, 117, 154
summary, 245–255
summary of ideas of God in "classical" literature (1760–1860), 126–127
summary of ideas of God in "mass" literature, 59–60, 95–96
summary of ideas of God on God's impotence and non-existence, 239–244
summary of ideas of God on impartiality of God and unity of mankind, 185–188
support the necessity for social adjustment, 15, 78, 116, 134–135, 139, 141, 143–145, 151
traditional patterns, 154, 163, 175, 195–197
universality of, 163, 171
vide: authors quoted
vide: J. Weldon Johnson, *God's Trombones*
vide: Literature, church school
vide: prayers
vide: sermons
vide: spirituals
I. L. D., 13
significance of, 13

Johnson, Fenton, 165
Johnson, Georgia Douglas, 184, 226 ff.
Bronze, 184

Johnson, James Weldon, 20 ff.; 26, 65 ff.; 160, 183, 205, 234 ff.; 243, 254
God's Trombones, 20–21, 65–68, 160
ideas of God, 65–68, 160
O Black and Unknown Bards, 20
Johnson, Mordecai, 214, 241 ff.
Jones, Absalom, 30, 32

King, Willis J., 171

Larsen, Nella, 220 ff.; 229, 242
Quicksand, 220–224, 229, 242
Literature, church school, 88 ff.
Bible, all parts equally good, 88
compensatory ideas, 90, 92
ethics and social righteousness, 94, 95
extent of literature, 88
ideas in quarterlies for young people and adults, 93 ff.
ideas of God, development of, 88–92
Literature, mass, 60 ff.
ideas of God, development of, (1860–1914), 60 ff.
ideas of God, development of, (1914 to 1937), 65 ff.
ideas of God, used to stimulate Negroes, 61
to perfect social change, 62
developed to get citizenship rights for Negroes, 64
vide: God's Trombones
vide: literature, church school
vide: prayers
vide: sermons, modern, (1760–1860)
vide: spirituals

Mackay, Claude, 182 ff.
To the White Friends, 182–183
Mathews, Shailer, 18
God, definition of, 18

268 INDEX

Matney, W. C., 12
Migration of Negroes, 3
Miller, Herbert, 16
Miller, Kelly
  Everlasting Stain, The, 164–167
  ideas of God, development of, 152, 164 ff.; 186 ff.; 197, 199 ff.
  Out of the House of Bondage, 166–167
Moton, Robert Russa, 168 ff.; 186 ff.; 201 ff.
Movement of Negroes, 3 ff.
N. A. A. C. P., 10 ff.
Negro, Business League, 12
Negro in World War, 8 ff.

"Othelle," 111
  ideas of God, development of, 111

Paul, Nathaniel, 41 ff.
  ideas of God, development of, 41ff
  ideas of God developed along social lines, 44
Payne, Daniel A., 48 ff.
  ideas of God, development of, 48 ff.
  ideas socially developed, 53
  objection to discrimination, 51–53
Pennington, J. W. C., 53 ff.
  ideas of God, development of 53–54
Pickens, William, 169
Popel, Esther, 205 ff.
Pragmatism, definition of, 14
Prayer, 192 ff.
Prayers, God-idea, 83 ff.
  anodyne for people, 86
  extent, 83
  other-worldly, 87–88
  summary, 83
Price, J. C., 61 ff.
  ideas of God, development of, 61–62
Purvis, Robert, 113

Reconstruction era, 2

Remond, Charles Leonard, 115
Revels, Hiram R., 63

Schuyler, George S., 236 ff.
Sermons, ideas of God, development of, 30 ff.: 59, 68 ff.
  advance of race, 59
  century, 1760–1860, 30 ff.
  compensatory ideas, 69, 71, 74
  constructive ideas, 76–78
  ideas stimulate social action, 81–83
  modern, 68 ff.
  other-worldly ideas, 69–70
  social righteousness, 78–80
Shackelford, T. H., 156 ff.; 190 ff.; 195 ff.; 246
  For Fifty and Two Hundred Years, 157–158
Smuts, J. C., 18
  God, definition of, 18
Spirituals, 19 ff.
  constructive ideas, 28–30
  compensatory ideas, 23–25
  development of compensatory ideas, 27–28
  origin of spirituals, 19–20, 27
  other-worldly ideas, 27–28
St. George's Church, 30, 32

Thurman, Howard, 174–176, 186
Traditional, definition of, 1

Urban League, National, 11 ff.

Vassa, Gustavus, 109 ff.
  ideas of God, development of, 109–110

Walker, C. T., 64
  ideas of God, development of, 64
Walker, David, 115 ff.
War, Civil, 1 ff.

War, World, 1 ff.; 17
Washington, Booker T., 2 ff.; 10 ff.; 139 ff.; 154 ff.; 168, 253
  ideas of God, development of, 139–146, 154–155
Watkins, Frances Ellen, 118 ff.
  To the Union Lovers of Cleveland, 120
Wheatley, Phyllis, 103 ff.; 109, 246
  ideas of God, development of, 103–106, 109
Whipper, William, 114

White, Walter, 209 ff.; 216 ff.; 225
  Fire in the Flint, 209–210, 225
White, William, 32
Wieman, H. N., 18
  God, definition of, 18
Work, John, 29
Work, Monroe, 7
  Negro, bibliography of, 7
Woodson, Carter G., 13, 211 ff.
Woofter, T. J., 5

DR. BENJAMIN E. MAYS is President Emeritus of Morehouse College, Atlanta, Georgia. He is co-author with Joseph William Nicholson of *The Negro's Church*.